D0741854

THE SECRET LIFE OF WAR

The Secret Life of War

Journeys Through Modern Conflict

Peter Beaumont

Harvill Secker
LONDON

Published by Harvill Secker 2009

2 4 6 8 10 9 7 5 3 1

Copyright © Peter Beaumont 2009

Peter Beaumont has asserted his right under the Copyright, Designs
and Patents Act 1988 to be identified as the author of this work

First published in Great Britain in 2009 by
HARVILL SECKER
Random House, 20 Vauxhall Bridge Road
London SW1V 2SA

www.rbooks.co.uk

Addresses for companies within The Random House Group Limited
can be found at: www.randomhouse.co.uk/offices.htm

The Random House Group Limited Reg. No. 954009

A CIP catalogue record for this book is available from the British Library

ISBN 9781846551574 (hardback)
ISBN 9781846551581 (trade paperback)

The Random House Group Limited supports The Forest Stewardship Council (FSC),
the leading international forest certification organisation. All our titles that are printed
on Greenpeace approved FSC certified paper carry the FSC logo. Our paper procurement
policy can be found at www.rbooks.co.uk/environment

Typeset in Filosofia Regular by Palimpsest Book Production Limited,
Grangemouth, Stirlingshire

Printed and bound in Great Britain by
Clays Ltd, St Ives PLC

I saw an angel standing in the sun, and he cried with a loud voice, saying to all the fowls that fly in the midst of heaven: Come and gather yourselves together unto the supper of the Great God; that ye may eat the flesh of kings, and the flesh of captains, and the flesh of mighty men, and the flesh of horses, and of them that sit on them, and the flesh of all men, both free and bond, both small and great.

Book of Revelation

For David and Margaret

Contents

Introduction

This book was in gestation for four years, and is the culmination of almost a decade and a half of travelling to war zones. It was finally written over a period of two years. With so many books concentrating on the politics and blame and ideology of recent conflicts, I felt passionately that there was a need for a reminder of how war is experienced personally in individuals' lives. I wanted to describe the sights, sounds and emotions and relate them not to history, but to what it is to be human. That is what I have sought to do, seeking out stories of the killers and victims, the innocent, the not so innocent and the guilty, to explain how conflict functions, altering everything it touches. It has not always been an easy process. Both the writing and the researching of this book have been painful. I have lost friends and colleagues and seen so many others I have come across damaged. I have intruded into moments of grief and anguish and fear yet almost always been received with grace and forbearance. It has also been a deeply personal journey. I have realised how much I have changed myself by writing about conflict, sometimes in ways I do not feel comfortable with. For that reason this is my own story as well.

I also knew from the beginning that I wanted to write a book about the nature of those kinds of modern conflicts I had encountered during my career – ambiguous, intractable, long-lasting and very largely unresolved affairs which amounted to chronic afflictions of violence. When I began I was clear that what I wished to do was to give back a voice – or rather voices – to those affected by war, free from the organising justifications of those who order conflict. This book belongs as much to those extraordinary voices as it belongs to me.

I have been anxious to convey – as far as possible – a sense of the immediacy of the things I saw as I saw them and the ideas as they occurred to me. The result is that the vast majority of these pages were first drafted *in situ* in guesthouses and hotels, on camp beds and bunks, from Gaza and Iraq to Afghanistan, either in my journal, note-books or on to my laptop. For the less recent sections I have relied on extensive notes and photographs that I took as well as dispatches written at the time. Armed with these, I hope I have faithfully reflected what I can recall.

Finally, and perhaps inevitably in a book of this nature, I have been forced to confront my own role as a witness – and therefore participant of a kind – in the conflicts I have visited. If I have learned anything, it is that there is no hiding behind the artificial conceit of the dispassionate observer. No excuse for editing out war's true, fundamental nature. No excuse for accepting that war is inevitable.

Kabul,
May 2008

Shape Shifting

In keeping with their biblical Four Horsemen of the Apocalypse theme, the [US] soldiers' Humvees are named War, Death, Famine and Pestilence. 'You mean I'm riding with Death?' asked a truck driver they were protecting.
Associated Press, September 2006

'You know haji?' Sergeant Garth Sizemore twists round to ask me. He employs the derogatory name American soldiers use for Iraqis, turning the term of respect for one who has made the pilgrimage to Mecca into something belittling instead. I do not like the ubiquity of this name among American soldiers, but I don't say so, uncomfortable in my silent acquiescence. 'He's a shape shifter – haji,' the sergeant says. It is not a question but a declaration. Sizemore is talking to me from his command position at the front of his Humvee. It is 2006 and we are riding a night patrol through Adhamiya, a Sunni stronghold in Baghdad close to the Tigris River, to check on the Iraqi police checkpoints and patrols and to ensure that the men on the street after curfew are real policemen and not killers attached to the Shia death squads hunting their Sunni neighbours. All in the vehicle know there is often no difference between police and executioners.

3

It is boring and dangerous work for the soldiers, checking ID cards and weapons permits on roads threatened by powerful home-made bombs and hidden gunmen. It is not a conversation: Sizemore requires no input from any of us. So I sit and listen as his words envelop me. My knees are pushed up tight against the back of his seat, bone jarring on metal. I can feel the front plate of my body armour digging into my overfull bladder.

Sizemore continues from where he is squeezed in behind his radio and the computerised console that allows each vehicle in the patrol to track the position of other US vehicles in the area. He is fishing for an audience, although I suspect his men have heard this one before. 'We mow haji down in a field of dirt. Yeh? Drill him full of bullets. When we go to find a body, a dog jumps up and runs away. You know . . . I'm not fucking kidding.' He coughs a dry, dusty laugh. Somewhere behind this story there is an unsettling reality for Sizemore that he disguises with this instant mythologising. There is stuff I would like to ask him but I fear it would break into this fairy tale, turn his words back into a desiccated, self-consciously wary exchange of question and answer.

It's near midnight, and Sizemore is getting into it. 'Did I tell you 'bout when we were fighting in Fallujah in 2004 in Operation Phantom Fury? Ha! We were fighting zombie hajis.' I am struck by his images – this combination of horror films and video games and an older folklore. 'We had this German captain.' Sizemore switches to a heavy accent that is actually less German than an accumulation of all pastiche foreign accents. 'Shit, heff you heard?'

4

Sizemore says in an Arnold Schwarzenegger-meets-Jean-Claude Van Damme patois, shifting the set of his shoulders slightly to occupy his new part. 'The hajis are taking zom drug so zey are not afraid. Ve're fighting zombies, so ve gotta shoot zem in ze head.' He is interrupted briefly by a voice that comes on the radio, a rustle of electrified vowels and consonants amidst the static that Sizemore seems somehow to understand.

'Did I tell you about the zombie cats of Fallujah?' he asks, returning to his theme a few minutes later, flashing me a wide grin so that I wonder if all this is leading to some huge wind-up. 'One night, we're in this house. Yeh? And we're silent 'cause we're in the middle of the fighting. An' everything is spooky. Really spooky because of the green tint of everything we are seeing through our night-vision goggles. And suddenly we start hearing this noise outside.' Sizemore pauses then suddenly howls. 'Eeeeeowwwww. Eeeeeeow. Eeeeeooooow. And I'm going shit, it's a zombie cat.' He laughs.

I'm laughing too. But in the vehicle's belly I understand that an experience is being reframed to make it easier for him to talk about, his war reinvented through the subtle alchemy of words. 'We're fighting . . .' He pauses, overcome by the seriousness of it. 'We lost some good guys back there,' he says with a brief, quiet intimacy that surprises me amid the banter. Sad and soft. 'You know, we shot this insurgent who had a bunch of weapons. And the Captain, well, he wants to go back and check for the guy's weapons the next day. So we go looking for him inside this house where we killed him. We go in there, and there he is, surrounded by his weapons. And there are these three fucking cats that are eating his face off. Eating his face . . .' There is a long moment of silence for dramatic effect. 'Zombie cats.' Sizemore waits for the inevitable guffaws before he becomes more introspective once again against the drone of the Humvee. 'You know. There's stuff from then I won't forget.'

Sizemore is a solid, handsome and bespectacled Kentuckian – likeable, even if I do not like the war he is fighting in. He is ruddy-faced and sweating under his helmet and the heavy body armour that squares off all the men into a uniform appearance to make them appear factory-constructed. He is careful with his soldiers. Checking, double-checking what they do. Swearing at them to keep them safe. But there is no guarantee of safety here – from the random, hidden rip tides of death and crippling injury. A few weeks later Sizemore will be dead himself, hit in the stomach by a sniper, the first of thirteen men in his unit to die in this deployment. A group who will suffer one of the heaviest casualty rates of the entire war. Pulled under at the age of thirty-one. His insistent voice silenced.

At one moment the driver almost propels us sideways over a steep bank. I know that rollovers, especially those into the rank canals of Iraq, have killed a lot of soldiers. I look out through armoured glass, thick and distorting as a porthole. We are on the very edge of a rubble-strewn drop off and Sizemore starts shouting at the soldier behind the wheel to pay attention. Later, when the driver starts to doze, he radios to the convoy leader for a safety stop – 'somewhere where we ain't gonna die,' he announces – to walk the driver round the car and bring him back out of the world of drooling, weird exhaustion dreams into which I am also drifting, suffocated by the Baghdad summer night, and the cloying warmth of the engine and gear box.

I step stupidly out of the Humvee into a night as warm as bathwater. My legs are wooden from being cramped in the vehicle's back. My feet numb as if frostbitten. In a single day I have clocked eight hours of back-to-back patrols in the suburbs of Baghdad, compressed in the back of Humvees, trying to get into Iraq again after a lengthy absence. Travelling with these soldiers the viewpoint observable is necessarily filtered. But it is not simply an outlook shaped by being American in a strange land, coloured by being the instruments of Occupation. Its outlines are described by preoccupations that are more discreet: the sum of these men's upbringings and experiences. Tonight – above all – it is Garth Sizemore's view.

I try to piss against the wheels with the other men but I am toxically tired. I am seeing things in the orange sodium glare of the streetlights. The light is a rarity in a city plagued by constant power cuts. Turning from the Humvee, I think I glimpse a large group of uniformed men sitting on a vehicle, watching us placidly from a distance of about one hundred metres. I stare and wonder why the others have not noticed them until I try to focus my gaze on the tableau and I am shocked to discover they are not there at all. I am looking at a concrete wall, drifting into a waking hallucination bred of tension and exhaustion, hovering on the edge of standing sleep.

I know about Sizemore's zombies or at least the drug he is referring to. I tell him how I had stumbled across it by chance two years before – an antipsychotic, also used in the treatment of Parkinson's disease, called Artane. I had heard rumours of strange prescription drugs being used by Iraq's criminal underground, some of whom were involved in the fledgling insurgency. The stories mentioned a drug that made you brave, impervious to fear. They said that criminals would take the drug, sometimes in tea, sometimes mixed with alcohol, before going to commit an armed robbery, kidnapping or shooting.

Months after his death, I find a picture of Garth Sizemore posted on the Internet among the sites set up as memorials to the American military dead. There are no such memorials for the uncounted Iraqi fallen. I am sitting in my flat in London, at last finished with Iraq after too many close calls in my last half-year, feeling my luck was running out. I had witnessed too the consequences of violent loss there strike the person closest to me. But it feels there is no escaping. I am checking facts on the day I discover Sizemore has been killed. In the space of a few minutes I am confronted with the whole aftermath of his death: the articles and interviews with his family; the details of his funeral; the address in the state congress. Pieces of a life I had no idea about. I can only find one picture. The photograph shows him – the squad leader as I remember him – standing slightly apart, his men hunkered with their weapons against a brick wall in a garbage-strewn street, clearing houses of insurgents during the battle for Fallujah. His broad face is instantly familiar but without a voice I find it hard to associate the image with the vividness of the personality I remember from that stifling, hallucinatory night.

I check his name against his unit again and again, against the dates I visited his brigade, hoping to find another Sizemore to take his place in the roster of the fallen, not even sure why it should matter to me. I can find no mistake. And it does matter. It is not because I had known this man in any meaningful sense. But in recording his memories and shaping them, a connection has been made. Words acting on words, sacrilising war by fashioning it into the stories we consume.

Observed from a distance, war is defined by its most visible phenomena – the killing, destruction and displacement. They are the solid things, assessable through numbers, statistics and dates – even the bald two-line report describing how Sizemore died. I dig it out more than once in an attempt to weigh the death of this one ordinary man against the heavy mass of war's attrition. But like the picture of the sergeant in Fallujah, these lines offer no insight permitting a deeper understanding. They are boringly, intentionally prosaic, skulking around the edges of his death. 'Garth D. Sizemore', they read: 'killed when his patrol came in contact with enemy forces using small arms fire during combat operations in Baghdad.'

They represent the aspect of conflict it is possible easily to map through its battles and altering front lines, the war of press conferences, statements and newspaper reports.

But conflict has another quality that exists at the margins of observable violence. A hinterland electric with words and stories, with the telling and retelling that enfolds war's central facts, it is this periphery that gives to conflict its real, deep and resonant meaning. Alive with voices like Sizemore's, searching for ways to describe their experience, it is imaginative and unreliable – dense with evasions, rumours, excuses, lies and hatreds. Yet even this unreliability is more truthful, more personal and more authentic than the cleaned up and sterile official version: real and human as it is in its failings.

As an observer I know that I am not exempt from the same tendency to remodel the experience of conflict, sitting and listening and applying my own interpretations and prejudices. I sample, filter and mix as I watch, effecting my own subtle, and not so subtle, alterations. I realise too that not only is it impossible to separate myself from the stories I collect but that it is necessary to channel those experiences through my own to try to render them in emotions and sensations that have meaning for me. Corrupting the data even as I download it, I become a tainted witness. The challenge becomes to be as honest as I can.

I know about Sizemore's 'zombie' drugs because of an encounter in the first year of the war in Iraq. I spool back, cross-referencing the meeting with Ala and his friends, six months after the invasion of 2003, to the conversation with Sizemore. I come across his little gang during the period of relative calm before the insurgency becomes widespread and ahead of the sectarian slaughter yet to come, living rough in the gardens of Baghdad, and hanging around the banks of the Tigris to beg and steal.

Ala thinks he is twenty years old; he says he is not quite sure. He leads a gaggle of ten- to fifteen-year-olds. He is taller than the rest, thin and intense, with a narrow face. His eyes are spaced and filmy with the lustre of a dead bird's. He is cleaner than the others and when he speaks the younger children quietly defer to him. Their faces are blackened with the smoke from the fires they sit around at night, their clothes stiff with body grease.

When I meet them, their home is the riverbank beside the Palestine Hotel. They beg outside the gates by the security checkpoint, crowding around, hungry and insistent, the youngest tugging at my clothes asking for food and money. I've heard a rumour that one of the older girls blows the soldiers for small change. Ala tells me that a week before, he and his friends had fished a bloated corpse out of the Tigris, hooking it with branches and hefting the stinking thing ashore. I think of a group of wasted Huckleberry Finns. Delivering the body to the police, in the hope of getting a reward for their grisly initiative, they complain that the officers laughed at them and sent them on their way. That was when bodies were rare – before the rivers and culverts became clogged with the rank cargoes of the dead, victims of Iraq's sectarian death squads.

They are bitter about this incident. They tell me that they need the money. Not to buy food or find a place to sleep, even to put clothes on their thin bodies. I know that. Instead, Ala and his gang live for drugs and need the money to get high. There is a word for Ala and his friends that I learn quickly. They are called the *capsiloun*: the pill people, part of a drug culture that, in Iraq, has its roots in violent criminality. Their drugs of choice – Artane, valium and other hypnotics, and powerful anti-epileptics like clonazepam – were the drugs available in Baghdad's Abu Ghraib prison, smuggled in by families or sold to inmates by corrupt doctors as a substitute for booze. Artane is the most popular. Its proper name, I learn later from a doctor, is benzhexol.

A bubble sheet purchased from a private pharmacy on prescription, I am told, costs 1,000 dinars. Almost nothing. My driver is uncomfortable that I am even talking to these children. He thinks they are as dangerous as anything in Baghdad and likely to rob us, or worse. When I first meet them at 10 a.m. they are already stoned, stinking of *tannar* – the paint thinners and glue that they mix and sniff in plastic bags. Ala tells me that a small medicine bottle filled with *tannar* costs a handful of change. The only girl with Ala's gang today, a skinny child in her early teens, is nursing a full bottle.

But what they really like, when they can get them, are *capsils*. They list the pills they can buy on the streets, especially by the Babb al-Sharq – the Eastern Gate. There are 'pinks' and 'Lebanese', 'eyebrows' and 'crosses', 'reds' and 'Syrians'. Mainly these are antidepressants, although sometimes they can find amphetamines. Some pharmacies sell to criminals and drug abusers, but not to the likes of Ala and his friends. For street kids, who buy the pills individually from the drug dealers, it costs a little more.

I enquire about Artane. I ask Ala to tell me how it feels, trying to relate it to my own experiences. When he explains it sounds like nothing I've ever come across. Taken in large doses, or dissolved in alcohol to speed up the effects, Artane brings on a rush of feelings of euphoria, encourages impulsive behaviour, easy provocation and, sometimes, vivid hallucinations. Most importantly of all for the carjackers, gunmen, bandits and muggers of Iraq's chaotic first months following its 'liberation', it removes the sense of fear.

Ala tells me his story, a garbled and random series of recollections. I notice too that there are things he does not tell me. Ala says he was released from Abu Ghraib under Saddam Hussein's general amnesty of non-political prisoners enacted before the US-led Coalition's invasion in March and April 2003. What he does not – will not – say is why he was in prison in the first place. I guess he is a thief. With nowhere to go, Ala ended up sleeping rough on Baghdad's streets.

I ask him what he likes about Artane. Mention of the drug again excites something unpleasantly hungry in his face. There is an odd arrogance as his words tumble out, as if to reinforce the difference between us, how I have not been admitted to this secret. 'It makes me feel brave,' he says cockily. 'It makes you want to attack people. It makes you more aggressive.' What is strange is that it is not supposed to work like this. When I return to London I ask a drugs specialist why these drugs are having the reverse effect to what is intended. He describes to me what he calls the 'paradoxical reaction'. When I research it I discover that some sedatives prescribed for adults, for example, will cause hyperactivity in children. In other psycho-actives, the paradoxical reaction is dose-related, with aggression and agitation more likely at higher levels of ingestion.

The outline of Ala's story is one I have heard before. With Saddam's release of between 40,000 and 75,000 convicted prisoners, a prison-based drug culture swamped the capital's streets. Imported like a corrupted file. The result was a citywide crime wave. At the time I speak to Ala and his friends, 80 per cent of criminals being picked up by the fledgling Iraqi Police Service appear to be under the influence of drugs. Referrals to the city's clinic for drug abuse have doubled in a handful of months. Later I hear of special teashops where you can go to have 'tea plus' – sweet Arabic *shay* served with a pill dissolved in the little glass. There is 'tea plus plus' as well – *shay* with a shot of alcohol as well as drugs. For a few dollars in those days you could watch a porn movie too. For a few more have sex. They are places that, like Ala and his friends, will disappear as the violent Sunni and Shia militias emerge to control vast areas of the city, high on their own trip of God and violence. I won't hear about the 'zombie' drug again until I meet Sizemore.

What I experience on arriving back in Iraq – or in the other conflict zones of the Middle East and Afghanistan – is a reaction as paradoxical as the aggression-fuelled high experienced by Ala and his friends

on Artane. It is my own unbidden shape shifting in response
to the proximity of conflict, a reordering of the chemicals
in the brain as powerful as the drugs the street children
take. It comes to me in a moment of epiphany one night,
sitting in the blacked-out silence of one of the lumbering
Rhino armoured buses that bounce their way nauseatingly
across the few miles from Baghdad International Airport
(BIAP) to the Green Zone. Pitching like a trawler. It is a
few months after riding with Sizemore and his men – after
his death, although I don't know it yet. Driving in convoy,
on roads threatened by Iraq's ubiquitous and powerful
bombs, I recognise it as an inexplicable feeling of content-
ment that spreads up warmly from my stomach like
morphine.

It reminds me of my handful of teenage experiments with
heroin: the sensation of curiosity mixed with detachment,
surroundings becoming luminous and defined as a Blake
print. But it is not opiates my brain is awash with in the
back of the Rhino; rather, powerful hormones. A therapist
I see a handful of times, Mark, a former journalist whose
expertise is dealing with those who cover conflict, explains
it to me at our first meeting. I am in his office at the top of
a tall, elegant building, not far from Regent's Park in
London, because I have started to feel panicky and anxious,
angry and alienated after one of my visits to Iraq. As he
shuffles his questionnaires Mark describes how the body's
chemicals can mimic opiates, and present the same problems of dependency. He explains how there are side effects
too, as with any chemical that has been ingested for too
long.

I find myself constructing taxonomies of the multiple changes that war effects on individuals and societies – in the physical and the emotional realms – discovering in these refashionings a savage and darkly compelling magic. And of all of conflict's transmutations, the most powerful is the first sudden initiation into the shuddering reality of violence itself.

I am sitting one morning with Lauren Frayer, a reporter with Associated Press, who has been in Iraq for four months of a one-year assignment. 'I just want to get the bad thing over and done with,' she says, out of the blue. We are on a base slimed with a cold, boot-sucking mud, whipped to the consistency of cake icing by the constant churning of vehicle tracks. When the sun comes, between the storms, it is baked dry into powder soft as children's paint. She is cupping her hands around a cardboard beaker of sour coffee, faced framed by curls. It is early spring 2007. In the way of these things we have been thrown together. While the rest of Iraq's press corps is covering the Baghdad Security Plan, the surge of 20,000 US troops designed to stabilise the capital and bring an end to the war, we had both noticed that the US casualties were sharply up in Diyala province, north of Baghdad, driven by fighters fleeing the capital. We had jumped on the same helicopter and found ourselves at 'Warhorse', a sprawling Forward Operating Base outside the provincial capital, Baqoubah, occupied by a group of US Cavalry. And now we are talking about the inevitability of confronting the combat up close, in the knowledge that four soldiers had died in the hours after we arrived. 'I know it is going to happen,' she says. 'I just want to have it done with and move on.'

We are in the Green Bean coffee shop, a kind of Starbucks behind blast walls supplying iced lattes and WiFi, double espressos and muffins – an illusion to anaesthetise the soldiers, just for a moment, to the fact of being in Iraq. By way of explanation, Frayer, a young New Yorker, tells me the story of a reporter from Agence France Presse for whom the 'bad thing' happened on his first day working in Iraq – on his first outing. It has been preying on her mind. She tells the story in a couple of jagged sentences. 'The soldier sitting next to him was shot by a sniper. The body fell into his lap,' she says. 'He carried on . . .' The words stumble on this telling, occupied by our shared knowledge that 'bad things' are the agents of change, that rearrange the shape of those who experience them. 'It is going to happen,' she says again with emphasis, almost to herself. 'Don't wish for it too much,' I say to fill the renewed silence as much as anything, regretting the glibness of my words. A few hours later the bad things begin.

We are walking down a rubbish-strewn road of com-pacted, cocoa-coloured dirt. The street into which I have followed a few dozen or so soldiers is, I notice, barely more than an alley, hemmed in on either side by two rows of low, white-painted single-storey houses. Here and there are pools of standing water, green-slicked with sewage, smelling acridly of stale piss and dirty washing. Entrances lead to hidden small courtyards that are fleetingly revealed as a few figures answer their doors, unwilling to poke bodies through the frames more than is necessary. They are glimpses of lives lived largely unseen by the US soldiers except when the doors are being hammered down in night-time raids.

The Bradley armoured cars in which we arrived have been left a little way behind us, parked where the street ends in an empty area dotted with a handful of skeletal trees. We are accompanying two columns on foot, a mixture of American and Iraqi troops, and a single Iraqi army Humvee, moving ever deeper into an area of narrow lanes. The helmet of one of the Iraqi soldiers, I notice with surprise, has been spray-painted a glittery gold.

It is, one of the US soldiers complains bitterly to me, a 'bullshit' mission. To ask the whereabouts of a local community leader and hand out the little 'tip' cards designed to persuade the residents to phone in information on the insurgents. To insist that there is nowhere that US troops can't go. But Buhriz, at the southern end of Baqoubah, is hostile territory, a stronghold of jihadi fighters. When the Cavalry first arrived and tried to push out the insurgents, the enemy stood and fought back – 'toe to toe' the soldiers say, pointing out the locations of the grim little battles in this neighbourhood that have become embedded in their personal histories. Veterans of heavy fighting in the campaigns in Fallujah and Najaf, they were surprised by the intensity of the combat. Now, a few weeks after those first engagements, the conflict has become a war of attrition in these claustrophobic alleys, a dirty confrontation of hidden bombs and snipers, of sudden, indiscriminate air strikes, of houses booby-trapped as giant bombs.

I'm a few hundred metres along the street when I sense a viral tension emanating from the soldiers' bodies. It is not a nervousness that is audible in their voices, but my brain picks up on the subtle physical signals – the rigid wariness and stretched expressions that describe not quite fear but a state of anxiety screwed one peg below. I feel it myself like the teeth-grinding edge of amphetamines when you want to fall asleep – a sensation of being pinned too powerfully and painfully in the now.

When it happens, there is a single crack. Almost not loud enough to be a thing able to kill or cripple. It sounds like a bullet. I know from having heard gunshots so many times before that it is a round being fired towards us. It is audible in two parts – first the air being displaced and then the muzzle crack – signifying an incoming round. A trick of perspective caused by an object moving faster than the speed of sound. I look around stupidly for confirmation from the soldiers' faces frozen in the midst of the same question, trying to assess its threat. The problem is that this noise is too solitary an event. It is neither quite close enough, nor distant enough, to be properly processed. To be reacted to or to be discounted. It is a meaningless piece of information, an event that on its own remains equivocal.

No matter how often it happens, how many times you experience the sudden onset of 'contact', the kinetic rush of metal and gas always seems to be a kind of cosmic impertinence. There is a voice, shouting nearby. 'Who fired? Who fired that shot?' I am aware of faces looking goofily around, and the sound of more yelling at the accompanying Iraqi soldiers in the hope it was an accidental discharge of a weapon. A second shot, closer this time, settles the matter, propelling the soldiers forward at a crouched run towards the source of the shooting. Someone is yelling: 'Go! Go! Go!' although it is not quite clear in what direction. It is not single shots now but bursts of automatic-weapons fire aimed at the street, vicious little suck-suck-sucks as each piece of passing metal warps the air, pulling a vacuum behind it. I am down in the dirt and I realise that Lauren is close by, on the ground as well. 'What do you want me to do?' she asks of one of the sergeants, trying to find out whether we should follow. He looks baffled by the question, not having any such option himself. 'You can do anything you like,' he answers blandly.

It seems best to stick with the counterattack rather than get left behind. By now I am following a small group of US soldiers along the right side of the street, shooting the advance with the two cameras slung around my neck, allowing me to frame the frightening circumstances of violence in the small, black-bordered box of the viewfinder. To manufacture an illusory distance. As ever, it feels weird to be running towards gunfire, legs a little drunk, surface of the world not quite solid. We crouch down by a half-built wall at a small crossroads that is being sectored by a cross-fire. The rounds are hitting the corner of the wall beside me, throwing up a haze of yellow dust. I'm conscious of the dust settling on my shoulders, the mouth-drying taste of it; the gold-painted helmet by my face reflecting the mid-morning sun like a mosque's dome. 'I'm hit,' the soldier two feet in front of me exclaims, as if remarking on something curious he'd just seen, but not moving out of the path of the bullets. He gropes at his thigh. When his hand comes away there is no blood. He has been hit by a piece of flying brick. When one of the Bradleys moves forward and fires its cannon to break the contact, I find myself sitting against a wall suddenly laughing at the ridiculousness of it all.

It is lesson re-learned. Most of the time contact is less awful than the anticipation of it. In the action and adrenaline, an occult layer is stripped away. What follows is the moment when war reveals itself: a busy-ness about staying alive even when you are curled up in a ditch or hiding in a basement. Minute movements and judgements take on massive necessity: lighting a cigarette, tying a shoelace or tightening helmet straps. Once I was pinned down by mortar and machine-gun fire in a snow-filled scrape on a hillside in Kosovo with a Dutch journalist. Concerned that her head was large and presented a better target than any of ours, she concentrated throughout the ambush on pushing her head just an extra millimetre into the snow and dirt behind my legs. So we get through.

There is something else, however, I have become aware of only over the years. Being conscious of it, it seems so obvious. It is that most days, as I venture out into the world of conflict, I catch myself attempting to anticipate what person I will be when confronted with contact. Each time the changes are different, layered into unfamiliar combinations. A couple of days later we are back in Buhriz, accompanying the Bradleys as they go in on a mission to clear insurgents from a section of the suburb. This time there is no doubt. I know there will be fighting. I get into the lead vehicle conscious that my relationship with fear defines my identity.

I am familiar with the main shapes of the experience at

least. There is a brave and reckless being that I recognise too well – infused with a sense of being unweighted and exhilarated, invulnerable amidst the violence. Its counterpart appears as frequently: a fearful, shrivelled self, clumsy and out of place, who lurches jaggedly across an uneven landscape dotted with pitfalls. Finally, there is the identity as blankly detached as a depressive, an empty watcher, grimly fatalistic. Today, there is none of the teeth grinding, no fear and no excitement. What I feel instead is this dull vacancy – as if I had been poured out, emptied – a consciousness without emotions that stares out of its shell. Sometimes I think it's best on days like this, when I become mechanical, recording what I see. It is only on days like this, in the suffocating longueurs between the scattered jolts of fighting, that I can fall asleep with the soldiers in the Bradley's back. Fall in with the rhythm of combat.

The fighting unravels in a day of spectral scenes seen through the gun camera monitors, flat as Chinese shadow puppetry but no less deadly for it. The figures of insurgents fire from behind human shields. I see a scared boy held by his arm by a gunman who peers around a corner. A few minutes later a woman and her three small children are pushed into the road in front of us so that a fighter with an RPG (rocket-propelled grenade) can try to fire his weapon from behind them at the vehicle I am in.

It is a day of deaths. Three men killed by my vehicle alone in one burst of fire, their bodies falling in front of us, bearded faces visible and eyes open to the sky. At first I think they are the scared little family group, and I am overtaken by a sudden sense of nausea and anger at the soldiers in my vehicle. It is a day of fatalities in the Bradley column too: a vast explosion engulfs one of the Iraqi Humvees a little way ahead that shakes the track and sends flames over the houses. Men die in the vehicle. Men writhe and die more slowly on the ground.

The question comes up: what does it do to you? I think what the askers really want to know is what is it like to die – to undergo that least knowable of transformations. It is a question born of a culture no longer familiar with death or serious injury except on the television screen, when it is distant and impersonal. There is no answer except to say I used to think I was immune to the self-inflicted damage of this voyeurism that has shown me the aftermath of suicide bombs and left the flesh of the victims adhering to my shoes; to the burned bodies, or bright flow of arterial blood. Not to the instant emotional shock that could leave me weeping when I turned away. Immune instead to its long-term effects – the adhesive nature of horror that attaches like fragments of white phosphorus to the consciousness and sizzles in.

In his consulting rooms Mark does the tests for post-traumatic stress disorder. I feel disappointed at how obvious the questions are, looking for hidden signs that will give me a heads-up. Hoping that there is more to know than the blindingly self-evident. But it is the same message my doctor delivered years ago. In the long run, sooner or later, war changes you and damages you. Mark says: 'The parts are wearing, but they haven't broken yet.' Then he

23

offers the possible outcomes. 'You get killed or otherwise messed up. You experience a breakdown you can't recover from. Or you get out of it. There are no other options.'

Before I covered my first war I tried to imagine what being in conflict would be like by sifting others' images, taken from films and literature, reportage and documentary. Now when I go, I find myself often unconsciously imagining an exit, or finding ways to push away reality. The soldiers do it in different ways, cranking up the boom boxes in their 'tracks' before they hit the gates – playing 'Bombtrack' or 'Bullet in the Head' by Rage Against the Machine; 'Sympathy for the Devil' by the Stones; 'The Ride of the Valkyries' or 'America, Fuck Yeah' from the movie *Team America*. Clichés. But occasionally I am surprised by something beautiful and serene. In the dark of early morning it is a string concerto gently bowing through the Bradley's 'hellhole' as the crew load up spare links of ammo for the 25mm chain gun under the floor plates.

Driving in Baghdad, I catch myself drifting into vivid daydreams. My car is a submarine, I find myself thinking one day, inching through the depths of the city's violent paranoia. I can only maintain the hull's integrity through the power of my concentration. I commit myself to rigid patterns of behaviour – like the soldiers' rituals before their patrols. I watch them touch the photo of a dead colleague that has become a totem; kiss crucifixes; lock themselves into the repetition of the same words – prayers or muttered imprecations in huddles of locked arms like football players.

As I travel 'low-profile' through the city in the car's back seat – 'soft skinned', not armoured – I have my own rules, more important to be stuck to than invested with practical value. Avoiding cracks in the pavement of conflict. Eye contact with those outside the car is forbidden. To connect properly is to be spotted, and that, I fear, means recognition as a foreigner, an *ijnabi*. If I don't look out, I try to tell myself, then no one can see me for what I am – an outsider, a valuable commodity.

These frightening journeys remind me how easy it once was to get around these streets in the days following the city's fall. Scenes return: a sheep standing on a carved, decaying wooden balcony in the old part of the city; boys walking hand in hand through the riverside amusement park on a wet Eid al-Adha festival; the Zayouna district on a Thursday afternoon, start of the weekend, with young men on powerful motorcycles drag-racing down the street.

I could visit the book market in Mutanabi Street and leaf through the yellowed pages – cowboy novels and cheap thrillers in English, old science textbooks, religious volumes and language primers. Buried among them, odd books that hinted at riskier reading going on under Saddam's regime: Ayn Rand's *The Fountainhead*, a few novels by Graham Greene, *The Day of the Jackal* and *The Scarlet Letter*. In those days, the possibilities of peace and violent collapse were locked in an equal race. You could go out for a pizza in the city's Arasat district where a musician

would entertain diners on a Spanish guitar. Or sit in the
street and eat *shawarma* sliced from the huge turning cylin-
ders of dripping meat. And hope against hope, for Iraq's
sake, that it might turn out for the best.

But even as 2003 turned into 2004, the violence was
intensifying. And the city and its life were being brutally
reshaped. Sectarian assassinations had started in the
western suburbs. The suicide bombers were beginning to
attack Shia targets, and in the Sunni Triangle the resistance
to the US Occupation was coalescing into an effective insurgency as fighters quickly learned how to confront American
armour with ever more sophisticated roadside bombs. But
still you could move around the country – to the holy cities
of Najaf and Kerbala to visit the grand mosques and wander
the lanes of the vast Shia necropolis on the desert's edge (a
dangerous place later, where the bodies of inter-Shia
factional violence were dumped). I could drive to dirty,
bustling Basra in the south, once a cosmopolitan port, later
to be run by the Shia militias. Fallujah too was only a forty-
five-minute journey, a violent place, but where the insurgent leaders were at first courteous and welcoming and
wanted to tell journalists their story.

But by the time the war entered its fifth year in 2007,
the country's horizons, those visible to Westerners at least,
had collapsed upon themselves like an imploding star,
super-heavy with the weight of communal, insurgent and
terrorist violence. First, it was independent travel outside
Baghdad that stopped. This ruled out even the risky runs
from the capital, my head wrapped in a *kefiyah*, driving
out through traffic-snarled and dangerous towns where

insurgent gangs would pay the cigarette boys who hawked their wares at cars' windows to call them if they saw a foreigner. I would close my eyes and will myself into a half-sleep. Then, slowly, it was travel within the capital itself. To the edgy suburbs first: Ghazaliya with its palm-lined streets, or Dora, overshadowed by its smoking power station. To Adhamiya's tangle of old lanes that finish abruptly at the Tigris, where the old men continued to play dominoes in the street even amid American raids. Places that I once strolled through.

Gradually, the well-heeled areas joined them: Mansour with its villas, gardens and private pools, which became a place of snipers and snatch gangs. Even 'safe' Karrada with its shops selling mobile phones, washing machines, satellite dishes and DVD players, and home to the National Theatre, became a place too dangerous in which to linger. So the city contracted neighbourhood by neighbourhood, until travel became a guerrilla operation launched from behind the guarded hotel 'compound' wall.

Compounds: the castles that squat ugly and blank-walled as prisons amid the capital and countryside. The civilian ones enclose clusters of hotels, occupied by journalists, NGOs and businessmen, guarded by snipers on the roofs and small private armies. Sandbagged and razor-wired, with posted warnings that guards were authorised to shoot to kill. The architecture of these fortresses brought with it a specialised imagery of division. If there is a defining physical feature of the new Iraq, it is not in grand new engineering projects. It is not even symbolised by the vastly expensive white elephant of the new US embassy rising

out of the Green Zone. Instead, it is the thousands of kilometres of poured, reinforced concrete, hundreds of millions
of dollars' worth of blast-resistant separation.

They accumulated and hardened like ancient reefs, abandoned by a retreating sea, the solid remainder left behind
by the dead ideas and failed projects, the blindly optimistic
words that the US-led Coalition brought with it. The Iraqis
know them simply as 'concretes', forming lanes, chicanes,
stockades and perimeters. As barriers that surround the
Green Zone and circle ministries, bases, compounds and
'outposts', police stations, provincial offices and checkpoints. They form walls within walls, standing in rings like
sarsen stones around the chapels and laundries, the
sleeping blocks and shops. As they have grown, they have
altered the country's physical appearance as powerfully as
the explosions that have brought down buildings and
villages, whole city centres.

When night comes, all is transformed again completely.
Outside, where the darkness pools, is doubly dangerous. It
is true for all conflicts. The night is an amplifier of risk,
the setting for the private, awful things to happen. And as
the war goes on the only way to see Baghdad at night, in
relative safety, is to view it from the air.

I take helicopters more times than I would like, always
conscious of the fragility of these machines. Once again the
fear is more in the anticipation. Airborne, I am hypnotised
by the unfolding scene viewed through the ever-present
dust wind-blasted on to the door panes of the Blackhawk.
Lights below diffract into soft haloes. Anxious not to lose the
sense of these journeys, I sketch one out in my notebook

one night — a dreamy, unravelling film show, my head swathed by the heat and wrapped in rotor noise muffled by earplugs. I am flying from 'LZ Washington' heading north out of Baghdad on a loop of the archipelago of vast US fire-bases that radiate from the centre. They are dark outposts in the night where the showing of white light is forbidden for fear of drawing mortars and snipers.

It is the once well-heeled suburbs I first see below me. In a city where electricity is one of the most valuable commodities, the light lapping around the houses is as great a signifier of status and wealth as the swimming pools or gardens. Light is a totem, helping those below believe they can ward off the terrors of the Baghdad night. Except it can't. And doesn't. Tonight is a night without too many power cuts and the lit districts merge into a homogeneous whole that unifies the blocks and warring neighbourhoods, Shia and Sunni. At first the light is ubiquitous, enveloping the streets and dusty parks, the roads and schools. The lines and planes of mosques and monuments and businesses are sharply defined by their harsh neon strips, green and white, the homes in a softer glow, while the sodium orange of the street lamps is reflected in the broad river bends that loop greasily like intestines through the city.

We are flying low enough for me to see into the yards of houses and the junk within them — tools and children's climbing frames in the bigger houses. I see chairs, tables, the generators themselves, dismantled vehicles, vats, crates and abandoned furniture. It is just before curfew, and a few cars crawl along the streets, pushing ahead of them their own twin pools, flickering vectors. Brake lights flash like nocturnal eyes. Apart from the cars, it is a landscape devoid of visible life, there is only the topography of the illuminated zones.

As we fly on towards Baghdad's outer suburbs, the darkness gradually encroaches in messy organic shapes. At first the shadows appear in ragged patches as the edge of the city frays into the night, marking out the poor, powerless, outlying neighbourhoods, and the beginnings of the palm groves, and irrigation ditches and fields. Solitary homes. In daylight the latter are dusty cubes roofed with corrugated metal with a yard behind for animals. They are dimly illuminated, a weak yellow brightness cast often from a single bulb hanging outside. The areas of darkness grow ever larger as we travel on. Then, suddenly, the light is gone. Darkness reigns.

But it is not a complete darkness. When my eyes become accustomed, I realise that it has different textures. The changing landscape resolves itself into shapes that then dissolve into the night. Around the date palm groves and fields, watered by black canals, the dark is deeper and velvety. Where the farms run out into the desert, it lightens. Here the deepest shadows are settled like the accumulation of blown dust into the dried-out wadis and into the lee sides of the low cliffs where the brick makers excavate their material. And dotted here and there are the most remote dwellings, like frontier cabins in the midst of the encircling night.

It occurs to me that these lonely, midnight desert homes, viewed from above, are a reflection of our understanding of Iraq, my understanding of conflict. We see only the brightest and most visible nodes, but not into the deeper darkness.

We are altered too in hidden ways we cannot recognise. There is a physiological reality that exists beyond the psychotherapist's questionnaires – a reorganisation of the base materials. It is a concrete, permanent and measurable transformation in the brain. War stresses acutely. And over time repeated exposure to acute stressors leads to detectable changes in the brain's architecture that both impair it and alter its functionality. The chemicals produced naturally in the body to help us confront threat, harm us too in the long run. Then they act as toxins on neurons. Nerve cell extensions in the hippocampus, an area important for memory and learning, become withered. Changes in the responsiveness of the area of the brain known as the amygdala, associated with behaviour, as well as structural changes in the medial prefrontal cortex, one of whose functions is related to signalling memory of fear, also take place. The consequence is a subtle rewiring of several interconnected brain functions that not only affects memory and learning, but our ability to control our emotional responses.

 Sergeant Sizemore is more right than he knows. We are all of us shape shifters – insurgents and soldiers, journalists and civilians. All are being shaped by conflict, and its trauma. Shaping ourselves in conscious ways or otherwise. We take a pill, put on an attitude or a disguise, we drink too deeply of the experience, and each one of us is reconfigured.

One evening, waiting for a helicopter to take me across the capital, I meet Melissa, a young American reservist from St Louis, at a helicopter pad close to Baghdad International Airport. A large camel spider is spotted clinging to one of the concrete T-barriers that separates the waiting area from the busy field. Soldiers waiting for their own flights gather to photograph the poisonous creature on mobile phones and pocket cameras, all of a sudden a bunch of giggling boys. Tonight, I know there will be a partial lunar eclipse, so we sit waiting for the shadow to pass across the moon.

Melissa is tired and edgy, her eyes red-rimmed. She tells me that in civilian life she worked on an HIV programme. Now she is soldiering in Iraq and has just returned from leave in Greece with her fiancé, also a soldier serving in Iraq. They have split up. 'He changed,' she says. 'You know, being here has been good for his confidence. But he is not the man I knew. I'm not saying he's a bad man. He's a good guy. Otherwise I wouldn't have been with him. But he's not the same man I wanted to share my life with. He's more aggressive, more egocentric.'

I find myself occupying a familiar role, the listening outsider, neutral, anonymous. 'You know, I like to talk. I'm not wild . . . But I miss having proper conversations like I would have with my girlfriends at work. We would have a coffee klatch in the morning and we would talk about stuff. Here no one says anything that isn't negative.'

Melissa looks at the quartered moon. 'It looks as though that is as far as it will get,' she says softly, a little disappointed. It is late and the soldiers waiting with us are growing tired. Two are draped long-limbed across their rucksacks. 'He's a surfer. My boyfriend. My fiancé.' She catches herself. 'My ex. We used to talk about what we would do when we left. How we would travel together. Then recently when he would talk about his plans it would be about himself. I said to him: "When you talk now it is all 'I' and not 'we'." It was like he was making his own space around him that did not involve us any more. He said he needed to do some things on his own after Iraq. But I couldn't accept that. It is not what we planned.' Melissa is close to crying.

I ask Melissa about her plans when she returns to America – whether she will go back to working for the charity. She shakes her head. 'I can be anything I want to be. I can become what I want.' It is a very American conviction, this idea of easy and utter change. The same notion that brought American and British soldiers to Iraq: the idea of an effortless transformation from dictatorship to a democracy. 'I've worked with AIDS. I've been a social worker and a counsellor. I would like to try something different. I'm interested in the area of alternative healing, holistic medicine. After the army I need to do something very different. Something for myself.'

I think about Melissa and feel sad for her, even as my own problems are dramatised one day leaving Iraq in the autumn of 2006. I've heard friends say how I have changed. But it is hard for me to understand it without seeing those changes underscored. Because I still feel intrinsically myself. I am driving from Amman's Queen Alia airport through a landscape of little valleys filled with the blocky white houses of the city's urban sprawl when it occurs. The sky is turning saffron with evening. My mind plays a trick. It is as if the houses and the hills themselves are burning, as I have seen towns and villages on fire. I feel nauseous and sweaty, my heart bursting. It's not the substance of this illusion that troubles me so much but my awareness of how easily it has broken through into my waking, conscious world.

This moment of dread dissipates almost as soon as I begin focusing on its details. Arriving at the Four Seasons Hotel, I think that it has passed. I go through the rituals of decompression that I hope will begin reorganising my responses for the world of offices and children, buses and bank queues. I hope. Because I know that when I return I drag war with me like something on my shoes.

In the hotel's pricey salon the hairdresser cuts my hair and shaves off the greying beard I have grown to try to pass unnoticed in Baghdad's streets. The smell of the hot towels and his cologne reminds me I am still dirty from my travels, so I head upstairs. In my room I pour a glass of wine and slip into a long bath in which I can immerse myself completely. It is only then that I notice that my hands are shaking uncontrollably with the powerful emotions of slipping out of war and back into the world of life. It is a transformation that at the time is beyond the dreams of most Iraqis. Beyond Garth Sizemore.

Clues

The four men are standing above me on a wall of crude mud bricks. I find it hard to make them out at first except as silhouettes framed against an opalescent winter sky, layered with clouds, absinthe swirled in a glass of water. As my car rounds the corner I see them more clearly, no longer dazzled by the light. They are bearded and, except for the central figure dominating the scene, wearing turbans and prayer caps. The exception is a lanky figure, a dark cloak thrown theatrically across one shoulder. What marks him out is not his height but the old Russian gas mask, smooth and rubbery, that he has pulled over his head, its eyepieces reflecting the sky like ship's portholes. I fire off a quick shot with my camera. Later, when I examine the photo carefully, I can see the faces better. One of the men is squatting, feral and hungry-looking, wearing a shit-eating grin. Another is solemnly serious. And then there is their leader: insect-like, blank and imperious behind his rubber snout and glittering eyes.

There is something else that is equally incongruous. Over the mask I can see he has placed a set of small headphones connected to a radio, which he is holding delicately, raised in one hand like a priest offering up the host. At least I think it is a radio. Years later, playing again with the image on my computer, I change the exposure, revealing the form behind the silhouettes, and blow it up. I discover my momentary impression has been wrong. It is something else he holds, a connector, perhaps, for a military transmitter, fat as a Mars Bar, with metal prongs protruding from its base.

The man stands as still as the statue of an alien prophet arranged before his apostles. There is something discomforting in the frozen nature of the tableau: being motionless, the men's passivity only underlines the impression they are studying me. I have the uncomfortable sensation of eyes staring at me through the mask, yet not being able to see Gas Mask Man's face. What he sees is – to him – as alien as the scene I am observing: we are looking at each other across a separation so deep and profound as to have almost no point of contact.

I'm in uncharted territory. I am overwhelmed by the feeling that I am out of my depth in a city seamed like a glacier's surface with hidden and unknowable risk, whose hollow bridges are the rapidly decaying arrogance of my confidence: that as a Western journalist I'm immune to harm. I wonder: how does he fit in? And come up with no answers that I care to contemplate for too long.

I am trying to keep my cool in Kandahar in southern Afghanistan, but the wildness here is unnerving. I am travelling through the still-burning embers of a kind of war that seems darkly unfamiliar to me. Outside the city the Americans are still engaging Taliban fleeing with their weapons; the battle for the Tora Bora caves, Osama bin Laden's alleged last redoubt, has just begun. The only visible Western troops are small groups of Special Forces.

The US-led war to bring about the ousting of the Taliban – the punishment for not delivering Osama bin Laden after the suicide attacks on the World Trade Center in New York and the Pentagon a handful of months before – is coming to an end. The Taliban's reclusive leader, Mullah Mohammed Omar, had refused US demands that bin Laden and other al-Qaeda leaders, who had been in Afghanistan in training camps since 1998, should be handed over for trial and the closure of their camps verified. He would not deliver them into non-Islamic hands. The 'War on Terror' had begun.

The media has poured into Afghanistan and its borders, to be around for the death or capture of bin Laden. But down here in the south there are no Northern Alliance forces, the loose affiliation of anti-Taliban fighters whom the majority of the reporters have been accompanying in their sweep through the country. Instead, this is where the Taliban began, capturing the city in 1994. Journalists are approaching it more cautiously. It feels like the Ground Zero of a different kind to the ruins of the Twin Towers in New York – the release point for a massive cultural, political and military temblor.

This is not, I realise, like the wars in the Balkans, where there were rudimentary, if ragged, front lines, and a kind of common European-ness to fall back on, described in conversations about football, popular music and film. There I had been able to map out the shifting geography of the conflicts. Here I have only a shadowy idea. I sense no connection to this place. No way of getting earthed. No instincts to rely upon. No one to trust confronted with 360 degrees of threat. And I feel no orientation is safe in a

37

place so recently vacated by the Taliban and their al-Qaeda allies.

And not everyone has gone. Not the Taliban at least. In the general pardon issued after Kandahar's surrender, most have simply retooled for a new reality, waiting for now to see how things turn out. So I swim through days made feverishly bright by a brain flooded with adrenaline. The sensation is similar to a lucid dream that has gone on too long: infuriating, boring and repetitive in its paranoia. The plummeting and stomach-sickening sensation of *déjà vu* is like the precursor to experiencing an epileptic fit: the feeling of balancing on the very edge, and tumbling.

But Kandahar is not a dream. It is a humming dynamo of violence both threatened, realised or imprinted with the memory of it. There are revenge shootings and rumours of other cruelties. Under the Taliban, Afghanistan was a cruel place whose interpretation of sharia law was famously brutal, not least to women. Victims were bulldozed under walls, flogged or shot to death in football stadiums. Landmines, a legacy of the war against the Soviet Union, litter the area – little plastic shapes scattered by helicopter and stuffed with high explosives – hidden by the drifting dirt. That danger is forcefully brought home when we rescue a television crew, stunned into immobility after their fixer stands on one of these mines, shredding his leg below the knee.

I am in a place where no boundaries – none that I understand, at least – exist. A place drowned for so many decades in conflict that critical social connections have been severed and lost.

It is brought home to me by a persistent irritation. The

youths who crowd round me during interviews jostle and push and try to grab my arse (as they do others) because I am wearing jeans. One day one of them manages to squeeze my balls, his hand snaking quickly and slyly between my legs from behind while I am in a crowd. I feel his fingers close around my testicles, cupping and squeezing them, until I turn and land a punch on the side of his head, suddenly terrified of the consequences, and aware of the appalled look on the face of my travelling companion, who thinks we will be killed in the ensuing brawl. There is a moment pregnant with possibilities of harm. Then the Afghan men join in, piling through the crowd of boys to thrash the youth with chopping blows, delivered from above like sabre slashes. The incident shocks me at first, until later an Afghan from the north laughs at the story and tells me the Kabuli joke about the south: how even the crows that fly over Kandahar cross their wings behind their backs.

And on top of the bizarrely jostling and sexualised atmosphere, there are the real threats. At one stage I am told that there are people who would like to kill us if we do not leave the city in a hurry. Several of us are called to an impromptu meeting at the compound we are staying in by a man speaking for the warlord-protector who is our host, who tells us we must leave. When I argue that I do not want to leave, it is this man who calls me aside and threatens me on the pretext that I have somehow offended him. His friends tell me he is a dangerous figure and I am hustled away – 'for my own safety'. Later I learn it has all been an elaborate charade. A television network with a reputation for such things has paid him to frighten other journalists out of the city, so that they can have the only images of American soldiers landing at the airport. No one is to be trusted.

A n old friend from the war in Kosovo comes to London from New York, a war reporter-turned-human rights worker. We sit in a Japanese restaurant around the corner from my office. She and her husband, who has also put covering wars behind him, are working on a project to educate reporters about the long-term psychological damage of covering conflict. The conversation turns personal. I push pieces of cooling chicken 'cutlet' around in a glutinous curry sauce. She asks me questions about what I know about the potential for damage, about my drinking and relationships. I am touched by her concern, knowing her own story – the friends lost in ambushes, murdered at checkpoints. People we knew. I am impressed: by her reinvention and that of her husband after two hard years.

I have come close so many times, always faltering at the same question. Who and what will I be if I give up? I understand at least what I don't want to be. Like the whisky-sodden sixty-year-old – a man I admire, who once slept on the floor of my room on the West Bank – still chasing wars. His age was not the issue, but an aura of neediness: to remain part of the adventure.

 veryone who has come to Afghanistan is hunting for answers: the Special Forces, the FBI and the accompanying spooks with their heavy beards and filthy clothing. The journalists too, all of them – like me –

are engaged in a vast scrabbling effort of turning over stones and collating scraps in the hope of establishing a fundamental connection to the events that started this.

The result is a kind of frenzied hunt, moving from site to site, from clue to clue, looking for any hint of a deeper explanation: fact, motive or even metaphor. Afghanistan has become a vast crime scene, littered with the forensic evidence not only of al-Qaeda's shocking and iconic moment of asymmetric warfare against the US, but also the ideas that gave birth to it. All of it is summed up in the image of one overarching outrage that points back, accusingly, to Afghanistan – a manifesto written in aviation fuel and bodies speaking of a comprehensive rejection of the West, its culture, its economics, politics of dominance and lifestyle.

For myself, I am interested in personalities not ideologies, in evidence of character and psychology told in ordinary details of lives, no matter how peripheral, to supply me with a clue to how this began. Even as I search I know this quest is grandly quixotic – that the understanding we seek is not to be found in the fragments here. And there is a notion, I suspect, that all of us subscribe to in different ways – a hidden conceit that by our excavations we can bind the wounds and mitigate the sight and sounds and smells of September 11. In some odd way, perhaps, reverse history.

It is the smell I still recall most vividly, arriving in Washington a week after the attacks: a toxic odour, sharp as a gigantic short-circuited electrical appliance – bitter on the palate – that inundated the early autumn air. A smell that drifted for miles from the Pentagon – where the third of al-Qaeda's hijacked planes came down — growing ever stronger as I skirted the scene of the attack.

One other memory persists, oddly inappropriately: it was the burning colour of the trees just turning in the hills outside DC as I drove the long miles down through Virginia to the naval base at Norfolk to stand and watch the great gathering of grey warships setting off for the war against al-Qaeda and the Taliban, a migration of steel and planes and cruise missiles.

This is why I am in Kandahar. To forge a connection between that attack and this dusty, distant city, as removed from the District of Columbia as separate planets in separate star systems. Specifically, I am in search of an impression of the personality of Mullah Omar from the things once touched and owned by the Taliban's reclusive leader. By al-Qaeda.

I had tumbled into Afghanistan without thinking too much about the consequences. After the weeks deliberating where I should be and what I should be doing, it comes down to an impetuous decision. Hearing that a handful of other journalists had driven to the border with visas that I do not have, I throw some bags into a car and race to overtake them. Then, while they queued and argued with the officials, I ignored the border guards and pushed my car past the barrier separating Afghanistan's southern desert from Pakistan into the no-man's-land between the border posts. On the wrong side of the border with nightfall approaching, no option remained but to continue, hoping the vehicles behind would catch up before too long.

My destination, a few hours away down roads littered with the detritus of three wars, was, until a few days ago, the Taliban's home base. Now the Taliban and its leader Mullah Omar have surrendered and melted away along with their al-Qaeda 'guests'. Or so the sketchy information from inside would have it. And I am racing through the dusk to reach the barely liberated city.

Darkness falls before the first headlights are visible behind us – one car, another, until finally we are travelling in a small convoy of half a dozen vehicles. I fall back and follow, relieved at no longer having to make decisions. Some of the overtaking cars have made connections in Kandahar with its new rulers, and my hope is that I can bullshit my way into the protection they have arranged. In the end it isn't necessary. As we approach the outskirts of the city, it is to be greeted by men waving from each corner and from impromptu checkpoints. They are the men loyal to the warlord Gul Agha Sherzai, who patrol the road in their pickups, flying his pennant from improvised flagpoles, armed with rocket launchers and assault rifles. Gul Agha Sherzai, it turns out, is in a power struggle for the city, although he controls the ground. We are there, his media guests, so that he can deliver a press conference and legitimise his claim.

The Taliban as an organised body has disappeared for now, and, despite the presence of the warlord's fighters, it has left a spooky and hostile city. While Mullah Omar and his senior lieutenants have fled, others have simply put their guns aside, and returned to their homes and villages. Driving into the city, my lights illuminate a gunman in their beams. He is young, not even eighteen, barely able to grow a beard, hairs visible as dark, individual tufts. He waves. As he does, I notice that he is still wearing the black turban of the Taliban, the end of which drapes down over his shoulder to settle on his rifle.

Our driver, a Kandahari who has been exiled throughout the years of the Taliban's rule in the desert city of Queta in Pakistan, not far from the border with Afghanistan, sticks his head out of the window and warns him that with his headdress he could be mistaken for an enemy by the anti-Taliban forces that now control the city. The young gunman grins shyly back at us as we are halted on the road. 'I was a Taliban last week,' he smiles, 'but I am a Taliban no longer.' I realise with a jolt that the Taliban's retreat from its centres, which I have been tracking on reports on the BBC's World Service, has not been as literal as I assumed. Instead, the situation is ambiguous. The risk is not that I will encounter a fleeing band but, rather, that thousands in the city have simply swapped sides.

But now it is daylight again. And I am on my way to the house of Mullah Omar, the Taliban's leader, which stands just outside the city. It is then that I see the man with the gas mask.

There are other questions that require answers. When I began travelling to wars I thought it was about bravery alone. I asked myself whether I had the courage to put myself in the position to write about warfare in the way that I desired. It became a test of my natural resistance. I recall that first journey from the dreary coastal city of Split in Croatia into central Bosnia during the Bosnian War in an old Lada Niva drilled with the holes made by the bullets that had pierced the driver's door, wounding its previous occupant. A journalist. The blood had been sluiced out; the car rented out again.

Those first encounters passed in passages of such fitful nerves that I doubted I was up to it, so scared I could barely work. But I returned, became used to the danger the more I saw of it, learning the rules of survival, rationalising the risk with the lies I told myself. And, gradually, I started being drawn closer to the core of violence itself. Where at first I reported from the edges about the causes and immediate consequences of conflict, I wanted soon to witness the violence itself to try to understand the emotional context of killing.

The reason for being pulled ever nearer, I believed, was that the writing about conflict I admired most was not written from the sidelines, but was the eyewitness accounts that followed, in their own way, the dictum of the great war photographer Robert Capa, who counselled: 'If your pictures aren't good enough, you're not close enough.' The same was true of writing — the essence could only be had through the closest observation. By being there. Now, later still, I have come to understand that, while there is a fundamental truth in that commandment, it also contains an element of affectation.

To be 'close enough', to be 'hardcore' (a word I had heard spoken by photographers) becomes an issue of identity. When I started out I insisted I was not a 'war reporter' but a reporter who sometimes covered wars. But as time went on I became what I had once treated with suspicion, the thing I was embarrassed to claim – a war reporter – who had bought into a whole baggage of attitudes, not least about covering fighting. Looking back, I understand at last how much those considerations reflect, with almost perfect symmetry, the soldier's deepest concern. It is not 'Will I be injured or killed?' But 'How will I perform under fire, in front of my friends and colleagues?' It is the question: 'How well will I do?'

What we call bravery is not simply a neutral attribute to be employed in pursuit of the truth. It can be a thing of necessity. Sometimes a duty. But often, in the reporter's line of work, it is selfish and self-serving. Then, courage becomes a status symbol in the group hierarchy, reflected in the war stories that reporters tell. Perhaps that is what bravery is most of the time: a performance, not as much about morality as we pretend but more concerned with how we want to feel about ourselves. Involving moments to be collected, arranged, and to be replayed, even if only privately, in the stories we rehearse inside our heads. There is something else about the business of being brave that I have understood more pressingly as the years have gone on: that my courage, like most people's, is a finite thing, to be used and to be worn out and exhausted. It not only has boundaries but an identifiable trajectory, a bell curve of knowledge both of the self and of the possible threats that peaks and diminishes after time.

When I reach it at last, it is evident that the word house does not do Mullah Omar's residence justice. It is not quite a palace, like those of Saddam and his entourage that I will later poke around in Baghdad, Mosul and Tikrit – all marble and vulgar, plated gold, matched with trite images of Saddam as Salahadin and other figures from Arab history. Rather it is a compound that is fit for a warrior-monk, and for the Taliban's reclusive warlord. I bump along the city's broken roads until the last houses run out at a narrow canal a couple of kilometres before the enclosure. Still it is not visible, screened from public curiosity – at least while the Taliban held sway – by trees and walls, set on a desert plain 1,000 metres above sea level.

To the far side of the grounds surrounding the house a line of dusty hills, capped by crumbling, yellow crags, rises in a crenellated ridge overlooking the desert floor. Further across – separated by a small pass from the main ridge – is a solitary and bulky sentinel of rock. I think the cliffs are sandstone at first until, crossing a pass between them, I can see that they are composed of a grey granite, striated with quartz bands, frosted evenly with dust. The effect is that the tops glow, burnt ochre, with the texture and colour of hashish resin.

The Afghans who stand guard around the compound – some of them former Taliban who quickly switched sides as the bombs rained in from the US planes and the Taliban's first incarnation fragmented – point out the location of the gun positions set up on the ridge to protect the compound's occupants. I try to make them out, but they are invisible in the hillsides. One of the men guarding the road introduces himself as Fakir Mohammed. He is wiry, with hollow cheeks and rotten teeth, and the long jaw and broad forehead of a saint in an Orthodox icon. He volunteers the information that Mullah Omar lived with his family, bodyguard and a personal retinue of 250 within the nearby walls. Fakir's colleague, Ramat Ullah, who is standing next to him, adds with a vicious smirk: 'He was very afraid. He lived here because he was afraid that someone in the city might try to kill him.'

The potholed road leads through the screening pines, a pretty plantation of Douglas firs, distributed among other conifers powerfully and sweetly smelling of resin in the cool air. The presence of the saplings, some of them shade trees planted beside the track, leads to me to speculate how much of this rough parkland is artifice, watered from the nearby canal. I am curious too whether the Taliban's leader walked among these woods, as I would like to, and whether he looked up at the mountains in the near distance from among the shadows of their trunks.

It is only when I am past the woods that the scale of Mullah Omar's house is revealed. I can see now that it is even more than a compound: it is the size of a small village, full of low buildings, many of them damaged by bomb and rocket strikes, which stretch for hundreds of metres in every direction. And as I walk, the compound reveals itself to be as complex as an Egyptian tomb. There are compounds within compounds, all them enclosed behind a vast brick wall almost five metres high. Towering above them all is the slender white minaret of Mullah

Omar's private mosque. From a distance it has a certain grace and elegance.

The men who have invaded the compound to wander in curious clusters through what was forbidden territory tell me that it was built two years ago by architects and engineers brought in from Pakistan. Its capacity, I estimate, is perhaps as many as 150 people. But when I get closer, I can see the decoration is gaudy, shabby and poor quality. There is nothing much to see. The guest lodgings, where senior Taliban and tribal leaders would have been housed, stands next door. Like the mosque, it is bare and Spartan, empty of any evidence for me.

What is more intriguing is the huge, ugly modern statue that squats opposite the mosque. It is a thing of odd knotted extrusions, like the exposed roots of an ancient bulldozed olive tree, or the body of some deep-sea creature washed up on the beach. There are horrible renderings too of palm trees that 'grow' out of the statue's sides and other things that drip like flowstone. For now, however, it has become a rookery for the bodyguard of the man soon to be Afghanistan's new interim Prime Minister, Hamid Karzai, invisible inside one of the buildings watched over by the US Special Forces as he receives visitors and delegations. Among the men, one sits on his perch with his head bent and cupped in his hands. If I were to ask there would be a story there. But I am not interested in the new. I am looking for a signpost to the past, not to the future.

I guess that the place I am looking for is among the rubble, beyond the mosque and the guest lodge, where I can see that the worst of the bomb damage begins. I clamber among the ruins, shocked by how even a few weeks of modern high-intensity war can render buildings into an archaeological site. I find stables, washrooms and living quarters, all framed by a vast courtyard painted with murals. I stop beside a young Afghan man with a rifle slung over his back to examine murals depicting an idealised rural Afghan landscape that line the wall of the stable yard. There is a lake and strange trees more like giant flowering plants. There are white flowers the shape of mushrooms, some white roses, and what look like cedars on the far shore. A tiny wave ripples on the lake. All images deliberately unreal. What is real, however, is the missile that has blown a hole through the scene tall as the armed youth, exposing the rough bricks so that fantasy frames the dirty hills beyond.

The central area covers a space three football pitches long and two wide. I poke around the stalls where Mullah Omar and his retinue kept their camels and horses. The stale, pungent fodder is still ankle-deep in places, scattered in drifts by the hot blast winds from the bombs that smashed into the compound. But the animals that once lived inside these quarters, better appointed than most Afghan homes, are gone – spirited away, or stolen. Perhaps even slaughtered for food. The bathrooms, too, are shattered. Now human shit dots the rubble. It is one of the sights and smells of war, the human turd, ignored by the poets and chroniclers of conflict. Where there are battles there is always shit. Excrement and empty bullet cases.

In some places there is a more unpleasant smell. One of the Afghan gunmen who now swarm about the compound, picking through the broken bricks and concrete looking for anything to loot, holds the end of his turban across his face. He tells me that there are bodies buried among the ruins, one beneath the heap where we are standing, another two close by. Then I catch it, that awful smell, hardwired into the human brain so it is tasted as it is smelled, bitter like a poison. I do not linger. Instead, I scramble in deeper, finding rooms with cots for children, bare rooms with single beds, kitchens and rooms full of inexplicable detritus. In one, its windows shattered, there are tourist posters scattered on the floor – depicting scenes of Alpine chalets, the Sydney Harbour Bridge and a mountain view printed with the English words: 'The most basic rule of economics is that bills always become due.'

At last I am led into something little more than a monk's cell in this stark, concrete mansion, which the compound's new guards inform me was Mullah Omar's bedroom. It is a small suite of private rooms painted in pink and green, that reminds me of the day room of the psychiatric ward I visited as a teenage volunteer. The cramped nature of his accommodation shows the contradictory nature of the man. In contrast to the enormous compound, it is a gloomy, damp little space he shared with one of his wives, sparsely furnished with a double bed of dark, highly varnished wood. There are a couple of small chandeliers, and cheap floor tiles.

If there were other possessions they have already been stolen. What remains is a solitary display cabinet with glass doors set into the wardrobe, fashioned from the same wood as the bed, in the style of hotel furnishing. It is empty too, save for the ammunition boxes of the fighters who now sleep here. I find them seated on what is said to have been the mullah's bed, reading, appropriately, the Koran.

There are pages from another Koran spread about the floor among the shards of broken glass. It is inconceivable that the Afghans here would have ripped out the pages and left them like this. Instead, it suggests to me a foreign hand and a certain stupid spite. Did one of the American soldiers guarding the compound do this? A petty act of frustration and retribution in having taken the compound but lost the man? I lift the pages from the floor and fold them carefully in my notebook to protect them for being trampled more. I am told it is Mullah Omar's Koran, but cannot believe he would have fled without his own. And the pages are made of a cheap paper that is already yellowing in the elements, to which the bomb blasts have opened the room.

It feels as if I have reached the centre of a maze, and arrived with the same sense of anticlimax. If this is it, then there is nothing here. Above the bed are the only two images in the room: framed lines from the Koran naming God as Allah and his prophet as Mohammed. My guide, a young man from Karzai's entourage who speaks good English, leads me out and up some concrete stairs covered in debris, past a tiny kitchen behind an ornate iron gate, and upwards to a terrace protected by panels of glass, some yellow, some clear. 'Omar liked to sleep up here sometimes,' my guide tells me. 'Sometimes he would take his breakfast here.' Yet I get no picture of him. No sense of connection to this spectral figure. Instead, a doubt is creeping in, triggered by the pages of 'Omar's Koran'. How much of this is true?

I ask myself how these men would know unless they were once part of his retinue? With each thing I see, he becomes paradoxically more distant.

Some of the gunmen produce a crude wooden ladder and take me on to the roof itself. From here I can see the full scale of Mullah Omar's fiefdom and the devastation wrought on the compound by the American bombing. A little way off, a vast pile of tractor tyres has fallen through the roof. They were heaped above a reception room for Mullah Omar's family, I am told, in the mistaken belief that a US bomb might bounce off them. It is a curiously childish notion. When the bomb flew in, weighing 1,000 lb or more, it simply punched right through.

There is nothing here at Mullah Omar's house but a footprint in the shifting dirt and the smell of death and human shit. If there were incriminating evidence here linking Mullah Omar directly to the September 11 attacks on New York and Washington, it has long since been whisked away. Others have already combed these ruins. This is attested to by the scorch marks left by the shotgun blasts, used by the US Special Forces to break the few locks with solid slugs they carry for the purpose. Whatever I had hoped for is not here. Instead it is as lacking in life and as etiolated as a skeleton excavated from the dust of the high desert. The things that this place says I already know from the cuttings in my laptop. And that is very little. The thousands of printed words occlude rather than reveal. They form an outline around the space where a personality should be. Bin Laden's friend Omar, the man blinded in one eye by shrapnel fighting the Soviets, who led the Taliban to power, was always a cipher whose power was expressed most meaningfully by his reclusive absence. In this house he seems no more in focus than in the single, blurred photograph that I have seen – of a thin, straggling figure wrapped in a cloak.

There are no hidden revelations here. Whatever I was seeking to explain what brought me to this war is as absent as the house's owner. No questions can be asked of scattered bricks and collapsed concrete. What I am seeing is war's surface reality, striking and obvious. It remains as hollow as a bombed-out building if I cannot connect with the life that once inhabited it. But I am not ready to give up on my search.

The brand new padlock and chain on the gates are discouraging at first. They stand out bright amid the dull colours of old wood and peeling paint and rust and dusty concrete. I yank at the lock in the vague hope that the mechanism will snick apart, but nothing budges. It is a few days after the encounter with the man in the gas mask, and I am standing at the entrance to one of al-Qaeda's training camps inside the city, hidden away among the bigger family compounds. The padlock and chain were placed here, I suspect, by one of the US and British Special Forces units scouring the city to secure al-Qaeda sites for further investigation. But the man we are with is anxious to get us in. In any case, in the chaotic aftermath of conflict

I have no qualms about breaking in. I had come nervously and after lengthy deliberation to the door of his house in a suburb of Kandahar because I had heard he had captured a foreign fighter from al-Qaeda whom he is torturing for his pleasure. He is polite but evasive when I ask about the captive. There is a hardness and cruelty about his face that tells me not push the questioning too far.

He says at first vaguely that his captive is 'gone now'. The 'now' I take to mean he was alive and is now dead. Pressed further, he smiles with a simulacrum of sweetness and says the man did not exist in the first place. It feels like an existential riddle. What I know, however, is that the man standing in front of me boasted to my driver a few hours earlier about 'his prisoner' and his cruel treatment of him. I know that he is lying and has probably already killed the man. I sense too that he knows I am aware of his deceit and that I have no power to force the issue of his lying. I am uncomfortable in his presence. In this large and violent city, with no help nearby, it is unwise to argue.

But this is why I have driven to this anonymous suburb – in the hope of meeting a live member of al-Qaeda, even one who has been beaten up. Standing here, however, I doubt my motives. Confronted by the smiling, boasting captor, I am not even sure what my plan is, in any case, if I am taken to meet his prisoner. Do I stare at him like an exotic and dangerous animal? And ask him what – and with what prospect of an answer? Where is Mullah Omar or Osama bin Laden? Did he know about the planned attack on the Twin Towers? How does he feel about that attack? Suddenly the prospect of these questions is as meaningless as the ruins of Mullah Omar's compound. So when the man 'who isn't holding him' asks me if I would like to see an al-Qaeda training camp he says is situated nearby, the distraction feels like relief.

The training camp is, it turns out, almost opposite his house, a compound much like his own, surrounded by a tall wall topped by a few strands of wire and guarded by the sealed double gate. I can see little beyond the metal doors, so my 'host' sends for a man to scale the wall who arrives after a few minutes with a ladder. I follow him over the wall and land on the other side in a small concrete courtyard. Broken paths wind among a few sad flowerbeds planted with diseased rose bushes. I ask our hard-faced host if there are any landmines. He shakes his head, almost offended by the suggestion, and I am curious how he would know. But when I walk across to examine some of the roses in the corner of the compound, the men shout to warn me about mines.

I collect myself and look properly around. The 'camp' is small in scale, a series of small rooms whose doors open on to a central area on three sides around the yard. I calculate that there is accommodation here for between twenty and thirty men, depending on how many of them shared the rooms. I am not sure what I was expecting – something bigger and more complicated to fit the image in my media-tised imagination of those behind September 11. But that is the very point of asymmetric warfare. A clip from an AK-47 assault rifle fired by a child can down a multimillion-dollar helicopter and its expensively trained crew; a cheaply improvised bomb placed by the road can destroy a Bradley fighting vehicle. It is the rebuke of the have-nots in the hierarchy of ownership of high-tech military technology to those who have.

The rooms are little bigger than cells, dark, windowless hidey holes with mud-brick walls, empty of possessions. There are some bowls and a handful of other eating utensils scattered among the bushes. I am still unsettled by the business with the mines. I am nervous too of other booby traps and tripwires and do not venture into the dingy cubicles. Until, that is, I notice the remains of bonfire spilling out of the entrance to a larger room set a little to one side.

When I enter the room, after running my hand tentatively around the doorframe to check for a trigger wired to a grenade, it is immediately obvious that the bonfire's fuel was a stack of paper piled as high as my waist and around two metres in circumference. It is made up of documents and school notebooks with their covers ripped off to hide the identities of whoever recently owned them. Which makes me question if al-Qaeda's recruits – the young Pakistanis, Chechens, Jordanians and even Europeans – who came to this camp, sat seriously on the ground with their biros when their training commenced and carefully outlined their names on the covers like good pupils. It is so strongly suggested that I can picture it: the bearded trainer handing out schoolbooks and pens on the first day of camp. The human traces reveal themselves, through the sympathy of my imagination. Not monsters or automatons, not aliens – these students – only people. Even such as these.

The fire itself has been a hurried job. While the books

and other documents in the centre are charred into fragile blackened leaves that crumble in my fingers those closer to the edge are almost untouched. Whoever constructed this pyre dumped the piles of paper on too quickly in his haste and smothered the blaze. When I disturb it, the thin sketchings of smoke still rising from the centre of the collapsing pyramid of paper suggest that whoever did this only recently made their escape.

I take some of the exercise books from the edge of the bonfire. Most are written in Arabic or in Urdu, but as I sift through the pile other nationalities emerge. My companion Daniel turns up a notebook written in Russian. Then my eye is drawn to an undamaged document. It is written in English. As I scan the words, the spellings and misspellings make it clear that the author has grown up in the UK. The writing is largely in two different-coloured pens – red and green biro – in an untidy hand that has not quite decided on its style. I flick through page after page and understand that these are the meticulously transcribed instructions for a van bomb: chemical formulae for making the explosives; annotated circuit diagrams; travel arrangements and instructions on how to live while the operation is being planned.

As I squat uncomfortably and read, a personality slowly emerges from behind the notes. I see him in the way I could not see Mullah Omar even in his ruined compound – a figure wavering between fear and determination. As I continue, this tutorial in the fine detail of commissioning mass murder, a record of lessons conducted by a master bomb maker and the English-speaking activist he is instructing, is transformed into a post-modernist tale. It is a murder mystery in which the murder has yet to occur.

Out of these scraps and diagrams, a young man (I assume) emerges. He is attentive, educated but not entirely competent. At first I think he must have a background in electrical engineering but then I see that he does not even know which way to wire one of the components and has to note the colour-coding marked on one side of it. I have a picture of him sitting in his small group, cross-legged on the ground, tired from the constant lectures, perhaps a little sick from the food. He is feeling dirty. His foot is going numb with pins and needles from the effort of sitting cross-legged for so long. At other times I sense a feeling of exhilaration and confidence as he thinks – 'I will do this'.

I read on. He makes mistakes in his practical exercises in building the circuitry for the radio remote detonator. He is corrected, revisiting his notes, adding observations in a smaller, neater hand, often underlined to put right his errors. It is too complicated for him, so his teacher points out details on the components for him to remember and he writes it down: 'head facing down, writing towards you'. His mind wanders. Sometimes the circuit diagrams are drawn in tight, tidy grids. Then the pen wanders into a messier scrawl, as he grows bored – I surmise – copying from the master diagram. And there is other stuff here. There are simplistic checklists, similar in tone to the documents found in the luggage of the September 11 suicide hijackers that tell him how to behave while living undercover.

Later, in the compound where I am staying I read and reread the document, not quite able to believe what I have

59

found. There are calculations in his spidery hand of how much boxes of detonators weigh, and how safely to handle the explosives so as not to trigger the main load, a van full of ANFO – an ammonium nitrate–fuel oil mix – the easily home-cooked explosive used by the IRA, FARC and ETA. He writes 'Business Plan' but what he means is something more deadly: 'Connect the wires properly,' he writes. 'Isolate connecting wires (Sellotape). Constantly refer to diag[ram], nobody work alone, const[ant] double checking.'

My man – for I feel oddly possessive about this insubstantial figure – is suddenly not alone. Behind the fragile assembly of this personality I have constructed, I sense even more insubstantial figures pressing, invisible to me but real nonetheless. And he is not concerned only with the engineering and chemistry that will make his bomb work. There is his cover to be prepared, which he sketches out in such vague details that I become more and more persuaded that he is very young. He tells himself he needs to travel and earn money, perhaps to fund the operation. He even suggests that he needs to find a girlfriend. While I know that this is his cover story, there is an odd tension here, something that does not quite sit with the seriousness of the bomb-making enterprise. It is as if all of these, the terrorist training camp included, are markers on a gap-year adventure that, if he can keep his nerve, will end in slaughter. Like a schoolboy, he lists and ticks off the attributes he will need to carry off his attack, that simply by being written out make me curious whether these are qualities he feels lacking in himself or whether he has been taken aside by his trainers to have his failings pointed out to him. He lists 'confidence', 'no panic' and 'don't be afraid'. Perhaps, in the act of being ticked, they are an assertion – confirmation to himself that he is up to the business of mass killing. It is that question again. *How will I do?* At setting off a massive bomb. In the city where I live.

I am in a pub near Sheffield when it does happen, having dinner after a day spent in the hills with no signal on my phone. Calling home, my wife is amazed I have not heard the news: a series of suicide explosions that have struck the Underground and London's buses. More then fifty dead. I can't believe the news at first while knowing it is true. When the information does sink in I sit thinking about the note-book and the camp while watching the images of the attacks on the pub's television. I think about the training camps, the ideology and indoctrination whose function was this end. The result is subtly different from how I imagined it would be. And yet the same.

There is another insistent little note that I come across as I flick through the pages in the training camp in Kandahar. It is as emphatically negated as the others are ticked: 'No *ijtihad*'. At first I do not understand what he means by this expression. When I look it up, I discover it is a word that refers to a movement of theological revision in Islam, a reinterpretation of Islamic principles by religious scholars that in the formal sense ceased centuries ago. When I delve deeper it begins to accrue complex levels of meaning, which boil down to an admonition delivered to the author – either by himself or by his trainers – not to try to reason about what he is doing, but to stick to what he has been taught in the fundamentalist religious training at the camp, and to his instructions. There will be no debate.

I am horribly aware that this is not a remote journalistic exercise. The references are opaque but I see them coalesce in front of my eyes. He reminds himself what to do on re-entering the UK via Waterloo. Then there are scribbled notes on how to find Moorgate in the City of London, a financial symbol as powerful in economic and cultural terms as the Twin Towers; a reminder to buy an A–Z and a business directory. There is no doubt what all this means. If there ever was, it is blown apart by a terse sentence: 'Connect load . . . Turn SF2 on. Leave as fast as you can.'

Blast Waves

But do you want to go?' That question. What do I want? I am sitting in a lay-by in the Peak District. It is too hot to climb, our plan for the afternoon. We had tried to squirrel our way into a band of shade beneath the cliffs to get out of the sun but even the rock was radiating a suffocating warmth. So we had abandoned it, our last effort to grab a few more pleasant hours together before being split up. Now we are pulled over in a car smelling of bodies and someone else's dog, crushed by the heat and the inevitability of an unplanned separation. A plan to spend a month's holiday showing Emily, my American partner, around Britain ahead of her going to Iraq for seven months, has disintegrated after two days of prevaricating. We are already heading back towards London, no longer driving to Scotland. It is clear to both of us that a decision has already been made. With the outbreak of war in Lebanon what I want is to be on a plane. I would simply prefer that I did not have to make a decision.

How many times have I found myself in this position? The missed Christmases and family birthdays. The months that add up to years spent apart from my children, my ex-wife — always with the vague promise to myself that next year, perhaps, I'll commit to a lifestyle more settled, more considerate. I recognise that it is largely a question of ego, a misplaced sense of self-importance – if it is a big story I should be there. There is the quiet drama of preparation to be enjoyed. Dragging out my body armour from the cupboard where it is stored, laying out the cables, checking my first-aid kit. Objects that litter my flat in boxes, crowding shelves, invested with a meaning beyond their actual function: the battered camera bodies, covered with black tape to seal the buttons from dust; sat phones, torches and knives; the heavy microphone. Things that attest to who I am, and want to be. Even the North Face duffel bag, constructed from heavy, black vinyl, is a badge, ubiquitous on the baggage carousels of the world's worst places, the same model toted by journalists and security details. There is a calming ritual to the assembly of these parts, an awareness that I am committed to a course of action. But for all my selfishness I know there is another part of me, a real portion that would rather not be heading to the airport, would prefer to stay at home and sustain relationships.

As the years go on there is a feeling that drags ever heavier: a special sensation of exhaustion; an anticipation of the tiredness to come. After doing this so long I feel my stamina for awfulness is being worn out. It is as if I have accumulated a reservoir of a soul-sick tiredness that – once back in the war zones – I can feel rising, a welling physical sensation that is greyly threatening and leaves me shattered and depressed.

Is this what I want? There are drifts of smoke rising like filaments of church incense in the near distance, soft, worn-out traces that struggle to be seen against the sea

haze. More sharply in focus are the rooftops and apartment blocks of Beirut spread out below me, intersecting
areas of brightness and shade defined by the late afternoon light, visible not as identifiable buildings but as
segments of colour. I see a digital picture blown up too
large, a vista of magnified pixels, revealing its architecture, the organising lines of a mysterious code. It is the
perspective of the sniper, the artillery observer, or of the
bomber strapped into the harness of his F-16 and diving
to ten thousand feet, and lower, to release his bomb. What
I cannot see, however, is the damage of the bomb strikes
and I am puzzled that so much energy from the air raids
of the night before could be expended for so little visible
effect.

Further in the distance there is more dense smoke visible
where I calculate Beirut's airport must be. Where this war
began. But none of it connects with the reality that I have
come to see. Instead, I am stuck with the idea in my head
from the television pictures of the Israeli raids that began
this war – monochrome images taken from bombsight
cameras of that first wave of Israeli jets attacking a surprised
city then released to the world's media. Homework turned
in. They showed the detonations on the international
airport's runways, expanding rapidly like accelerated
images of opening flowers. Symmetrical. Awful. And beautiful.

It is the afternoon after I have arrived to cover Israel's
short, brutal summer war against Hizbollah in Lebanon in
2006 – thirty-three days and nights of bombs, rockets and
coastal shelling. I have driven up into the hills overlooking

Beirut with two friends, looking for a gallery seat from which to watch the bombing for a few hours. Together we sit on a brambly ridge of red earth above the southern suburbs looking down towards the airport and beyond to the Mediterranean, a shimmering backdrop behind the runways. Two of us are new in town, a little late arriving for the war. I am anxious that it may be winding down before I have had a chance to see it. What feels necessary, sitting among the fragrant bushes, is an affirmation of violence: to make the conflict real. We smoke cigarettes, waiting for Israeli jets to appear and strike the jumble of apartment blocks below – the place where Hizbollah's fighters are. But Israel has announced a slowing of its air attacks on the capital to allow the evacuation of foreign passport holders in the flotilla of warships and ferries we can see sitting far out from the harbour.

I am not passive and neutral in this violence. I have a horrible investment in something happening to justify my being there. Not just my travel, and Emily deserted, friend-less in a strange city. I need something to happen, not simply as a justification of these decisions. Without a war I feel my identity diminished. My being here will be fraudulent. If a bomb falls, I will be 'working'. But this evening the sky remains silent. I experience a shaming disappoint-ment.

When I sort out my orientation in the city, it turns out the smoking buildings are located in Haret Hreik, the most bombed of the southern suburbs. It is next to the airport where the war began in earnest with the Israeli raids on the runways in retaliation for a Hizbollah raid along the border.

The following morning I go down to join Hizbollah's daily media tour of the previous night's destruction – for in the end, after night has fallen, the jets have come. It feels fake, shuffling through rubble and broken glass that crunches under my boots with sixty or so other journalists, led by a couple of young men from the movement's political wing who herd us in a school crocodile through the destruction. But then a corner is turned and there is no avoiding the devastation that the falling bombs have delivered. I write in my notebook: 'Twelve-storey building to my left – four ground floors scorched where cars had flamed and burned. Cars scattered around an open area capped by a collapsed motorway bridge. Beyond, in a rough semicircle more housing blocks. One painted a brick colour. Rest cream and green. Whole floors blown out.'

There is a rattling on a balcony above. Someone is beginning to clean up the ruins of their home. I watch a middle-aged man, the sleeves of his shirt carefully rolled up, working a broom amid the broken glass and concrete, pushing the pieces through the bars to fall in a dusty cascade on to the street. I feel a moment of guilt at the cold business of observation, broken only by a sudden tension in the air. The Hizbollah guides are sprinting and shouting: 'Khatar!' (Danger) 'F-sataash!' (F-16). And so I run.

I am still confronted with the question I asked myself in wars before: in Afghanistan and Kosovo and Bosnia. The same question troubles me now, in Lebanon. I know that it is not enough simply to ask: What is war? It is how to relate, in a way that feels honest and satisfactory, what I have seen and felt and give a shape to it. The constraints of reporting – the clinical assessment of facts and of conversations gathered – is no longer enough.

At first I thought it was possible, with time and application, to assemble an understanding of conflict by following the clues and the signposts: politics and history, psychology and social impact. All I have assembled through this gathering of knowledge is a thing stuck together from its broken parts. Its animate existence lies elsewhere. Not in the large concepts but in the fine detail of lives lived amidst violence. I am driven back to a single image from the Second World War diaries of the Russian novelist and reporter Vasily Grossman: he is travelling to the front for the first time where he encounters a startled chicken fleeing from an army clerk's office during an attack, its wings stained dark with ink.

We talk too often about war as an alien sphere, divorced from ordinary life. We describe conflict in its specialised grammar of planning and battles, objectives won and lost, legitimacy and war crimes, with a familiar litany of damaged places, characters and societies. What is missing is the texture: how conflict smells and feels and tastes; how people go about their lives, and what happens in their heads. Too often the life of war is absent from our descriptions – the ink is scrubbed from the feathers.

he first intimation of violence is usually anticipation. Not fear. Instead, it jabs at the consciousness in pinpricks. Niggling questions that unfold into moments of concern then fade into the static of an internal voice, talking too loud, too fast, as it moves on to new anxieties. It is present the instant you cross into a war zone. In the dark of the Lebanese night the taxi driver who has agreed to ferry me to Beirut from the Syrian border stops the car occasionally to consult with the other drivers in our small convoy. He is a big man, with a belly that hangs over his jeans. It is the height of summer and humid. Although it is past midnight my flesh sticks to the plastic where my arms touch seats broken into uncomfortable shapes by the thousands of passengers who have used them. They no longer seem to fit the human body. A physical displacement to match my mental state.

I wind down the window of the old yellow Mercedes to let in some air. I can see little. The few bomb craters that we pass, where the Israeli jets have hit the road close to the border, identify themselves only by what they are not: dark vacancies where there should be tarmac, roads and the up-ramps to bridge spans. As we pass them, our head-lamps briefly illuminate a few trucks. They look as if they have been crazily parked, jack-knifed at odd angles. But even that quick glance reveals that they have been burned and wrecked. There is one word in Arabic that I do under-stand from the taxi drivers' intense conversations as we make our stop—start progress towards Beirut, a word that emphasises that this is new and dangerous terrain. It means 'missile'.

The war I am entering is not the one I had anticipated. A year before, in the aftermath of the assassination of Lebanon's Prime Minister Rafik Hariri in a massive car bomb blamed on the Syrian security services, which once controlled this country, it had seemed that inter-communal violence was the biggest risk. No one, least of all Hizbollah, the heavily armed Shia movement, anticipated that their actions would trigger a war with Israel by the ambush and kidnapping of Israeli soldiers across the border to trade for prisoners. Part of a tit for tat of mutal violence and retribution.

The road after the Masnaa border crossing, on the route from Damascus to Beirut, is denied to us by bomb damage, so our journey winds in a long diversion around the ruined bridges and motorways. Their wrecked shapes appear out of the night, illuminated in a flat, smashed contrast, as if painted by Picasso. Apart from the damage and the diversions, it appears freakishly normal as we pass through villages and then hit the road to the coast that will take us south to Beirut. There are porch lights shining in on homes and restaurants. In ordinary times, the driver lets me know, the journey from Damascus to Beirut takes less than three hours. Tonight it will take six.

I would like to sleep. Sometimes I drift off. Then the stupidity of this night journey overwhelms me: we are nocturnal prey scuttling beneath the hunting F-16s with their laser-guided bombs. That sense is reinforced when I notice, after a while, that on some sections of the journey the other drivers in their yellow cabs are hanging back while we drive ahead, looping down the mountain roads. They are letting my car go first to test the safety of the route. Because my driver is the only vehicle with a paying passenger tonight, the others have decided he should take the risks for all of them. If any bombs are going to fall, then they should fall on him.

A blast from an explosion works like this. When certain materials – petrol fumes, gas or even dust – mix in air in the right proportions they can be detonated. In chemistry, this is known as the explosive limit. The flammable material burns in the oxygen, causing an instantaneous and massive heating of the air in the immediate vicinity. The air expands at supersonic speed, creating a blast wave that moves with the force of something solid. The same principles apply to a 1000 lb bomb dropped by an F-16, to a missile or to an artillery shell. The only difference is how the explosive materials are contained and shaped, designed to maximise the lethal and destructive power. As the blast wave moves away from its immediate source, it fragments any objects in its path, including its own casing, hurling them outwards.

Societies in conflict have their own explosive limits. It occurs when the fuel of hatred, of fear of the other, victimisation or sense of hopelessness builds to its critical moment. Then the parts required for the reaction become perfect and dangerous. It can be built like a bomb through politics and propaganda, the careful management of a group's cultural identity so that it explodes into sectarianism or mass murder.

The 'refugee moment' is one of these limits. Social scientists and anthropologists talk of a 'kinetic model' of refugee dispersal resulting from an overwhelming rush of fear, sometimes hysterical in nature, where the final process of deciding to flee is compressed, often into a handful of hours or even minutes, with no notion of the consequences. People will stay in their homes until the meter of what is bearable reaches a certain point. It may be an increase in the level of hostility, or the depletion of resources. It may be that a deadline they have given themselves for the situation to calm down has passed, or it may be a rumour that they are 'next' to be bombed or massacred or overrun. When that limit is passed, it requires almost nothing to trigger a fugue state in the group psychology – a cascading, exponential collapse of confidence. It begins with individuals and spreads to family groups and villages and towns. It is the panicked perception, 'If I don't flee now, I might not escape', that spreads like a shock wave until whole communities are atomised and forced violently outwards.

When the bomb comes down, the air shudders with the energy of its explosion, billions of energised particles in motion. I feel the last spasm of the blast wind across a kilometre of rooftops, rank with an odour of burned explosives that catches in my throat. There is just enough time as the Israeli jet dives in to release the bomb, suddenly visible, to take cover and hope I'm not too close. Hadi Fakih, a paediatrician at the Sheikh Gharib Harb hospital in the city of Nabatiyeh, thirty kilometres from the border, ducks with his colleagues behind a wall. A fluttering of white coats and scrubs. There are no children in his hospital these days – there are only a handful in the city, the children of fighters who will not send their families away – so he spends his time working on the few emergency cases brought in. Later, I learn they are largely fighters whom we are kept assiduously away from. His cases are, he says, a textbook listing of the effects of high explosives on the human body. He recites, like a student being tested: 'lacerations and crushing injuries . . . and burns . . .' He halts, not from the struggle to remember, but from the exhausting business of treatment in a war zone.

'Usually the bombing starts after midnight. Usually it hits apartment houses. So I get up at 3 a.m. That's when the casualties start coming in. Until seven. We're used to it now. I sleep in the afternoon.' It is afternoon now, however, and Hadi is awake. Although he is young – just thirty – his skin has the translucent, sweaty look of illness, wasted with tiredness. A camera with a long zoom lens is passed from hand to hand to examine the smoking shell of the building high on a green ridge in a neighbourhood called Harouf-tul. One of the porters says it was once a home for handicapped children.

Hadi continues. 'Yesterday it was injuries from flying glass. A bomb hit near a three-storey apartment block and there was still a family in the first floor.' After so many days of bombing he struggles to recall even something so recent. '. . . a broken leg. And burns . . . All kinds, you know . . .' Hadi says with genuine puzzlement words I have heard before, not just from Lebanese civilians but also from appalled European diplomats: 'I don't know how they choose the areas they bomb. They seem to me to be civilian areas.'

Hadi talks about his wife Lina and six-month-old son, Ali, who are now in the neighbouring city of Sidon. 'I kept them with me here in Nabatiyeh for nine days. Then the electricity and water in the area where we live ran out. The people who are still here are crowded together in small houses.' They talk three times a day by telephone. But Nabatiyeh is not a safe place. Hadi knows that and so does his wife. What happens here is reported daily on the local radio and television. The night before we meet was a bad one. It is the reason I came – in search of the bodies from Israeli raids that hit two family houses. So Hadi and Lina speak on their mobiles and tell each other loving lies of reassurance.

A daylight bombing raid so close by has sucked the air out of our conversation. The words that are left come sluggish with the special enervation of fear, an unreal feeling like the weakening creep of hypothermia or heat exhaustion. An artillery barrage opens up on the villages to Nabatiyeh's south, towards the border, with a ferocious intensity that continues throughout the day. Each bracketed set dazes me more, a flurry of boxer's punches. I say my goodbyes to the doctors and I leave to wander a city that growls and thunders like the calving of icebergs from the blasts beyond the hills. At a bombed aid station is the husk of a burned ambulance, its brakes melted to glittering silver puddles that have solidified as they have run towards the drain. I touch a smooth hardened surface and drag my finger across one, captivated.

Nabatiyeh is largely a ghost town, exuding the science-fiction emptiness peculiar to areas where there is fighting and the people have gone. All the soft tissue of life has been dissolved, leaving behind only the hard carapace: houses, cars and powerless streetlights. Not totally empty. On one street, a handful of tough-looking men, Hizbollah fighters, slip into a house with looks that discourage us from knocking at the door to talk to them. Instead, I tour the city's hospitals, as oddly silent as the city itself, still searching for the dead and injured. No one wants to talk until at last I am directed to the Ghandour hospital. It is here that the women and children who have stayed behind are hiding. Every night around four hundred squeeze into the basement. Many are now too frightened to leave at all and sleep in exhausted little clusters on blankets on the floor or on thin mattresses. Other sit, stunned, in chairs after another sleepless night of fear.

I ask about wounded fighters and I am told that none have been brought in. But then my driver overhears the hospital's guards discussing how we can be kept away from the fighters being treated somewhere within the hospital's depths. Instead, I am led upstairs to meet twenty-one-year-old Shireen Hamza. A pale blue cap covers her head and she sits stiffly immobile on the bed as though she no longer knows how to arrange her limbs. The night before, two Israeli bombs hit her house and that of a neighbour killing her father Ahmed, aged fifty-eight, her brother, Mohammed, aged nineteen, and her forty-five-year-old mother as well as three neighbours, fighters, as I later over-hear. She lists the names of the dead and the survivors and I mark them with crosses and circles. 'We heard the first air strike,' she says, shuffling recollections so that they fit, pieces in a scattered jigsaw. 'I was screaming, but no one could hear me. Then there was the second air strike and I knew my brother was dead and my father was lying there under the bricks. I said: "Please don't go to sleep!" So . . . what happened?' She is confused. 'I thought it was a long time. I was on the floor. I woke up and the second raid came so fast and people ran away. My home is on one floor. But the neighbours' house was levelled. The house was levelled. And we are ordinary civilians. We stayed here because my dad is a man who is not easily scared. My mum was scared. But we thought . . . we are ordinary civilians. No one is going to kill us.'

As we are leaving Nabatiyeh I visit the bomb-damaged souk, a place of once beautiful old buildings. In places the bomb blasts have sucked out the shop fronts' metal shutters into pregnant, buckled shapes. In others the same explosions have sliced open the metal with white-hot fragments. A handful of old men are sitting in one street near the souk's centre selling ratty vegetables that no one comes to buy. I chat to them for a while and they persuade my friends, two Americans who live in Beirut, to take a cat that has been abandoned by its owners. It is a famished calico kitten that crawls around the back of the car as we drive back to Beirut. Strange refugee.

Back in the capital, we stop at the vet, Canycat. As the young owner examines the kitten he directs me to the huge terraces of wooden cages that line his shop. A whole wall of cats in boxes. They are mainly older cats – black, cream, ginger and grey. They sit miserably confined, or fight to find an exit, or paw at the cages above and below. All have been abandoned as their owners fled. An elderly woman who has remained, and who has brought her cat in to be wormed, tsk-tsks that Beirut has come to this.

Blast injuries, as Dr Hadi Fakih can tell you, fall into three main categories. The first kind of wound is caused by proximity to the huge pressure of the blast wave. I remember a course that I once went on designed to teach me how to survive in conflict zones. It was held in a house in the English countryside owned by a religious foundation, whose quietly introverted students would stroll the grounds while we were subjected to vigorous and noisy scenarios involving snipers, explosions, kidnappings and wounds that squirted fake arterial blood from hidden tubes. In the classroom, one winter's morning, the former Marine teaching the first-aid course using a teacher's white board explained the closest zone of an explosion – where primary injuries take place. 'If you're 'ere,' he said with a certain gruesome relish, indicating the innermost circle he had drawn, 'then there ain't nothing left of you.'

Except, of course, there is. I've seen it. The veal-coloured scraps, peculiarly translucent, turning slowly grey, plastered against walls and on to roofs and cars, sticking unbidden to your boots; the fragments of jaw and skull and bone that are flung to sit hidden in gardens, gutters and playgrounds. In the primary blast area, the gases move like a solid object. When they hit the chest, the sternum and ribcage are driven forcefully back into the spine, compressing the lungs. The diaphragm is pushed upwards by the gut, squeezing the heart and lungs still more. Internal haemorrhaging occurs, but less obvious are the constellations of air bubbles forced into the bloodstream that can linger for up to half an hour in the main arteries. Tissues of different densities are sheared one from the other by the movement of the blast wave. Tendons, muscle and even bone are tugged and stretched beyond the limits of their tensile strength and snap, pulling limbs from bodies.

But it is the secondary effect of the blast that is the most obvious and often the most deadly: injuries sustained through shrapnel – war's biggest killer. It is not just fragments of the weapon itself. The blast wave turns ordinary objects into lethal projectiles: splinters of trees, car parts and plumbing fixtures, bricks, shattered sinks and kitchen implements; pens, keys, the glass from picture frames, tools, ornaments, pieces of human bone. Finally, there is the third kind of injury, sustained from being thrown by the blast wind – that breaks limbs and cracks open skulls.

One day in the hospital in Tyre I meet two shy young women whose faces have been blast-damaged. Particles of dirt have been driven by the explosion under their skin to pit and pepper it like dark acne. Their faces are swollen, fluid-filled and yellow as if they have been punched repeatedly. One has a black eye. They are terrified that their looks have been ruined and hide their faces behind screening, embarrassed fingers until my friend Stephanie Sinclair sits down and holds their hands for an hour and gently tells them how wounds heal and that their faces will recover.

t first I make Beirut my base, watching as Lebanon fragments beneath the bombing into a broken mirror whose shards reflect the fragile sectarian identity fixed since the country's fifteen-year-long civil war bled out in 1990. As the disintegration of war takes hold under the Israeli bombing runs, the roads are cut, leaving Beirut separated from the south and from the Bekaa Valley to the east. Its neighbourhoods, Christian, Shia and Sunni, draw back into themselves, separated by their old hostilities. Those displaced from the south, and from the big Shia suburbs of Beirut, have become like shrapnel, violently scattered by the fighting, so many pieces tearing open Lebanon's old wounds. The displacement of the fighting sets up the dynamic for new tensions and for new conflict.

The capital itself seems to have been sandblasted clean of its dirty vitality. The heaving nightclubs have been emptied of the girls with their surgically uniform noses and breasts. The Saudi princes, who come to Beirut for the summer to drink and fuck, have long gone, their boats abandoned in the marina. The well-heeled Lebanese, who cannot or choose not to leave, or who do not have a second passport to join the anxious, grumbling queues of fleeing foreigners waiting down at the harbour to be ferried to the warships, head for their villas in the mountains, or check out to Syria to sit out the war and count their losses.

I wander down the Corniche, the city's seafront esplanade of hotels and ice-cream shops, to find it emptied by the fear of shelling by the Israeli warships and Apache helicopters that have struck along the coast. Further back from the seafront, in a safer location (in the collective judgement of the city) – around the area known as Hamra – there are cars still cruising the streets while, in the cafés, elegant Lebanese sit reading *L'Orient-Le Jour* and the *Daily Star*, with an attempt at insouciance. It is the affectation of a city that has survived the depredations of long civil war that this one is merely an inconvenience. But one eye is on the television.

It is the same story in Gemayze and Achrafieh in the city's Christian east. My friend Mitch, a bluff exile from D.C. who has made his home in Beirut, telephones me one morning to report the comment delivered by his Christian baker when asked for breakfast croissants. 'No croissants 'til this war is over,' the baker snaps back. A statement of fact, it is also a challenge to the conflict's suspension of the trappings of civilised life: war is not a country for eating pastries in. There is a dangerous fuck-you attitude in these Christian neighbourhoods too. Not towards the war but directed at the Shia, whom they blame for bringing another war to Lebanon just when things seemed to be improving. In the Starbucks in Gemayze, there are young Christian guys with gelled hair, tight T-shirts and arms pumped up from pushing weights, who loathe the Shia guerrillas of Hizbollah. They are children and grand-children of the Phalangists – the *Kataeb* – whose supporters ignited the flames of the civil war three decades before. They watch the news and cheer the Israeli bombs as they crash into their own city and shout '*Yallah*!' – 'Let's go!' They will only get angry with the Israelis later, when bombs start landing close to their neighbourhoods. When the petrol for their cars runs out. And when the last major highway out of town is cut.

There are rumours. Some of them turn out to be true.

Of subtly undermining text messages transmitted from
Israel that ask: Do you feel Hizbollah is to blame? Press 1
for 'yes' and 2 for 'no'; of fliers dropped by aircraft in the
south demanding that the villages 'evacuate', and of a voice
that breaks through on the radio channels delivering the
same warnings. I hear it one day as my car is weaving
through the bomb craters that pock the coastal highway
heading south. It intrudes into the news, metallic, harsh
and alien, demanding: 'Where is Hassan Nasrallah
[Hizbollah's leader]?' I hear stories of collaborators too,
men paid by Israel to toss plastic discs next to Hizbollah
buildings that emit a signal the bomber crews can see.

I make an audit of the bodies I have seen as an
exercise in assessing the damage that it has done
to my psyche. If I have a count of the corpses then,
perhaps, I might have a better understanding of what I have
become over the years and of the filth that has stuck to me.
It is largely a tally of blast victims. The fifty dead after the
car bombing at Kerbala in central Iraq, spilling out of
the morgue into the dust outside; not even a full tally of the
dead that day. Then there were the bodies dragged out of
the flaming ruins of the Mount Lebanon Hotel in Baghdad
that exploded a few hundred metres from where I was
passing, so close that I arrived on the scene clutching the
bottle of wine I was taking to dinner with friends nearby.
There were the dismembered bodies, impossible to count,
covered with carpets, scattered about the highway the
evening we drove into the same city in our little convoy

during the invasion of Iraq. I stop counting when I reach three hundred.

By an act of will, I make the observation of violent death a deliberately mechanical process. Blink. An emotional curtain comes down like a camera shutter. The distance is preserved while I go about the business of looking. Of course, it is delusional. Because once seen and once recorded, the image does not go away. It becomes as vividly a feature of my mental landscape as the birth of my two children. Imprinted in the cells. Recorded. Because death – even that of scores of strangers – demands too much attention. And so I can remember exactly how this body lay. How this hand was curled. This body bent. The smell.

There are the sounds too that become hardwired into my brain: the muffled sound that a walking suicide bomber makes when his explosives go off, a 'dum' lower and much quieter in the register than the emphatic smash of the car bomb. There is the elongated zizzz of a tear-gas grenade as it corkscrews through the air; the flat crack of plastic baton rounds. Some events are memorialised by the sounds they leave behind as aural after-images: the humming of my car's tyres on a road imprinted with the heavy, chequered tracks of a tank that has passed over it and gone. Laid down as if on acetate. The noises have their own decodable grammar and meaning. In time, I can tell the difference between incoming and outgoing mortar fire; the relative proximity of bullets; distinguish between the incontinent spray of happy fire, and the disciplined tick-tick of the firing range near my hotel in Baghdad, where the American soldiers zero their weapons' sights. The latter is instantly distinguishable from the jazzy bop and rim shots of real contact – angry, improvised and random. For years, it is this noise that troubles me so deeply that I avoid fireworks displays, jump at sharp noise. Until even that response is worn and tired and elicits only an instinctive hunching of my shoulders.

O ne morning I hear that refugees are gathering in Sidon, a little north of the besieged southern city of Tyre. Heading out of the city I notice that the flags left over from the World Cup, which the Lebanese passionately followed – German, French, Brazilian, Swedish – have been co-opted for war use. Hung on to buildings and flown from cars, they signal a message to the Israeli jets: 'Please don't hit us, we have other passports and identities than Lebanese.' They are a reminder of something else. Of what happened to Lebanon during its bloody fifteen-year civil war. Three times as many Lebanese reside abroad as do within its borders, an emigrant community that swelled in the war years with the flight of a significant new minority. Hundreds of thousands left, many of whom returned in the 1990s. These flags tell of a people scattered by violence who returned to rebuild their country during the uncertain years of peace that followed. They speak of exile and second passports, split loyalties. Mark out the fragile lines of potential fragmentation – a country scored by a glasscutter, waiting for a new impact.

With the main coastal highway bridges bombed, the only way south is across the mountains. An hour into the journey I see the first of them – cars, dusty and packed with people.

The flags they are trailing now are largely white: T-shirts, sheets wrapped over the roofs like shrouds, pillow cases, towels and scraps of cloth held in hands, wrapped around heads or tied to aerials and sticks. At first they come in ones and twos, then we meet the first of the convoys. It becomes clear. The journey time from the south, the villages within range of the Israeli tanks and mechanised artillery, means that all of the cars have converged on the road north at the same time from across the border area south of the Litani River – Hizbollah's stronghold and home to their rocket bunkers that point at Israel.

On this day tens of thousands of Shia refugees are fleeing. Car after car, they creep slowly, husbanding their precious petrol, their faces still anxious with the fear they have transported with them from the smashed villages on the border. It is an expression I have grown to know and understand. Sometimes it is a pained look on the point of panic. Most often it is an intense, grim concentration – the hyper-vigilance of war. Through the windows, women in head-scarves peer out through the reflections with the faces of the drowned.

Where there are traffic jams I lean out of the window of our car to ask where they have come from, how long their journey, and why they have fled. They shout out their homes in voices croaking with dehydration. Many are from villages around Tyre, fleeing days of air strikes, artillery barrages and naval gunfire. Others name towns, villages and cities south of the Litani, right on the border with Israel itself. Kfar Kila, Aita Chaab and Bint Jbiel. For now they are simply names on a map. I have no sense of their physical reality.

They tell of days of attacks, of sheltering in basements, of fear and thirst and hunger, and finally of the awful decision to abandon their homes and make a run for it.

The gorges become deeper as we climb, hemmed in by orange limestone crags, their bases hollowed out into deep caves millennia ago by the river at the valley bottom. Every now and then, entering one of the little Druze hamlets and towns that straddle these mountains, there is a makeshift cardboard sign fixed to a lamp post indicating in heavily scrawled handwriting the turns to take to Beirut – in one direction – or south to Sidon and Tyre. As if all the close geography of this tiny country has been broken up and hastily reconstituted on this single stretch of twisting road. At the last village before dropping again to the coast a group of baggy-trouser-wearing Druze stand at a road junction, warily watching the tide of Shia villagers. And then they wave us down to a sea that seems to be on fire. It is the burning power plant at Jieh. I stop to take pictures of the flames and the black smoke, a conflagration so intense that one of the plant's neighbours who has sent his family to safety in Beirut tells me that when he and his brother drove lorryloads of sand to try to suffocate the blaze it turned to glass.

What everyone really wants are stories from the front. Despite the attacks on areas like Haret Hreik, the scene in Beirut – in the media's collective judgement – lacks authenticity. The balcony of one hotel, overlooking the southern suburbs above the airport, has been appropriated by television journalists looking for the equivalent of the porn film's money shot – a bomb exploding in the densely packed blocks behind them as they speak on air. The besieged city of Tyre too, a place that has dominated the news, has been transformed after two weeks of war into a media clusterfuck. Packs of reporters roam the city in cars trying to outwit each other for some obscure exclusive, or ambush arriving refugees from the villages to the south, mobbing the stunned families for news from the border. One day I travel down in search of an apartment house that has been atomised by an Israeli bomb. But when I get there, there is only rubble, dust and curious onlookers. It is already packaged up, done with, ancient news.

War reporting, like any other kind of journalism, requires a familiar rota of drama, the clichéd set pieces that turn history and human misery into soap opera. The simple ideas that fit into a minute-long broadcast or into eight hundred words are a kind of awful entertainment most of the time. A reinforcement of how fortunate we are to be able to afford the luxury of distant sympathy or anger. The child without his limbs who has lost his family; the once pretty girl without a face; the brave soldier who risked all to save a comrade. It requires monsters and angels. What it would rather not deal with are the grey and murky areas that have the texture of real life. None of us is immune.

Once, right at the end of Angola's long civil war, I travelled from the ruined city of Quito – the country's Stalingrad, it had been labelled – on roads threatened by mines and ambush up to the great ruined metal bridge that sagged into the Kwanza River, to acquire one such hackneyed image: a human head planted on a pole at a checkpoint. A friend had seen it a day before. By the time I reached the river the head had been removed. The pole was there. It was a little grisly at one end, but now stood bare. Headless.

Eventually there seems no option but to head south to the border. I am not interested in being stuck with the pack in Tyre or doing hotel journalism from the comfort of Beirut. That leaves the border – the war's hidden and most dangerous front – where no one is reporting. Down there, we have heard, Israeli ground troops are crossing into Lebanon in ever larger formations, into the green and rocky valleys where Hizbollah's bunkers are hidden. My travelling companions, Joao Silva, a photographer on the *New York Times*, and his reporter, want to cover the fighting at first hand. This time the fear of jets is not imagined. It is real and palpable as we head down the Bekaa Valley. We watch jets come in to strike a junction ahead of us, a wooded hollow whose dry summer grass ignites from a raid designed to hole the road. Diverted on to a mountain track, we skirt a dozen of these craters, watching artillery hit the far side of the valley. Until at last we are sitting beneath a willow tree a handful of kilometres from the border.

A few minutes earlier we had passed the 'Bomb Café' on the outskirts of Marjeyoun, decorated with a large mock-up of one of Hizbollah's missiles protruding from one wall. I am not surprised it is deserted. No one in his right mind would want to drink coffee and eat chicken sandwiches inside a building with a gaudy rocket sticking from its roof. Not when there are hundreds of missiles flying daily out of Lebanon – across these hills – and into Israel. Not when I can hear the real things whooshing above our heads from their hidden launching sites, invisible except for the occasional helix of hanging smoke. Under the sheltering branches of the willow, Joao measures out the last few kilometres to the border with a cigarette and his thumb for scale. Two kilometres. We have arrived.

Ahead of us I can see the village of Kfar Kila straddling the border itself. Artillery shells are exploding above the village and on the mountain to our right, site of the Beaufort Castle, pulverising the white limestone bluffs. Originally a Crusader fortress, it was occupied by the PLO before being captured by the Israelis in 1982 during the civil war. Phosphorous flares are being fired, suggesting the presence of Israeli troops in the olive groves beyond the village where the border is. White streamers that wriggle up into the air like spermatozoa and fall on to the olive groves, setting the trees on fire.

The border here is shaped like a finger that pokes sharply into Lebanon. Looking at the map I realise that means Israel is also to my left across a small, flat valley that rises to a low ridge. The border is so close that Kfar Kila overlooks the red-tiled roofs of the kibbutz town of Metulla, staging point for the Israel Defense Forces on this sector of the front. The presence of the Israelis on the nearby ridge is quickly confirmed. The binocular flashes of the Israeli artillery spotters wink from time to time. I am close enough, too, to see Israeli cars parked neatly in a line on the road leading to the kibbutz. I know that there are friends of mine a few hundred metres distant inside Metulla, other journalists covering the war on the Israeli side, accompanying the tank crews, watching the rounds go out as we see them come in. My phone shows Orange Israel not a Lebanese service. I could call them but I am nervous who might listen in.

We drive the last few hundred yards into the village at high speed. The street is deserted at first, and then a handful of villagers appear from a house. Accompanying them is Yamen Hassan who has come from the neighbouring town to rescue anyone that he can find. He is a slight, tough and tattooed young man in a blue T-shirt who appears at first unfazed by the surrounding violence. He announces calmly that there are Israeli troops advancing on our end of the village, and asks if I would like to see. We duck between buildings to the final house overlooking the fruit groves on the plain. Among the trees, not far distant, I can see a small unit of Israeli soldiers darting from tree to tree, approaching the western outskirts of the village in an attempt to outflank its defenders.

Hassan tells me he has come to Kfar Kila to pick up some families he knows who have been trapped beneath the Israeli bombardment for the last few days. But he has been halted on its outskirts by three Israeli tanks that have entered with a larger group of soldiers and there has been fierce fighting to push them back. I have arrived at last where the war is being fought, at close quarters, on the ground. 'I am crazy,' he tells me with a grin. 'But I am not so crazy that I'll go any further in.'

As we speak, an unmanned Predator drone armed with Hellfire missiles drifts across the road in front of us, banking above the houses to underline his point. In any case, Hassan now has different passengers to take out of the village: Mousab Rida, a garbage collector and his wife, Zainub, who, on hearing that Israeli soldiers are creeping through the trees towards their home, have now decided to flee after remaining through long days of shelling. As Zainub packs a few belongings on to a tractor-trailer for her husband to take out of what was once home to 12,000 people, she begins to shake and weep. It is what I have come to see, a cruel anthropologist in search of the breaking point, the very instant of fracture. As Zainub weeps and Mousab ties down their possessions on the cart, we quickly start taking pictures. 'I've had enough,' says Mousab. 'My wife is just too scared for us to stay.'

The only place to stay is a hotel, empty of guests save us. Bored, I climb down a ladder into a pool drained of water. The blue-painted bottom, where it has been exposed to the sun, has cracked and bubbled into hard blisters that pop beneath my shoes. One of the staff has put a cat into the pool that cries to be let out. Hizbollah fires a salvo of missiles from its hidden positions on the slopes of the hill nearby. After five minutes Israeli jets appear: hitting the hillside six times on the first evening. The nearest bombs explode a few hundred metres away. This close, the cooling, fragrant air sounds like a huge, cracked bell ringing with the detonations.

It crosses my mind that this building is on a clipboard in the Defense Ministry in Tel Aviv, a GPS location typed on a target list. It is no safer to be inside the hotel than out of it. I take a basketball from the hotel's sports locker and shoot hoops with Osama, the driver, as a distraction. The ball splats on the gravel court as we crash into each other and sweat and pant as the bombs explode, close enough to loosen a window frame on the hotel's second floor. It is not a good place to sleep, but there is nowhere else.

When Emily calls I think I detect anger in her voice although she tries to hide it. Not for the first time I am confronted by the selfishness of my choices. I am thrown back to the memory of the furious demand from my son during the invasion of Iraq, shortly after I had crossed the border: 'Come home.'

The most dangerous game is the daily one of hide and seek we play entering Kfar Kila. Probing deeper and deeper into the village in search of its hiding residents and the invisible fighters. One day an Israeli shell flies over the car, exploding in a grove on the other side of the road. Whether it is aimed at us or not, I do not know. What is certain is that the village is being shelled on a regular basis. I know too that the fighters are all around us. I can see and hear their missiles being launched from almost every side. Sitting underneath the willow tree one day and screwing up the courage to go in, I suddenly see Hizbollah mortar fire being directed from a brush-covered ridge a hundred metres in front of me, a series of thumps and detonations of brown dust.

One afternoon, by chance leaving the village, I see three fighters walking down from the olive groves on the slopes above Kfar Kila, carrying a heavy bag between them. Despite the intensity of the bombardment they have daily endured, their walk is jaunty and they return a wave with embarrassed grins like schoolboys caught doing something naughty. Otherwise, the fighters are absent. Until on the third day I meet Ibrahim Yahia.

He is in the courtyard next to the willow tree smoking a water pipe and drinking tea. It is immediately clear he is no civilian. Not just from his muddy boots and dirty combats; he has the soldier's acrid smell of old sweat and long-slept-in clothes. He motions me to sit down and offers round the pipe. We try to introduce ourselves as journalists but he grins from under his black beard and tells us that he knows. 'We've been watching you,' he explains. He says he is twenty-six-years old, a farmer and a fighter in the Islamic Resistance, which Hizbollah leads. He is not a member of Hizbollah, but another group, Amal.

He tells us about the battle two days before that we had witnessed fragments of. How the Israelis had tried to take the village with three tanks and infantry in a pincer movement. Ibrahim and his colleagues fought them to a standstill for two days. In that battle, one tank was disabled, by Israel's account – three according to Hizbollah's – before the Israeli troops pulled back from Kfar Kila across the fence, burning the olive groves as they left, to resume the business of hurling high explosives against the ridges above the village. 'If they want to come again, they'll come,' he says sombrely. 'Then we'll fight them.'

Ibrahim guides us through the groves to the middle of the village, a journey made even more uncomfortable by having a fighter in the car. There are smashed and ruined buildings, some of them scorched. He takes us to a white-painted concrete house with a balcony at the upper end of the village. On the wall behind the balcony he points out a large red stain, where one of the local fighters died. I look through homes damaged by shellfire. In one, blackened by flames, I find a huge set of crockery in boxes, a wedding set, strewn by the blast across the floor in drifts, like seashells on a North Sea beach. The pieces are coated with fine, gritty soot. When I pick one up and brush off the smuts I notice that it is decorated with a little rose.

The hot lick of the explosion has set an ironing board, left leaning against a wall, so suddenly on fire that it has stencilled a sharp, greasy shadow on the wallpaper even as the ironing board has been knocked down. A shell hole perforates the wall. Ibrahim tells me it is his parents' home. He leads me into a small yard on a terrace close to the house to show me the family's Friesian cow. It has been blinded in one eye by a sliver of shrapnel. It bucks and kicks as he gently holds its rope halter. As it moves a stream of blood pours from a nostril.

The few hundred who have stayed have barricaded themselves into stone basements. They appear in a lull in the shelling, blinking in the glare. The women chat and smoke in the street. Bread is distributed, brought in by an ambulance driver from neighbouring Marjeyoun. The children play. Then a shell flies in, exploding somewhere to our left, scattering the families to their basements once again.

Hate Studies

Watch this! . . . The tank is coming. Coming . . . Coming . . . Coming. Then . . . Watch!' Ahmad glances over his shoulder to make sure I am following the action on the computer with him. It's how boys talk. It is what my own son does playing *World of Warcraft* or *Ghost Recon*. 'It explodes!' Ahmad says triumphantly with a large grin. He slides to one side on his chair and restarts the video shot by a hidden cameraman, whose hands are shaking with fear and excitement.

The Israeli armoured personnel carrier is bumping over some rubble, unsteady as a toy. There are a few seconds of footage and then suddenly the tank is engulfed in a ball of flame. Then black. The abrupt ending of this little film is for a simple reason: if it were to carry on it would show the APC grinding on, undamaged. But that is not the issue. The point for both those who shot the footage and for Ahmad is that it shows the coincidence of tank and explosion, a rare thing in the history of the Palestinian struggle. What it represents is not the image of an armoured vehicle being destroyed, but the *possibility* that one day a vehicle like this *might* be destroyed.

Ahmad knows this. He scrolls back again carefully and points out how you can see that the explosion is unfortunately to one side. 'If it had been underneath the tank,' he tells me with his serious child's face, 'the tank would have gone.' Except it wouldn't. I can see, even in these poor-quality images, that the blast lacks any deadly force. It is more of a giant firework than a tank killer, the blast dispersed rather than channelled lethally into the armour. Ahmad has not finished with his show-and-tell. And the folder that he opens on his desktop next is the one that he has actually brought me into his bedroom to see – his library dedicated to images of al-Qaeda. Now Ahmad is quietly shy. I am not sure of the reaction he wants from me or how he feels himself about these pictures. Whether, perhaps, he is a little confused, even ashamed.

He clicks on the folders, a flowering of pixels that snap open, abrupt as evening primrose petals, into picture layered on picture, showing faces that have become as familiar and iconic as those of pop stars for many of this generation of young Middle Eastern boys. There is the headshot of Mohammed Atta taken from his Florida driver's licence, with his brushed black hair and lazy eye, the features of the man who piloted the first plane to crash into the World Trade Center at 8.46 a.m. on September 11. And with him, staring out, mug shots of the other suicide hijackers – collectible as football cards. Other images show the rest of the memorabilia of al-Qaeda: Osama bin Laden with his lieutenants sitting cross-legged on the ground; a picture of an American dollar with bin Laden's face where George Washington's should be. Finally, there are the towers of the World Trade Center in flames – and the falling body of one of those who chose to jump rather than burn. Ahmad, swapping pictures with other boys on his slow internet connection, has acquired the full set.

The bedroom is in Rafah, at the southernmost point of the Gaza Strip. Ahmad is seventeen, still a boy. I have been staying with his family, eating their food and sleeping on their floor. As far as I can judge these things, I would say Ahmad is not a bad boy. He seems affectionate and curious, studious and keen to please. It is simply that in the circum- stances of his life he is acquiring the habits of hating. My visit is in 2003, more than two years into the Second Intifada – the al-Aqsa uprising – which began in September 2000. The Israeli settlements in Gaza, which will eventually be evacuated by Prime Minister Ariel Sharon, are still under Occupation. Gaza, too, has yet to descend into the anarchy of clan warfare that will trigger the violent takeover of the Strip by Hamas in 2007. For now the conflict is between Palestinians and Israelis. And children are at the front line.

On his desk there is a framed picture of his cousin, Haisam Said Natat. He does not have to explain what it signifies. I have seen enough of these pictures to know Haisam is dead. The boy in the picture has two guns crossed against his chest and a black headband. A martyr. A *shaheed*. 'Sha-heeeed': you hear it shouted on the funeral marches. There is a tangible quality about the frozen expressions of these young boys and men that always affected me, although for years I struggled to fathom precisely what it was. Then one day it came: what they reminded me of were the publicity pictures that my father had printed as a young actor in search of work to send to theatrical agents.

It is the same quality of deliberate invention I can see in these pictures. The conscious effort to imitate the thing you wish to be. But bent and twisted. As if all the teenage struggle for identity and independence had been channelled into death. The boys smile grimly, look 'hard' or scowl into the camera with a terrible bravado. A few smile cockily. All of the pictures are infected with an identical aura of fatalism. These portraits assume a kind of glamour that I know will be understood by those who look at them. Not by me. As an outsider, shocked by the attrition to Palestinian children and youth in this ragged on–off conflict, it does not speak to me, as it does to Palestinian boys, of power, courage or sacrifice – only of an inevitably hopeless outcome.

And Haisam made it. He paid the door price for admission to the gang of Palestine's dead warrior children, commemorated by this cheap photo. Ahmad tells me, without much emotion, that Haisam was killed attacking Israeli soldiers. He shrugs when I ask him for details. As if that matters, his gesture says. In the reckoning of these things, perhaps it doesn't. The logic of conflict does not require knowledge of stories as I do. Too much knowledge militates against participation in violence. Ahmad blandly reels off a list of names, as if mentioning participants at a family gathering, until I understand he has lost seven relatives and friends to the violence of the *intifada*. Killed by the Israelis. Among them is the boy whose face serves as his screensaver.

There are other pictures in Ahmad's tiny bedroom: posters of Michael Jackson and the Backstreet Boys,

smiling down, glossily counterfeit. Ahmad has a final
folder of images on his computer that he wants to show
me from his collection – a face as iconic as Mohammed
Atta's. There, shiny-haired and sleek, is Diana, Princess
of Wales. 'Dee-a-na,' he pronounces it, and asks me what
I thought of her. When I tell him that I covered her funeral,
Ahmad wants to know every detail. I wonder whether for
Ahmad (as for so many) she is another martyr in his collection of the dead, only made of a softer material. He seems
not so different from the milling crowds on that long night
outside Westminster Abbey, projecting their longings and
disappointments on to somebody else's life. On to their
death.

Ahmad has another video downloaded on to his
computer that speaks of life and a different possibility.
'Watch this,' he says, with the same insistence as when he
showed me the picture of the tank being attacked. 'Do you
like it?' His slender shoulders are shaking with laughter.
I realise that I am watching the actor Rowan Atkinson
twisting his rubber face and tangling his elastic limbs as
Mr Bean. There is the paradox: al-Qaeda and Diana,
Michael Jackson and Mr Bean – which to ascribe greatest
importance to? I ask Ahmad how he can be into the
Backstreet Boys and still admire the September 11 attackers.
He looks as baffled by the question as I feel. 'But I don't hate
American culture,' he explains earnestly. 'What I hate is what
their politics are doing. They are helping Israel with money,
tanks and guns against the Palestinian people. So I support
those who support us in our struggle like al-Qaeda.' It does
not answer the question.

I think about the contradictions represented by Ahmad. How much of his attitude is youthful bravura? How much of it is formed by his experiences? How much by his culture? What I am certain of is that in Israel Ahmad would be seen as hateful, a hater, and a product of hatred. Yet in his room it is more complicated, throwing me back to a question that has troubled me for years: about the genesis of hostility and the formulation of attitudes that make violence possible.

Sleeping in Ahmad's house is not such an easy thing. The bedroom next to his has a wall adjoining the street covered with a thin bed sheet. I pull it aside to reveal that the bricks behind it have been blown out, an opening through which the sounds of conflict break in. When darkness comes the Palestinian boys sneak out to throw blast bombs at the Israeli soldiers in their steel-plated towers. It is a deadly game, vividly audible behind the cotton wall, that begins the nightly exchange of bullets between the soldiers and the shooters on the roofs – the soundtrack to Ahmad's life – the alarming rip of bullets, persistent as drumming rain, traversing the street outside. A Palestinian tells me later with a bitter laugh that it is the 'Rafah lullaby'. The first detonation jars me out of my sleep. After a while my friend Sharon, who has been sent to sleep in the room with the missing wall, to be separate from the driver and myself, emerges with a stunned look on her face. She is in a long nightie that comes down to her feet, supplied by the family. Dragging her mattress she announces that, even at the risk of offending our hosts, she'll curl up on the floor with us.

In Northern Ireland, as the three-decade-long Troubles wound down, Paul Connolly, a professor at the University of Ulster, invited both Protestant and Catholic children aged between three and six years old to play a series of games designed to study how sectarian attitudes were formed. He showed them images of football shirts that marked the communal divide – concentric patterns coloured for the national flags of the UK and Ireland. He asked them questions too about how they felt about contemporary events. He discovered that by the age of three Catholic children were already twice as likely to say that they were hostile to a police force regarded as being pro-British as Protestant children, who identified with the police as protectors against terrorist violence. By the age of six a third of children identified clearly with one of the two communities. A significant minority was already making sectarian statements.

Connolly came to a critical conclusion: that the first stirrings of sectarianism – the habit of inter-communal hate – were born not in school or from watching television, but came from the family, community and culture. And while Connolly's cut-off point was young, others who have looked at the problem believe that the most virulent forms of prejudice and nationalism begin to be established by the age of eight, their views hardening in mid-teens. This same tendency for early hostility has been noted too in Israel and the Occupied Palestinian Territories. When Daniel Bar-Tal of Tel Aviv University asked what 'Arab' meant to Israeli children, he discovered that by the age of two to three years they were developing stereotypical conceptions of the word, which by six and older was becoming associated with ideas of violence and criminality.

Why is the concept of hatred so difficult to tackle objectively? Is it because we think about the word itself in loaded terms? Implicit in its meaning and use are strong connotations of moral judgement. It is not good to hate. Haters are necessarily bad. Being the object of hate suggests a state of victimhood and recourse to a justified reaction. When we say that 'we hate' it is reserved for dark and uncontrolled feelings. Yet we all hate.

Although we think of hate as an extreme, incontinent emotion, what makes us prone to hatred is at the centre of human experience, hardwired into how we make categorical distinctions. Learning is not simply about acquiring factual knowledge. It is also about processing it. In a world that should overwhelm us with the constant roar of stimulus and information, our brain constructs short cuts. We lump objects, ideas, words, social relationships into manageable categories for easy handling. Discriminating in all of our thought processes, including all our social interactions. We prefer those most like us – who share the same nationality or social status, are members of our families or groups or speak like us – while developing stereotypes associated with outsiders. Those negative models, developed when we are very young, far from being modified as our intellectual capacity develops, are just as often reinforced.

And while this tendency to preference explains, in some measure, our ability to form socially sustaining communities, it is also mirrored in a darker aspect. Implicit in preference is that someone else should be excluded: that different rules and considerations should apply. Even regarding acceptance of their entitlement to equal human rights. When this prejudice is combined with a strongly negative experience of actions performed by the other group in the course of a long conflict, that discrimination is easily expressed as the most dangerous kind of hate.

Ultimately – as Connolly demonstrated – we view the world through the medium of the culture in which we are moulded. And in intractable conflicts, like that between Israelis and Palestinians, involving a struggle for the same physical space, the competing cultures themselves – the defining software – become altered. The result, as in every war, is a culture that expresses itself in a narrow and rigid repertoire of scripts required for surviving the challenges conflict throws up. A 'culture of conflict'. It is as monotonous as it is repetitive and harsh, reinforcing the same few recurring themes: unity, suspicion of outsiders, penalisation of spies and collaborators. At the same time new virtues are promoted, prominent among them the virtues of sacrifice and struggle.

Displacing the peacetime culture, it throws up new models for behaviour: from conversation to play and the rules governing the use of permissive violence. In the latter, a destructive feedback loop is created. Young people who see violence being used in what they believe is a 'legitimate' context are more likely to be attracted to it. To be drawn into it. To believe that violence is just. In Palestinian society, that legitimisation is supplied by the notion of the rightness of 'resistance against Israel' and the long struggle to establish its own state.

Early during the Second Intifada I learn from the Palestinian boys that perfume and menthol toothpaste and raw onions are useful for tear gas. The *shabab*, the tough kids who throw stones at the Israeli soldiers, give me a demonstration. They spread a little paste beneath their eyes like a quarterback, and rub it in to soothe the burning.

When the gas drifts in, in its strangling, eye-scouring tendrils, the boys sprinkle perfume on the scarves they wrap around their faces. A lucky handful own swimming goggles. When it gets too bad they emerge from the stinging mist, eyes rimmed pink and swollen, their clothes and faces blackened by the tyres they burn to screen themselves with their own smoke from the Israelis. At the *shawarma* shop down by the City Inn in Ramallah, Palestinian 'capital' of the West Bank, a place I nickname the Intifada Café, the wife of the owner – a Palestinian-American who returned when things started looking up after the Oslo Accords of 1993 – soaks wads of cotton wool from a bottle of cheap fragrance. Tender as an aunt, she dabs it beneath the eyes of the younger children. The alcohol breaks up the chemicals, she says. The older boys take the soaking wads and help themselves, or stuff the rolled cotton wool up their nostrils, before heading out again into the fray.

It looks a stupid game at first: a mixture of bravado and taunting. But it is a battle. Few of the kids are strong enough or bold enough to hurl a stone that will reach the Israeli troops and hurt them. That is not the point. The point is to be present and participate, to be part of the struggle, a reinforcing process that echoes, in its own informal way, the initiation into martial and national values of Israel's compulsory military service. At first they hang out. Backs are slapped. Slings compared and examined. Stones picked up and turned in hands. The big boys swan up with a certain swagger, arms thrown round shoulders.

When there are enough of them, the boys load their slings and burst out of the pack, in ones and twos. It is then that the bored Israeli soldiers fire back with powerful, plastic-coated rounds. They are bone-breakers to be shot into legs, ricocheted off the tarmac. That is the theory. The standing orders. But the soldiers, some of them little older than teenagers themselves, ignore orders or, following more brutal ones, fire at the children's heads and straight into their bodies. Then the boys go down, to be lifted and dragged out, limbs spastic and eyes rolling like cattle in the slaughterhouse, stunned with a hammer. An ululating wail goes from the pack, a call to the ambulances that wait daily for their cargoes of the injured. One day, following an ambulance's stretcher crew rushing to pick up a felled boy, one of the plastic-sheathed rounds skims the skull of my friend Bryan, who stumbles right in front of me, his hair parted with a blister where it grazed his skin.

But sometimes the soldiers use live rounds and the Palestinian men use the distraction of the stone throwers to fire on the Israeli soldiers, inviting missiles and cannon fire in return. I am caught one day in such an exchange, struggling out of the café, horribly hungover and with liquid bowels, clutching a chicken sandwich to eat while I watch the clash. I am halfway across the street when the heavy cannon rounds begin flying towards the boys where I am standing. I hit the ground, my sandwich still in one hand. And crawl towards the kerb, towards a sliver of cover. As I do my troubled guts squirt out a little jet of shit.

Once I saw a boy shot down so close to me I could have touched him as he ran past to throw his stone. The shots from the Israeli soldiers were coming with a pitter-patter frequency. So I had retreated to a doorway where I could watch the action, a spectator at a match. He was a skinny little kid who came up to my shoulders, in a sports shirt so big so it drooped long over his hips like a tennis dress. I remember his face: sharp eyes, with a lock of hair that fell across his forehead.

If I allow myself to forget the circumstances, it is one of those moments suffused with the confident self-awareness of late childhood: the bowler running up to the crease, desperate to be observed; the gymnast in flight; the centre-forward shooting for goal. The other boys are shouting. Taunting the soldiers. He runs forward for his throw. He is in front of me. Foot back, back curved, his arm whipping forward the weighted sling from far behind, hips turning into the shot as his arm extends. I hear the *whoo-whup* of the sling stretching to its limit and the accelerating stone. There is perfection in his movement. He senses the eyes of his watching peers, exaggerating the movements, to insist upon his skill. His bravery. Then the tension that holds the arc together – arm, spine and weight placed on the back foot – is suddenly destroyed. He is elastic, his weight falling on to a leg that cannot support him. A foot turns oddly and crumples as he falls. I feel suddenly nauseous. For some reason another image comes into my mind – that of the youth who fell off the middle diving board on to the poolside when I was a child: the same rolling eyes; the same bloodied, yellowing face.

When I talk to the boys I get a litany of fragmented sentences and half-finished thoughts: about 'the need to fight the Israelis', 'to end the Occupation'. Boys posing as men, they jostle for attention, are sullenly shy, or else aggressive. Some show off. But the significance is not so much in the words as in the attitudes they strike – in the excited imitation of adult violence. For all play is a kind of ritual, and a way of learning about the world. This is no different. Except that the world they are learning to be part of is one with a perilous set of rules.

I recall my own childhood games, and see them reflected in the prism of these children's, amplified and made deadly. 'Who wants to play war? Who wants to play war?' The chant of the playground. Then, British schoolboys still used to form up into 'English' and 'German' gangs, running around with imaginary guns and grenades. 'Brrrrpp. Brrrrrppp. You're dead! You're dead! Lie down!' You do, squirming for effect. One day I asked my father, a child during the Second World War from a naval family, what games he played when he was evacuated to the Somerset countryside while real bombs fell on his home city of Portsmouth, killing family members. Not war, he said. But – just once – after he had learned that his father had died in India in 1941, they played at 'funerals', until they were caught and slapped so hard they never played that game again.

As a teenager I played more dangerous games, not very different from the games the boys of Gaza play: making noisy little pipe bombs from the gunpowder we scooped out of fireworks, or from home-made explosives. We tried making nitro-glycerine one day with acids stolen from the school lab, but found it too complicated. Once we even managed to lay our hands on a .22 bullet and crammed it into a sawn off car aerial, gripped in a vice in a friend's garden, then hit with a hammer. They were games designed to challenge authority and take risks. The crucial difference was that no one was going to kill us.

The Palestinian children of Gaza and the West Bank — those too small to be throwing stones — play *intifada* with their guns made out of plastic (if they can afford it) or of painted wood. I am surprised to learn that for some of the children it is no bad thing to get picked as an Israeli for these games. The Israelis are stronger — so the logic goes.

I'm walking through 'O' Block, one of Rafah's UN-run camps, looking for the boys I heard throwing blast bombs near Ahmad's house the night before. The houses here are not like Ahmad's large villa with its nice sofas, its glass chandeliers, computer and its exterior walls dressed to look like white marble. They are small and square and pokey, with thin mattresses stacked up out of the way that are brought down at night. A woman calls us into her home to offer us tea. She slices pale cucumbers into oblong sections, squatting on her stone floor, washing them in a standpipe in a street where the waste runs in open sewers. Children crowd around and follow everywhere I go. Ehab Abu-Taha falls in as my guide. He is cocky and famished looking, lighting one cigarette off another. I take him for sixteen. The other younger boys who appear in the narrow lanes and alleyways defer to him, as he knocks on doors or calls to them to ask if they have a pipe bomb we can see. One runs to fetch the broken tail fin of a home-made Qassam rocket of the kind fired out of Gaza into the Israeli towns just to the north. But firing them, I know, is an adult occupation.

I ask Ehab if he throws bombs at the Israelis himself and he is immediately put out. He tells me he is twenty-three. Throwing bombs, he insists somewhat sulkily, is something children do, not older teenagers, and certainly not adults. The mood passes and he asks me if I would like to see the ruins of what was once his family home, on the front line of 'O' Block. It is here that the Israelis are building a tall metal wall that sinks as deeply into the dusty earth as it rises out of it – five metres tall – red as a girder. It is designed, say the Israelis, to stop the weapons-smuggling tunnels coming in from the Egyptian border to the south. And as the wall has risen, the armoured Israeli bulldozers have demolished entire rows of houses to create a 'death zone' in front of the wall, Ehab's house among them. I will see the same wall again after it has been cut and blown down by the militant group Hamas in 2008 – kilometres of bent and twisted metal.

For now, the D9 armoured Caterpillar bulldozers have

crushed and pushed the concrete from the houses close to the wall into sad, fractured dunes: sections of stair and segments of window or doorframe still identifiable. The shell of Ehab's house still remains for now. We pick our way between roofless walls painted a pale blue. On the rubble-covered floor, we find the remains of the exploded bombs: twisted and ruptured tubes of metal, discarded like spent cigarettes.

Suddenly Ehab spots a boy he recognises, a local child returning from one of the UN camp schools. He is a barefoot boy of ten or so, and is sent running to fetch a bomb to show me. He tells me he has thrown pipe bombs 'four times'. When he skids back into view five minutes later, out of breath and his face damp with sweat, he has the tube stuffed into his purple school rucksack. He takes it out: a section of scaffolding pipe of the kind that supports the roofs of many of the poorer houses. It has been sawn down to six inches long, welded at both ends and drilled with a hole to take the home-made explosives and a rudimentary fuse. A bomb this size, says Ehab, would cost seven shekels to buy (about $1.50). The best ones, he tells me, cost $2. He hands it to me. I weigh it carefully. It is heavier than I had anticipated. Cool to the touch. When I come to leave Israel at Ben Gurion airport the traces of explosives transferred first to my fingers and then to the keyboard of my laptop will show a residual trace on one of the scanners. The reading is ambiguous enough to get me through, but worrying. An older hand later advises me that if I ever touch things like that again, I should vacuum the keys.

The boy says there is a shortage at the moment.

Palestinian security officials have been told to close down the metal shops that turn out the bombs. But he says that you can still get them if you know where to go. The real problem is that $2 is a lot when families struggle to raise the $100 a month they need to rent a house away from the front line. So the boys scavenge among the rubble under the Israeli guns for stuff that they can sell. Three sections of aluminium curtain rail will raise a shekel. Otherwise they admit they earn pennies by running messages for the older gunmen. The boy leads us down an alley close to the front line and asks us if he should throw it. I tell him no, but ask him to tell us what he does when he goes out at night to throw a bomb.

The 'game' goes like this. The boys creep through the streets and into the hollow shells of the abandoned build- ings on the front line. They get into the rubble and dirt of no-man's-land beyond – an area of demolished houses and bulldozed dirt seventy-five metres across. Then they crawl through the rat-infested ruins, among boulders of concrete and sheets of fallen asbestos roofing that were once attached to someone's home. When they are close enough to the Israeli patrols, they toss their bombs. The pipe bombs are crude things to make and cruder still to use. The boys light the petrol-soaked fuses with their cigarettes. When the fuse is almost down, they throw the bomb. Sometimes the bombs go off too early. In Rafah there are children who have been peppered with fragments from their own home-made grenades and who have lost hands and eyes.

The thing that everyone insists on is that throwing bombs is child's play. The bombs make a loud noise but don't do too much harm, they claim. The Israelis don't even bother firing back at the bomb throwers that much any more, say locals, not like during the first months of the *intifada*. A father – who asks not to be identified – tells me seriously that it allows the boys to let off steam. For those trapped in the camp, he says, it fulfils a psychological need. As he tells it, it is a form of self-expression. The Israelis paint it rather differently; when it is reported, it is as a 'terrorist' throwing a bomb.

On a pile of rubble opposite the wrecked remains of the Salahadeen mosque, opposite the Israelis' huge new metal wall, I come across Mustafa Kamil Abu Nada, aged eleven, and his friend Fairaz Mohammed el Sharkawi, aged ten. They tell me they have come to watch the Israeli demolition operations and maybe throw a stone. I am with a Palestinian journalist, Mohammed Joudah, a resident of Rafah and father of two children. He suddenly gets angry with the boys. 'It is not a circus here,' he snaps. 'Who sent you here?' The boys tell him that no one sent them. Joudah is exasperated but they stay.

A few minutes later they are joined by a ten-year-old girl who lives nearby who also comes to 'look around'. She tells me about her interests as she plays amid the rubble. 'I like skipping. And drawing. And French! And I have a doll I play with. And my dad breeds birds.' She says it is the first time she has come to this spot. I ask her if she is bothered by the gunfire that crashes through Rafah's night. She looks a little embarrassed. 'Sometimes I wet myself,' she says. When I ask her what she would most like she says: 'Peace with the Israelis.' She does not think it will happen. One of the armoured bulldozers fires a warning shot above our heads, the bullet cracking like a whip. I duck but the children are unfazed, too accustomed to the sound of it.

re the stories about violence the children tell me so different from those of the adults? I am not so certain. For thirteen years, I have recorded the excuses and justifications of a dozen different conflicts, the propaganda and subtly and not so subtly reordered histories. With each conflict I have learned the words of the new scripts. But beyond the individual details, there emerges a universal quality, speaking of a reality we would rather not acknowledge: that the processes of hatred are inseparable from our human natures. The way we view groups outside our own, social psychologists have long recognised, is regulated by the tension between two competing kinds of perception: between empathy and what is called cognition, our intellectual capacity to understand the other's position. It defines our attitudes and commands behaviour. In the constant to and fro between the two, it is empathy, or rather the lack of it, which is the more powerful actor. It is hostility's engine.

After the war in Bosnia I returned to the devastated southern city of Mostar, divided along the line of the turquoise Neretva River into a Croat west and a Muslim east, a place of beautiful old Ottoman architecture, whose most celebrated edifice was the Stari Most bridge, blown up by the Croats. My translator on the Croat side of the river was a little older than Ahmad, a smart and pretty Catholic girl who asked naïvely uncomfortable questions. They were hostile and racist yet curious, as if the substance in the mould still had to set and harden. Did the Muslim girls smell differently from the way she did? She had heard they were not as clean as Croats. Did I feel safe among the Muslims on the other bank? Wasn't it better to be among the Croats? She asked about the photographer I was working with – was he a Jew? She thought he must be because of his name. How different were Jews?

She told me her own story. How her brother had been badly wounded in one leg during the fighting for the city and was now a bitter drunk. Her mother had worked in the big department store on the wide boulevard, close to the river. I had been there. The building had been on the front line, scoured by the anti-aircraft fire the Croats had poured down from the surrounding hills where they had set their guns among the limestone reefs, bare and white as bones. Even the trees on the once elegant street had been amputated to ugly stumps by the intensity of the bombardment. Intrigued, one day I took her to the shop where her mother had worked in the hope of eliciting a sympathetic reaction. As we drove past the ruined buildings, she became silent and, for a moment, close to tears. 'How did it make you feel?' I asked when we returned. 'It made me sad to see it,' she said, then added angrily: 'but I am not sorry that it happened!' The same dynamic was evident in the attitudes of Palestinian and Israeli youths surveyed on a large scale in 2004. It found that although both sides could legitimise the other's story on

an intellectual level, when it came to emotional understanding and empathy, the teenagers expressed similar high
levels of anger.

And conflict works even against this intellectual understanding. War, by its very nature, insists on denying the
other group's 'justifying' story. It demands the imposition
of a shared view of past, present and future as a mechanism
for the interpretation of motives and events. Cultures in
conflict create common reservoirs of explanatory stories
and attitudes, and an insistence on superior traits. The
enemy is dirty and lazy, murderous and untrustworthy in
negotiations. His beliefs are brutal and uncultured. At worst
he is sub-human – an insect to be stamped on. The history
and legitimacy of the claims of the rival group must be
picked apart, denied. Destroyed.

In the conflict between the Israelis and the Palestinians,
the result has been the creation of competing and mutually exclusive national accounts of suffering, victimisation
and martyrdom deployed to justify the continuation of
violence. It explains why Zionist history for so long
attempted to deny the original existence of Palestinians on
the land, and why so many Palestinians continue to deny
that Israel exists. On the Israeli side, the conflict's narrative has its centre of gravity in the Holocaust and the struggle
for a Jewish homeland free from persecution. It is held up
in national monuments, in myths, history, archaeology,
education and national ceremonies; encapsulated in an
obsessive concern for national security regardless of the
social cost. Those attitudes are mirrored on the Palestinian
side, whose own icon of suffering – equivalent to the

Holocaust in Arab terms – is the Nakba, 'the Catastrophe' of 1948, the year of Israel's creation that drove so many from their homes. It is only the iconography that is different in expressing the continuing Palestinian fight for national identity, and its endless thwarting: the keys held by the displaced refugees; martyr posters; murals that celebrate the struggle.

I am chatting with Ahmad's father, Khaled, one evening. He worked abroad as a teacher for fifteen years and speaks excellent English. His is a conservative and religious household, not unusual for Gaza, and he is strict with his teenage boys and elder daughters, insisting they work hard at school. He shows me his son Yahir's English exam that he has sat today. He tells me proudly his son has scored 100 per cent. As we sit drinking coffee, he complains about the parents who leave their children to be educated by 'the street' – whose boys throw blast bombs at the Israelis. He tells me of the argument he had with his son Mohammed when he came home from school carrying a bomb. Despite his disapproval, I can't help noticing in pride of place in the front room a framed picture of Mohammed wearing the uniform of the militant and holding an assault rifle. When the children bring the picture for me to see, which they do several times during the evening, Khaled offers no comment.

He is telling me a story that has the ring of an old saying about it. 'I asked an old Palestinian once, "Is four children enough?" And he said: "No! The Jordanians will kill one. The Israelis will kill one, and the Egyptians will kill another. Time will take the last . . ."' It triggers a moment of reflection. 'When children are young here, they have huge freedom. Then they become teenagers, and they realise that they are trapped. That,' he says, 'is when you see them start joining actions against the Israelis. Because of our situation, the children interfere.'

Khaled tells me at last that Mohammed is 'interested' in *jihad.* He says it as if his son was keen on football or collecting stamps. A short and stocky boy with a crew cut, Mohammed bounces around the house in a baggy shirt, worn loose from his trousers. He hands me his picture as a would-be 'martyr' and spells out not quite correctly 'Kash-al-ni-kov' in slow syllables. He sits on the sofa, still for a minute, and I ask what he wants to be when he grows up. Khaled encourages him to speak English. 'I want to be an engineer . . .' He lapses into Arabic. 'Speak English,' his father interrupts. 'I would like to travel the Arab world. The Gulf. Germany. The US . . .' 'Why?' asks the father, ever the teacher. 'To learn and marry.' Then in staccato English, he adds : 'Tank. Apache. Helicopter. I want to liberate the Palestinians from the IDF [the Israeli army]. Now Israel is top of the mountain. Some day it will come down.'

Khaled and his wife are not avoiding the issue – they just don't see Mohammed's infatuation with the gunmen as anything to be concerned about. When Khaled says his son is 'interested' in *jihad* that is exactly what he means. It is Mohammed's interest, just as other boys in other places might have an interest in music or skateboarding. It goes without comment or notice because it is what teenage boys in Gaza do. Because men in conflict are co-opted into the struggle, boys on the edge of manhood replicate what their adult models do. Where men hurt other men, boys emulate it.

I take a bumpy drive down the potholed main road that runs through the heart of Rafah, following Israel's iron wall towards the sand dunes and Rafah's West Camp in an area known as Tal el-Sultan. Here the houses end and the golden humps of sand begin, the same sand that is lifted by the wind and blown across Gaza. It is beautiful in a dirty kind of way under its huge coastal sky but in the nature of a cliff edge.

Over the dunes in one direction is the Egyptian border. Across a field, more sand than vegetation, is another kind of border. It is the fence of the Israeli settlement of Slawe. It will be dismantled with all of Gaza's other settlements on the orders of Israel's Prime Minister, Ariel Sharon, after Israel's withdrawal in 2005. For now, however, it still stands, its greenhouses visible from the road. I watch as the Israeli military patrol cars, their aerials like spines, race along the settlement's security road to halt just as suddenly in their staccato charges. Warning shots are fired. The threat encroaches on the intervening space: an invisible invader of the football pitches where the older boys come to play; of the municipal well where the younger children are sent to fetch water; and of the few poor allotments that line the road. Poisonous as gas.

I am drawn to the last apartment block on the corner of

the road directly opposite Slawe. It is low, a handful of storeys of badly laid and flaking concrete. The ramshackle impression is reinforced by the damage that has been done to the building. Around each window are scores of bullet holes, the pitted sores of war's infection. There is evidence of heavier ordnance, splashes of cannon fire that have squirted hot metal through the flimsy breeze blocks into the rooms behind. And hanging from the windows, like so much laundry, are the children who live within. Once, my Palestinian guide tells me, this was a much sought-after place to live. In a tiny territory teeming with 1.4 million people, enclosed on three sides by walls and fences, and by a Mediterranean patrolled by Israeli gunboats on the other, it was valued. Its windows opened on to Gaza's greatest luxury: empty space.

The children, a dozen of them, belong to Zahira Samir Ibrahim, who lives on the second floor. Her husband, whose brother lives on the ground floor with his own family, is being treated in Egypt for cancer. With so many children and no wage earner, Zahira stays on in the building, unable to afford the rent on a safer – and more expensive – home away from the front line. In places under siege, I have learned, safety has its own economy measured in metres and dollars. I am not so naïve that I do not understand why this building has been so heavily hit. At night the gunmen enter it and fire at the settlement, and the Israeli soldiers and settlers fire back.

Zahira shows me up the stairs. Where there are external windows opening on the staircase the residents have piled breeze blocks, so when the shooting starts they have some psychological protection as they crawl on their hands and knees down to a ground-floor safe room with a concrete ceiling and no windows. Zahira's son Mohammed squeezes into her bedroom with a crowd of other children. He is five. The other children tell me that when the firing starts Mohammed hides in his mother's cupboard. They open it up and I see that it is packed almost to bursting with the family's clothes. Mohammed burrows towards the back. I think about the darkness, the soft textures, and the reassuring scent of family. Safety has a smell.

Saher, a twelve-year-old boy who lives with his father on the top floor, pushes in. He is an angry child who starts asking me questions to which I have no answers. 'When is this going to be finished?' he demands. 'Why is it taking so long? Why do they hate us?' When I talk to his father he admits his son wants to be a fighter. 'I can't guarantee what my son is doing any more. Suddenly he feels he can do anything. And he has cut his parents out of it. It has all started happening in the last two years. He heard that there was supposed to be a peace in the Palestinian lands, but in those two years all he has seen is shootings, shelling and assassination.'

There is something else going on with these Palestinian children. Kirsten Zaat, an official with the United Nations Children's Fund, who has observed what is happening, explains it to me one day. She says children as young as eight and nine feel that the adult world has failed them and that they are now 'responsible' for bringing the Palestinian struggle to its conclusion. It is, she says, a widespread problem and increasingly pernicious. She tells me about one of the Palestinian Authority's most senior negotiators in the peace process, whose fifteen-year-old son refuses to talk to him because the father believes in negotiations, not violence. 'They have lost trust in the adults who have been leading them for so long,' she says. 'Now when their parents tell them "Don't throw stones" the children's response is that their parents are not committed to the struggle to end the occupation.'

This fracturing between the generations has led to an increase in lawlessness previously unheard of in Palestinian society. 'For the first time in places like Jenin and Nablus we are coming across teenage street gangs,' says Zaat. 'What is happening is frightening Palestinian officials. We try and sit down and talk to these kids and tell them there are other ways to struggle – to get educated and politically involved. You tell them to train to be a doctor or a teacher. But when you say that, the kids turn around and say "Bullshit". They know that even if they do that the likelihood is that they will not get a job. And if they do there will be no money for their wages.'

This breakdown in family authority, Zaat believes, has combined dangerously with a problem of Palestinian society's own making: the celebration of the martyr during this *intifada*. Suicide bombers, teenage gunmen, stone throwers and those simply caught in the crossfire have all been elevated to this status of *shaheed* – like Ahmad's cousin whose picture sits upon his desk. Boys carry photographs of the martyrs – their friends or classmates who have died – on necklaces they wear beneath their clothes. 'Originally it was a defence mechanism for Palestinian society,' says Zaat. 'Where violence became so much a part of life, then society embraced it and celebrated it. The problem is that it has created a culture celebrating violent death.' I hear the same view expressed by Iyad Sarraj, a Gaza psychologist. He describes the creation of a new culture of conflict by Palestinian children in response to what they view as the older generation's powerlessness, the frequent humiliations. As the celebration of the young martyrs has gained wide social acceptance, so it has become impossible to criticise their sacrifice.

I finish my visit to Rafah at the cemetery. A couple of children are playing near one grave. When they see us, other children come running among the plots to meet us. A blustery wind carries a few spots of rain. You can tell the 'martyrs'' graves by the elaborate marble slabs that have been laid across them. The oldest boy says he will show me the martyrs and runs off down the sandy paths. I notice a tiny fresh grave, piled high with sand, with truncated concrete posts at each end. I learn it is the grave of Hamid al-Masry, a two-and-a-half-year-old child who lived in 'J' Block on Rafah's front line, shot and killed a few months earlier as he tried to flee with his parents when Israeli troops fired on their area.

By coincidence, I had encountered his parents two days before. His father, Asad, had shown me two certificates that he had been given to mark the killing of his child. I had seen them before, one of them awarded to each *shaheed* by the government of Saddam Hussein of Iraq. I asked him then about his six-year-old, Khalil, who had been leading Hamid by the hand when he was shot. How was he coping with his brother's loss? 'When he hears the shooting he runs into my arms,' said Asad. 'He talks about his brother daily. He talks about the Israelis. He says he's frightened of them. And he says he hates them.'

Weapons

The two sergeants are talking outside the briefing room at a Forward Operating Base in east Baghdad. We are waiting for a late-night ride to one of the new combat outposts set up by the US Army to take the war to Shia militant groups on their home turf. After days of travelling I am so tired that I can taste it in my mouth, stale as dirty laundry. It is July 2007. Outside, a katabatic evening wind blows strong and hot as a hair drier. Where I am sitting it is rancid and oppressive even with the air conditioning. Bundled up in my body armour, I can smell the odours seeping off me, organic and rotten. Beads of sweat stop–start in their descent down my spine into the small of my back, ticking like a water clock into a gathering pool. The skin on my feet, I am aware, is slowly turning white at the extremities from being constantly wet with sweat inside my trainers. Already it is flaking and cracking painfully under the soles and between my toes.

I rouse myself from the chafing, squirming discomfort to listen to the soldiers. The smaller sergeant, a young Asian in his mid-twenties with a boyish and cheerful face, is weighed down with rows of ammunition pouches hanging from a harness around his neck on armour even bulkier than mine with its high collar, groin flap and side plates. There is so much equipment that only his face under his helmet is visible as a reminder of his humanity. All the rest is boots and gloves, webbing and armour. Clipped on top of that: ammo clips, radio and weapons – all metal and sharp angles. He reminds me of a story told to me by several Iraqis: of how some parents have told their children that the American soldiers are not human at all, but a species of robot.

I don't notice it at first, but the bigger and older of the two sergeants does. He spots the handle of a knife sticking out of the Asian sergeant's ammo pouches, a blade slotted neatly between two rifle magazines. The older man's hand shoots out and grabs it. He flips it in his fingers. I can see at once that the knife is a brutally pared-down affair, a simple handle with a series of large holes drilled in it to reduce the weight. He examines the lock knife's short, curved black blade then sticks it at the owner playfully. He lunges a knee and thrusts forward like a fencer, a tall man with a neatly clipped moustache, turning grey, ramrod-straight in the way he holds himself.

'You keep that there and someone else is gonna pull it out and use it on you.' I can't hear what is said next. The banter comes and goes in odd, disjointed snatches shushed out by the air con's noise. Their muffled voices, dipping in and out beneath this interference, remind me of the soundtrack of one of the poor quality, pirate DVDs that everybody watches in Iraq, myself included – Harry Potter films and horror films, *Die Hard*, and grimly perfunctory porn movies, all thrusting cocks and grimaces. I try instead to read the name on the bigger man's jacket. It begins with B. But I am not quite close enough. The rest is as difficult to make out as the words that he is speaking.

His voice drops once again below the irregular rattling of the air con – a sound that defines Iraq (when the electricity is on), a collection of sounds labouring against the summer heat. Sometimes it is a laboured wheezing or the tick-ticking of the diesel engine of a black London cab. At other times it whooshes so that at night, when I close my eyes, I can imagine it reassuringly as the wind blustering on one of the Peak District's long grit-stone outcrops, and think of home. '. . . Close. Close enough . . .' the older sergeant says, as his voice builds again in volume. He is miming out an event, a pantomime of violence in which he takes both parts. He is holding an imaginary weapon against the smaller man's chest. Curling his finger round a trigger. 'Boom.' He jerks his hands as if accommodating the recoil of a shotgun. 'Boom. Boom. Three times in the chest.' He is laughing, I think. But it is a noise that comes from deep inside – jerky and random like the convulsing diaphragm of a dying man expelling air for the last time.

He is turning, cranking his head back in an exaggerated motion. From the actions, it is clear that someone is slashing at his neck with a knife. The sergeant is stepping back again. He moves his head like a boxer dodging a punch. Boom. Another shot is fired. I sense another death has taken place, another killing in this empire of the dead and dying. It is over and the older man is stiffly still, nodding his head in gentle affirmation of a fact known only to him. The two men are standing together silently considering the moral of this story, while the smaller man slides his knife back where it belongs. 'What pisses me off,' the taller of the two adds thoughtfully after a few beats, 'is that some of the guys got no recognition for their kills for months when they got home.' The men both nod at the wisdom of his comment, and the injustice of the bureaucracy.

Conversations that never seem to finish. Reiterated, universal, passing from voice to voice, soldier to soldier. They are themes that rise and fall in war's looped sound-track. In the language of this country: the place that is America in Iraq. Like the sergeants' voices they peak for a moment over the background noise until I am aware of them and I wonder why I did not pick up on them before. It is, perhaps, because they are said so casually. And there is one subject pre-eminent – killing.

War's most dreadful secret, banal and terrible at the same time, is not that men kill – that much is obvious – or even that many men enjoy their killing. That too has been well documented. It is more insidious than that. There exists a widespread envy of those who kill, and especially those who kill and kill again. There is bitter resentment among men when others claim their kills, or their kills are denied. That deems some men 'luckier' to have the opportunity to kill more than others.

Soldiers bitching. Another outpost, infested with rats that crawl across useless ceiling ducts that are connected to nothing in a former police station half-ruined by a bomb. The talk is about the young Texan lieutenant who has just left to lead a Small Kill Team on an overnight ambush, pale-faced and tired. Top of his class at school, the soldiers say with pride. From what they say it is evident he likes killing and is motivated by opportunities to kill. His men like and respect him, admire his bravery, but sitting on their cots they resent him grabbing all the opportunities to rack them up.

An activity so full of paradoxes, its meanings are hard to mine and even more difficult to understand. Killing, as Joanna Bourke explained in her study of combat, *An Intimate History of Killing*, for very many men is an exciting and pleasurable activity as well as a taboo. Being exciting, it is hidden on return to a civilian life that regards permissive killing, even in the high heat of conflict, as something 'to be done', an experience to be endured. But it is different in proximity to the battlefield – among your 'buddies' – where all ordinary rules are deliberately suspended. There it becomes obvious that the business of killing is easily assimilated into the story-worlds that define men's lives. It is integrated into all the other stories that I hear when the men are sitting in their hooches, or round their Saturday night barbecue pits with their cigars, drinking non-alcoholic beer or Gatorade with a shot of illicit spirits occasionally mixed in, after smoking a discreet bowl of hash. Then they talk about sex and cars and films; holidays and children. And sometimes combat and killing.

A few days after the performance with the knife, I am sitting with two soldiers on a base up north near Mosul. 'Don't use our real names,' says DC, a handsome paratrooper from the New York suburbs, a good enough soldier, it seems, but with a troubled history that has seen him busted down from sergeant and made up again. 'I don't fucking care,' his friend Andy interrupts, grinning a spacey

smile: 'I'm so far out of my fucking bubble.' I am listening
to their theories of life. Mainly they involve emotionless
sex and racing cars and motorbikes. They talk about how
to tune the engine of a Harley, about drag bikes, crashes
and the tactics for midget car racing. They tell me how fat
girls are always a dead cert, and best picked up at the ice-
cream counter at Wal-Mart at 2 a.m. 'Those are the ones
you know who really hate themselves,' says DC. About the
competitions back at their home base in Texas to see who
can pick up and fuck the fattest women. 'We had a ton, once,
in the same room,' says DC, grinning. He whistles, trying
to see if I am shocked. About queuing to fuck the same
woman with your buddies. Rotisserie, they call it. They talk
about getting wasted back home, and driving pickup trucks
with oversized wheels, and fleeing from the cops. Finally,
the conversation turns to Iraq and getting stoned and
heading out into the Red Zone behind the sights of a big
gun, weaving together the strands of sex and violence until
all human life seems as consumable as different cuts of
meat.

It is the first time that any of the American soldiers I
have come across have spoken directly about taking drugs,
although I have heard rumours. The random drug tests keep
it underground, discreet, unlike Vietnam. But they are off
duty and garrulous at the end of a day in which their unit
has not been required to go outside the wire, drinking coffee
at one of the cafés the army has placed on the bigger bases.
Most of the soldiers I talk to want to get out of Iraq as quickly
as they can. Not DC. 'Why are you in such a fucking hurry
to get back home?' he demands of his friend. 'What's back

there? Nothing. This is it,' he says emphatically. 'Ain't nothing better in the world. Take a big hit on the bong and then get all dressed up and get behind my gun. And then it's: "Come on, fuckers, fire at me" so I can shoot up the streets.'

T here is a game with guns I know some of the young soldiers play in Iraq called 'Do You Trust Me?' An unloaded weapon is pointed at the head. The trigger pulled. Not Russian roulette, just a buddy game with guns. The point is that people forget to clear their weapons and accidents happen. That's what the question means. I never see it. It is too private a ritual for outsiders.

Knives, however, are ubiquitous and visible. I am aware, all of sudden, of the same knife everywhere, brought into sharp focus by the sergeant's performance. I see it clipped into jackets and combat pants. One afternoon I stop discreetly to watch a group of soldiers trying to throw and stick a couple of the blades into a sheet of plywood that they have laid against one of their CHUs – the containerised housing units that have been dragged into the country, stacked on the back of trucks. They are in shorts and trainers, a bunch of giggling kids, jumping up and squealing to protect their feet when the knives – inevitably – bounce back towards them off the hard, compacted wood.

On another occasion a smart and studiously polite woman soldier shows me her knife. She says she bought it after she came across graffiti in one of the plastic porta-potties outside the command centre where she works announcing that the writer 'would like to fuck' her. She tells me she tried to scrub it out. Three times. Three times it returned, the letters creeping across the plastic. 'I know it is someone I work with,' she explains. 'It feels like I'm being stalked.' So she went to the PX military store and bought two knives, sliding one blade inside a desert boot and another into her pocket.

After a while I want to handle this knife, and get a sense of its potential. But I am reluctant to ask to look at one, embarrassed. The alternative that I settle on is to buy one from one of the warehouse-sized stores to be found on the larger bases that sell everything from chewing tobacco, DVDs and snacks to bras, cars and televisions. I find the knife in an aisle selling military equipment, buckles, badges and rucksacks. It comes in two sizes and I choose the smaller, not certain it will be legal to take it home to the UK.

As it turns out it is a Special Forces tactical knife, designed by Kit Carson, a name that means nothing to me. But when I look it up on the Internet later, I see it described as a 'classic design', offered for sale alongside other blades whose names I do recognise – fetishised little objects from novels about crime and serial killers that I have read, like the Sypderco blades beloved of Hannibal Lecter. It feels like an act of transgression buying this object, and I hide my new purchase at the bottom of a basketful of Pringles and Gatorade, expecting to be challenged. I am not sure why, but I fear that I have crossed over into the world of people who own blades designed for injury and death.

Fiddling with the knife, back in my CHU, it is the colour

that bothers me. The bare, black metal of the blade and handle is unsettling – as if intended to be hidden and secret. Its stark utility – an edge and handle, nothing more – contrasts with the knives I have owned in my adult life which have all been ambiguous in nature, fulfilling multiple roles: Swiss Army knives and Leathermen, or knives with spoons and forks attached that break down into rudimentary dining sets. This is a very different kind of blade. I can see immediately that it is a well-made knife when I take it out of its packaging. I tell myself it will be useful for mountaineering – a sturdy, light and compact tool, good for cutting abseil slings, the sharp blade excellent for camping and picnics. I also know that is not entirely its intent. It talks of a different kind of functionality.

Folded into its curving black frame, the knife is ten centimetres long, the blade three or so in width, tapering at the end to form the chiselled angle of a dagger point. Close to the handle I run my thumb over a set of deep saw-like serrations, so sharp I can feel the points tugging at my skin. The whole effect is shark-like, sleek and full of teeth, so much so that I wonder whether it was intended in its design. Playing with the knife, I discover that one half of the thumb guard, which I had taken to be part of the handle, in fact forms part of the blade, fashioned so that the knife can be flicked open to the locked position with a quick push of the finger, swivelling on a pivot. It is not a flick knife – there is no spring – but if I flick my wrist in the right way, it will swing smoothly open and snick into its lock. It is an object of a stark simplicity, long and strong enough to punch through muscle and gristle, to find an artery. Sharp enough to cut a throat.

But there is a mystery here. No one in Iraq uses a knife to fight. No one wants to get that close when they can blast Iraqis at a convenient and safe distance with weapons that have made killing people simple. Yet the knife exerts a peculiar fixation, far more so than the soldiers' personal weapons which are carried like tools, useful but invisible despite being in plain sight. I see men run with them during PT, take them to the showers and cinema and church, prop them by the table during meals. There are some men – 'geardos' the other soldiers call them – who lavish attention on their assault rifles, weighing them down with additional gadgets bought from magazines and the Internet – special sights and extra torches. They are the minority. The knife is different.

For earlier generations of soldiers it was the bayonet that was the fetishised instrument of violence, more fantasised about than actually employed. But cultures change. Now it is the Special Forces' dagger that is the badge of close and personal killing, symbol in the military imagination of the true warrior ethos.

I come across the knife again in the western Iraq town of Tal Afar. The translator sitting next to me in the back of the Humvee has it clipped to her body armour. The sergeant major in command of the vehicle, Briggs, asks to see it. 'You know how to use this thing?' he asks the woman, Rhoz, a Kurdish émigrée from Tennessee who tells me she likes military equipment. She is a pretty young woman with dark eyes, an open face and a lustrous black bob of hair who is upset that a stray dog she befriended on the base disappeared while she was on leave, almost certainly shot, as the men slyly suggest, by the Military Police. Everyone is more interested in Rhoz's knife than in her missing puppy. Briggs continues: ''Cos if you don't know how to use it you'll hurt yourself. It can close on your hand if you're not careful. I know a guy who lost a finger like that. If you're gonna use this on someone, you got to hold it the right way.' Briggs turns the knife in his hand and spells it out in slow sentences.

'See. This here is a collapsible knife. You use it like this,' he says, his fingers curled around the handle, 'an' you stab somebody, then the force maybe is gonna break the clasp and the blade's gonna fold on to your fingers.' He looks around at Rhoz and smiles. It is a pleasant, ordinary smile. 'You want to hold it like this,' he flips it over and shows how he has placed his fingers. 'But you want a knife – then what you really want is a K-Bar.' We are stopped for a while and the driver hands his over. It is a long and solid dagger, perhaps eight inches of blade in a fixed handle. 'You use this like you use a bayonet,' says Briggs. 'Stick it in and twist it around.' He hands it to Rhoz, adding seriously, 'I don't want to see that knife clipped on your armour, 'less you know how to use it.'

I ask Briggs if he knows of anyone who ever used his bayonet. I ask because I interviewed a man who used one in the Falklands War, during the battle for Mount Tumbledown, and I remember his description of the horror of using the weapon. I want to know how much of this stuff about weapons that stab and cut is bullshit. 'Not here,' he says at first. There is a pause. 'No. Wait on. I knew one guy who used it to kill two Iraqis, protecting his colonel in close-quarters fighting.' The K-Bar belongs to the driver, Hunt, a ruddy Kentuckian, whose face is purple and sweating. I ask him if he's ever used his knife. 'Not in Iraq. Not in the army. But I used a knife, coupla times before.' The talk of stabbing seems to trigger recollections of past violence in his life. 'My mom stabbed me once,' he says, without explanation. 'An' my brother shot me with a .22 when I was sleeping. You know we was just playing fighting. But I hurt him. And he said: "I'm gonna shoot you when you are asleep." An' he shot me.'

Favourite objects reflect the owners' preoccupations. They act as props in the performances that are our lives. They reinforce our special sense of self, and have subtle meanings both for ourselves and for those observing us, reminding people who we are and what our values are. In martial societies, the investing of weapons with meanings is deliberately encouraged. Soldiers in training are encouraged to form a relationship with their personal weapon. Their tanks are stencilled with nicknames. The most cherished object, however, is often the knife.

The knives are handled and played with in a way that verges on the autoerotic. Stabbing – some have observed – has a sexual meaning, penetrating the victim. The rareness of the knife's employment in combat, and the bloodily violent implications when it is, are suggestive of the particular ruthlessness of what was once called valour.

To be so close, and in such hazard, recollects martial traditions from duelling to hand-to-hand combat. But that is not the whole picture. The knife's symbolism is given further weight in popular culture, in the way these knives are advertised as being designed for an elite cadre of Special Forces, two words that have a powerful, almost obsessive resonance in modern culture, depicted endlessly in films and magazines and books as the modern warrior ideal. And the fixation with the knife in the US military signifies something else: it is as much a social indicator as a cultural one, reflecting accurately the economic, educational and ethnic nature of the groups from which the military largely recruits, groups that have the highest history of weapon-carrying in adolescence. Largely involving knives.

The business of carrying weapons reinforces how much of an outsider I am in this world. I am a visitor in war, even when accompanying troops through combat. It is possible for me to share the risks. Without a weapon, the soldiers remind me I am other to them, to be kept at a distance and not quite to be trusted in the real conversations fighters have with each other. Not about dying – people will often talk about their dead and injured friends – but killing. I am left instead to pick at snatches and suggestions. I have seen men kill. I have seen a gunner fire the cannon of his vehicle thinking he has killed civilians by mistake and, as he has looked down to his friends for reassurance, seen the sick and lonely look on his face turning to something approaching happiness on realising the bodies were men holding guns. I have heard soldiers rib a friend who had killed a child in error and seen his face colour with embarrassment while they laughed. Until he laughed also.

I am not without a map in this. Studies by military psychologists help me understand, describing in minute detail the framework of the act of killing, and the relationship between different weapons and the experience. What emerges is a mathematical connection between the type of weapon used and the remorse that most men feel after the kill. It exists as a dense and complicated moral algorithm. Resolved into its most simple form it dictates that the closer you are to your victim – killing with a bayonet, a K-Bar, or with your rifle in close-quarters combat – the more desperate and human the victim appears after you have taken his life; the more likely it is that the soldier will later feel a sense of shame.

Remorse, or the degree of it at least, becomes a matter of centimetres and metres and kilometres – a scale of guilt calibrated on a slide rule. According to this equation, to shoot from a distance is better than to shoot from close quarters; to shoot at close quarters is better than to use a knife. To slash or cut or bludgeon is easier than to stab. Worst of all is to stab with a K-Bar or bayonet. Given the fixation on knives, it is counter-intuitive.

The gradations are part of a well-recognised cycle of emotional responses that accompany the act of killing. In his study of how soldiers kill, *On Killing*, Lt Col. Dave Grossman, a former US Army ranger and lecturer in psychology at West Point, identifies a cycle of emotional responses associated with different weapons systems from aircraft to knives. I come across the book by chance in the office of a tough Ranger-tabbed chaplain who has a signed poster on his wall from Rush Limbaugh, the conservative shock jock. He lends me the book, and as I tote it round the base it is suddenly the focus of comments. They come largely from officers who, seeing me with it in my hand, come over to introduce themselves and remark how good it is or tell me they have a copy. They are quietly, intensely respectful of Grossman's views. For some, the comments are made with the same casually serious voice with which many of them say grace when sitting down to eat, until I think of it as a bloody missal, a guide to permissive murder.

I read the book with a renewed curiosity, racing through the pages while lying on my cot and trying to imagine the impact on those soldiers of these words when they first read them. I imagine them, grappling with Grossman's similes as he compares the nervous moments of preparing to shoot one's first man with that of the hunter shooting his first buck. But it is an alien and distant comparison for me. The experience of killing animals on the farm when I was a child – rabbits and pigeons blasted with my grand-father's shotgun, or snared with a wire noose and brained messily on a nearby rock or on my boot – lacks any kind of emotional resonance. They seemed rather perfunctory acts. My memory is of the struggle to manage a shotgun. Instead, I am left looking for my own metaphors of violence. Only when I think about the fights I have been in do I get the faintest bitter flavour of it, a taste like distant tear gas.

Killing goes like this: there is concern, in the first instance, with the idea of it, followed by the act itself passing in a blur of adrenaline. Next, argues Grossman, comes a period of mental reconciliation that begins with feelings of exhilaration and excitement, followed by shame, and finally an acceptance and rationalisation mediated by different social mechanisms (it was necessary or justified; the de-legitimisation of the victim's claim to humanity; the idea of following of orders). It is only when the process of rationalisation fails that the risk of suffering post-traumatic stress disorder rises sharply.

But what seems straightforward is actually far more complex. It is defined not only by personality, the level of training, cultural background and the feeling of the just-ness or otherwise of the cause, but by the technical means by which the killing is accomplished. It is why it is easier for snipers and pilots and the operators of stand-off weapons systems to kill with less remorse, less psychological damage.

Still, for those of us who have not killed, and have no desire to kill, it remains unfathomable. Flying into Iraq on one occasion I encounter David Finkel of the *Washington Post*, who puts his finger on the problem. It was not how a sniper made his first kill, he suggested, as we waited for the helicopters that would take us out to units we were visiting. There is training, the encouragement of *esprit de corps*, the drilling in of orders and necessity that deals with that. There is a sense of curiosity too. Perhaps, most power-fully, a feeling of curiosity. It was not that which puzzled Finkel. It was how, having done it once, a soldier could do it the second time. Watching the red mist of matter blown through the body. Seeing someone die. And knowing you had done what cannot be undone.

In war all life is negotiated around weapons. Societies are reordered into sharply defined new hierarchies: into those who have weapons and those who have not. A man with a gun can walk to the front of the bread or petrol queue. With his militia friends he can take over a petrol station if he likes and reorganise the distribution while skimming money off the top. With a rifle you can order a woman to have sex. Weapons redistribute wealth through 'taxes', protection rackets and straight theft. Scores can be settled, under the cover of generalised violence.

A gun can be a lever in the political system. An armed group can take over a hospital ward, and later a whole hospital, as happened across Iraq, thus grabbing control of a key part of social provision for a political party. Having a gun confers small benefits too. In the Baghdad traffic jams – the *izdiham* – the way through is cleared by those who have weapons. A new topography is imposed upon the city by armed checkpoints and men with guns, which ways are open, which ways closed. Weapons censor, blocking out argument, debate, verbal exchange. Those with guns can speak. They have opinions and deliver orders and instructions. Those without are required to be silent.

Early on, in the first few weeks after the fall of Baghdad, a US soldier pulls a rifle on me as I try to reach the Sheraton Hotel, the entrance to which he is blocking. I argue that I am staying in the hotel and that the car park, which he is preventing access to, is where I leave my car for safety. But he is new to the detail. Perhaps a little dumb and lacking in confidence, a youth for whom possession of a rifle is a replacement for thinking. I try to get him to turn around to see the other cars parked beyond the wire, but he is not listening. I can see his face through the wind-screen, angry and scared at the same time because I am not doing what I'm told; because I am in breach of the unwritten contract between the armed and the unarmed. He presses the weapon almost on to the glass in front of me. He is uncertain, shaky, and shuffles to get a better, wider firing stance, his hip pushed into my car's front bumper. The sights obscure his face, until all that is left is the visible fact of the gun, the compact and worn 'o' of the barrel's end that is echoed in a little, desperate, deflating 'oh' inside of me when I realise that he might really fire.

The mere suggestion of a weapon is sometimes enough to trigger the same unsettling emotions. It is not the sensation of contact, the wild, druggy adrenaline rush experienced under fire. Instead it is fluttering and flat, a sense of abruptly being diminished. Like the moment of hearing tragic news about a friend, as if all possibilities had been at once extinguished.

You can spot men who are carrying guns sometimes from the way they hold themselves. As the war goes on, I find that Iraqis learn it like a second nature. Eventually I learn it too. Not long before the first battle of Fallujah, I turn up in the city with a friend and *Observer* colleague, Gary Calton, to do an interview. Three months before, I had spent almost every other day for a month travelling back-wards and forwards to Fallujah, meeting insurgents and interviewing families, money changers and shopkeepers, former Ba'athists. I had felt safe with the connections I had developed.

Overconfident, at first I don't notice how things have changed – subtle signals of new tensions and dangers. We are waiting for a meeting. Killing time, we decide to cross the road to grab a bite in a nearby restaurant. But something is wrong. The food takes too long to come; others are being served quickly and eating. Two waiters hover too attentively beside the table, watchful and smiling awkwardly. It occurs to me at last that someone has told them to keep an eye on us. Nervous, I insist we leave the meal half-eaten on the table. We cross the road again to check on the progress of the interview with the 'general', our connection in the city, in whose shop I feel safe. But we are not safe. Not yet.

Traversing the road's raised median, I am aware of a muscular man in his late twenties wearing a tracksuit, who hovers at a distance, quietly talking to Iraqis on the pavement. As we approach where he is standing, I notice him fiddling with the elastic band of his trousers. In an instant I realise he has a pistol on his hip. I whisper to Gary. And at that moment he turns to walk directly at us, the breeze lifting the corner of his jacket to reveal the dark nub of a grip. It is not our final encounter with the man. Forty minutes later, as I am conducting the interview, he appears outside the shop with three other men, long weapons hidden clumsily beneath their jackets, waiting for us to leave. In the end it is only the general's influence that saves us from whatever they intended.

The knives I fear most are out in the *malhalas*, Iraq's dreary and dusty neighbourhoods that sprawl, massive and uniform, out of its urban centres. They are not the toys the American soldiers play with, dreaming their martial dreams, but the blades used by an absolute minority of Iraqis, the head choppers allied to al-Qaeda in Iraq, who employ butchers' knives made for slaughtering sheep and cattle to decapitate Iraqis and foreign hostages who fall into their hands. They are beheadings that exert a fascination on many Iraqis, unexplainable either by the Koranic exhortation to 'smite the infidel in the neck', or as political acts designed to inspire terror through the horror of the spectacle. For some who watch them, collect them on their hard drives, it is clear they do have a political and religious meaning. But most who watch them in the Internet cafés or who save them on their telephones across Iraq do so because they want to see a killing.

I avoid these grotesque performances until one day, to demonstrate a point, an Iraqi guard at a human rights organisation is called in to show me one of the clips saved on his mobile phone. I am supposed to be watching the murder of an Iraqi woman, but as he cups the phone in his hand and presses play to reveal a jumpy and bleached set of images, it is clear that the hostage is a dark, smooth-skinned man with faint, fatty breasts. What I am seeing is the decapitation of a Nepalese hostage in 2004, one of twelve murdered by the same jihadi group.

The video moves quickly to the murder. I tell myself at first that I am watching it for journalistic reasons. But I understand the curiosity as well. There is in these images a horribly compelling appeal. Perhaps it is the knowledge that in a few seconds a life will end. I wonder about the quickness of it and the pain. I am curious about the killer too – whether his hands will shake with excitement or with fear and fumble it.

A man lies on the floor, shirtless. His hands are bound behind his back with a broad white cloth. The same cloth, bloody on one side, is bound over his eyes. A second man in combats, his face carefully concealed by a cap, bends down over the prisoner. Quickly and methodically he begins to cut his throat. But what stays with me is not the dying hostage's last moments, breathing through a severed and quivering neck, nor the moans nor the unreally red arterial blood, nor even the theatrical dumping of the head. Instead it is the killer's use of his knife. It is a perfunctory sawing that probes deeply at the victim's throat as the executioner holds his head, looking for tendons and muscles to sever.

It is too easy for such a dreadful act: like skinning fish, or a butcher cutting fat off meat. I think: murder should be more emotionally charged, angry and physical, exultant or fearful, not this offhand snipping and slicing. I realise too that I have seen this before, watching the father of a Palestinian family cut just this way through the throat of a startled, hobbled ox held by his sons on a Gaza pavement, slicing and digging, to bleed it for a feast.

he head choppers understand that fear is the most powerful weapon in asymmetric war. Out in the Red Zone – out in the 'Red', a word laden with connotations of blood and danger, the real Iraq beyond the concrete walls, barbed wire fences and checkpoints – the Iraqi fighters have no multimillion-dollar weapons. There are no M1A1 tanks or Humvees, no Apache helicopters or Warthogs with cannons that rip trees and buildings, cars and people to pieces. There are no systems at all. No chance of military victory in the conventional sense. There is only the ability to frighten through the medium of death. The men who ambush from the palm groves and from amid dense networks of canals, from out of empty, ruined buildings eviscerated by dozens of fire fights, have no night sights or coded combat radios, no satellite vehicle-tracking systems. What weapons do exist in addition to rifles and RPGs are cheaply terrible affairs, fashioned out of scrap and the military detritus of an Iraq awash with mortar and artillery shells. Or they are the devastatingly simple explosively formed penetrators (EFPs) – tubes that fire a slug through the US armour.

They are not only destructive. They function on the slow attrition of nerves, operating both on the minds of the soldiers who patrol the roads, as well as on the political space, on the imagination and tolerance of the US and British publics who receive the shipments of the dead and maimed. Who, in the democratic sphere, have a say in the cost–benefit analysis of all this slaughter. And these different kinds of bomb are the most successful weapons in Iraq not because they are the most effective killer, but because they are so cheap and simple, costing a few hundred dollars to produce and able to destroy vehicles and men in which hundreds of thousands have been invested.

I am shown one of the steel slugs fired from an EFP while visiting a small US military training team marooned in the heart of Sadr City, Baghdad's vast, impoverished Shia slum. They are twenty US soldiers with 30,000 rounds of ammunition stacked in the corridors of their small outpost, entirely surrounded, a Fort Apache of fearful anticipation. The slug is a disc of machined metal the width of an ashtray, thick as a bar of soap. The weight pressing on my palm has a horribly suggestive force, dense and obscene, that pulls at the muscles and tendons of my wrist as I heft it. I imagine its mass being driven through the thick plating of vehicles, spalling glass and steel in its rushing path into tumbling, jagged fragments that hack at limbs and heads and torsos. Imagining it, I am afraid.

When I look more closely I can see that the slug is bevelled on one side to form a shallow hollow, like the surface of a blood corpuscle observed beneath a microscope. A US Army explosives expert, a major with the engineers with whom I share a billet for a week, sits down next to me on my cot with his books and explains the physics of it. He is one of two engineers staying in my room in the basement of one of Saddam Hussein's former intelligence headquarters, a multi-storey concrete building, whose upper floors – now sagging – were hit by a cruise missile. The other man is middle-aged: tall with stooped shoulders, a reticent civilian with a straggling moustache. He speaks little and is fetched at all times of the night by his military minders. Eventually it becomes clear that he is looking for a new version of the weapon.

Most of what the major says makes no sense to me. He

talks about equations, coefficients, vectors and thrust with a hobbyist's enthusiasm. But he is happy to have an audience and I am just as happy to listen. The device, he explains patiently, works in two different ways, depending on the material out of which the slug is fashioned. If it is steel, as it is blasted from the tube the heavy slug is forced inside out around the weakness in the metal created by the pressed indentation. The result is a crude, hollow bullet that punches a hole and then fragments as it enters the target. More dangerous, he explains, is the softer, copper version. When it is fired, the heat of the explosion turns the copper molten. Then the bevelled shaping in the slug creates a superheated jet of metal.

If you spend enough time on Iraq's roads you come across victims. One time it is a Humvee that is hit, travelling in a convoy to an outpost in the southern Baghdad district of Zafraniyah. It is early and I'm half asleep when I hear word of an attack using an EFP. When I reach the scene there are already a dozen military vehicles. The damaged Humvee has been pulled over to one side. I can quickly see that the slug has gone through the armoured glass next to one of the vehicle's rear seats. The glass around the entry point is crazed like a frozen puddle stamped with a boot. The undamaged glass on the other side is bloody. There is a tense and angry silence about the soldiers who mill around. Some run off looking for Iraqis to arrest. A few hold up the traffic. For the rest there is nothing much to do, except consider the circumstances that left the gunner standing on the gearbox dead, while the colonel next to him survived.

There is another type of bomb. It is more common than

the EFP. Most of the US soldiers who go out beyond the wire have been blown up by one, some several times, or at least have been brushed by its scalding breath. I meet men who have been hit five, six and seven times. Usually it is an old artillery shell or two, or a cluster of mortars wired together, looted from Saddam Hussein's vast stockpiles that the US military left unsecured for months after the invasion. There are rare crews I meet that have been hit twice in a single day. Mainly it is the aftermath I see: junctions cratered to moonscapes where the bombers have returned again and again; vehicle repair pounds full of Bradleys, Humvees, even tanks that have been torn violently apart. In this military world of acronyms, it is called an IED, an 'improvised explosive device'. And in the ordering of things that explode in Iraq there are a whole host of different classes. There are devices that are vehicle-borne (car and truck bombs) and within that a sub-class of suicide car bombs. There are bombs carried by donkeys. There are suicide bombs that are simply vests worn by walking attackers. But most common is the bomb buried in culverts and in potholes.

They are often visible to the naked eye: the slight thread of a command wire snaking out of holes and rubbish dumps, crawling out of culverts, so that a horrible decision is made in these places on a daily basis: to stop and call the bomb disposal team, or to drive on. Most times, if a triggerman is not visible the vehicles continue. My mind finds a way of dealing with it. At first, travelling in military convoys, the fear of these things is utterly exhausting. The anticipation is felt physically. It is not being hit that becomes the issue, but where in the body the fragments might strike. I worry about the Kevlar sides to my body armour, where I would take the blast, lacking the ceramic side plates of the US soldiers' armour. I worry about the flak jacket sitting too high on my waist, exposing my liver, about my unprotected legs and groin, the location of large arteries. You cannot live like that. And while I wonder at the sangfroid of the soldiers, after a time my body imposes the same stillness. It is a fraught calmness I recognise from bad moments in mountaineering, a fatalistic feeling of acceptance. Not bravery, or resilience, but the process of being conditioned like a lab rat.

In the end even those of us who do not carry weapons are forced to address the meaning of their use. Two guns are sitting in an Adidas sports bag on my bedroom floor in the Hamra Hotel. It is later – much later – in the war. As it gets ever more dangerous, I accept that if I wish to work unembedded no option remains but to hire armed local guards to ride with me. It is an uncomfortable decision, not least because I have no illusions about whether two guards will make an ambush any more survivable. What is clear is that when everybody else has guards, not to have them marks me out as the soft option for any would-be kidnapper.

I employ Ayman and Thair, and a second driver to follow in a 'chase car'. At the day's end, the two men tuck their pistols in their waists, shake my hand and prepare to leave. They don't want to carry their rifles, which are illegal without a proper permit, back and forth to work each day. So Ayman, the older of the two, delivers the sports bag containing the two weapons to my room for the night. After a while I begin to feel that the weapons sit in my room with an unspoken permission attached to them: if things go very badly wrong, then use them. Except that I do not want anything to do with the guns. Even having them in my room instils in me a deep sense of uneasiness. I feel embarrassed by their presence, as if they were porn mags beneath my bed.

I did not always feel this way. I learned to shoot at school as a cadet. Then, guns seemed exciting and glamorous. To fire them as a fifteen-year-old boy was to enter a club with a small membership. My school, founded by Henry VIII, had a little range round the back of the bike sheds, stacked with sand, where we could fire .22 Martini rifles of First World War vintage and older – bolt-action rifles with wooden stocks polished from generations of handling. Later we were given Lee–Enfields, and on a trip to an army training camp in Cornwall we were allowed to fire pistols and sub-machine guns and given blank rounds with which to crawl among the steep-faced dunes in a mock attack that ended in the equally mock execution of my history teacher.

I feel the AKs in my room, morosely silent visitors. Although I do not like touching guns as an adult, I know how these weapons work and their peculiarities. I have seen them fired and stripped and fought with. I have seen them used as hammers and levers to break locks and doors, used as clubs and barriers. Mostly I have been afraid of them. I have had their bullets shot at me, or travelled in pickup trucks with bored teenagers who do not know how to make the weapons safe. I know that the safety is counter-intuitive, going from safe to fully automatic and only then to single fire. I know too that they have a reputation for recoiling heavily, so that when fired on fully automatic the weapon tends to climb away from the target after the first three shots.

One night I cannot sleep and I feel that it is the guns that are responsible. It is a bad time in Baghdad and the conversation in the Hamra Hotel has come round to what-ifs: how long the few journalists left in the hotel will be able to continue working and what would happen in an evacuation of the hotel; how long the security on the perimeter could hold out before the Quick Reaction Force could mount a rescue mission from the Green Zone. The times talked about seem long. The guns beg a question that I understand must be resolved.

It is past 1 a.m. I slip out from underneath the thin, uncomfortable sheets to stand in my bare feet. I pull a chair to the centre of the narrow room and set it facing the door. My bare back glues to the wooden frame as I sit there in the dark, looking at the faint lump that is the bag – until I drag it to me and unzip it. By now, my eyes are acclimatised to a purple darkness illuminated only by the light outside my window. It is enough to see the worn black metal and cracked wood, the grey duct tape wound round the doubled magazines to hold them together for rapid changing of the clips.

Gently I take one of the rifles from the bag and lay it on my lap. I can smell the faint tangy odour of oil. I let it sit there for a few seconds – no more. But then I know that it is done. As I return the rifle to its bag I understand for the first time in over a decade of covering conflicts that I would use this weapon if I had to. I know too the implications of that realisation – that my time covering wars is grinding slowly to an end. I have been compromised by fear. Corrupted by what conflict means.

Terror

The shoes from the shop window have been scattered by the bomb across the pavement of Jerusalem's Jaffa Road. A single black loafer, shipwrecked on its side, lies separated by floes of glass from lace-ups, tan women's flats and cream court shoes, still stiff, waxy and factory-polished from the box. I halt in my progress past the smashed shop fronts and mannequins now open to the air, wigless from the blast and bald as cancer patients. If I bend down I know I will be able to smell the odour of new shoes, the stockroom perfume of leather and rubber, naptha and lanoline, ethyls and gum Arabic. It is, briefly, a reassuring thought: to connect with a world distant from violence, and with the Saturday job of my schooldays when I sold shoes like these. I notice a solitary suede knee boot, deflated as a discarded Saturday-night condom, hanging from what remains of the glass in the shoe shop's window, caught on a shard in the bottom of a pink wood frame.

The flickering strobes on the white ambulances ink a faint scarlet wash on to the winter light as the men from ZAKA – the *Zihuy Korbanot Ason* (Disaster Victim Identification) – work their scrapers gingerly and respectfully over the pavement and the walls. ZAKA: the body-part men, collecting the human fragments from a suicide bombing for burial. Most are Orthodox Jews, religious men who volunteer for this hard duty out of conviction. 'True kindness' they call themselves, working to ensure that no part, not even blood, is left behind unburied. One in particular catches my eye, a little younger than the rest, moon-faced and heavy-set with a dark beard and side curls. He squats carefully, his fluorescent bib over his white shirt, the strings of his *tzitzit* fringes hanging on black trousers. He supports himself with one hand on a meaty thigh among the shards of glass, some bloodied. With the other he slices his tool delicately, methodically, at a piece of flesh. I am struck at once by the intimacy of it amidst the urgency. There is the sound of plastic on concrete, the shuffling of glass, as he scoops, as carefully as lifting a poached egg from a pan. I notice that his tool is the same implement I use to clear the frost from my car windscreen. His face is blandly impassive as he works, the only expression a screw of concentration as he bags the fragment, then begins scanning the scene again for other pieces to collect.

The air is heavy with the sourness of recent death. Once, I tried to break this smell into its parts by writing down the different elements I could detect. A sick perfumier. What I found was the bacterial odour of old fridges, the sharp tang of butchers' shops, soiled nappies. It reminds me too – in a way I cannot quite fathom – of the astringent smell of the milking parlour at my grandfather's farm. All mingled. The brain knows it for what it is: a unique challenge to the idea of our living selves. I try to breathe only through my mouth. But no matter how hard I try, some of the odour always infiltrates, triggering a short circuit from nose to palate, tripping the gag reflex and leaving a dirty taste that lingers far too long. It is like the children's game where you endeavour to manoeuvre a loop of wire around a bigger metal coil without touching, without making the electrical connection that will power the buzzer. With this smell, the buzzer always sounds.

I have missed breakfast and my stomach is acid and churning with hunger. I wonder how I can still feel the desire to eat, seeing and smelling this. But I realise that I am famished. A photographer friend shooting the scene jokes grimly about not being able to eat meat for a while. Perversely, however, I want nothing more than a *shawarma* sandwich, as if eating could erase the taste, and expunge the reality of violent death. There is a buzz among the Israeli police and journalists that I am slow to catch on to. The forensics guys in their white overalls and yellow boots are working on a severed arm lying across the kerb. The bomber's arm is just visible where they are kneeling. It is still clad in a pullover sleeve disconnected at the same point as the limb. They are attempting to get a print. The hand is small, the bloom of the flesh already turned waxy. Finally I understand what the excitement is about. It is a female limb – the hand of the first Palestinian woman to have become a suicide bomber.

For a while the Israeli spokesmen and lobbyists attempt to insist on a descriptive formulation that emphasises only the element of murder, erasing the idea of the sacrifice – no matter how pointless – inherent in a suicide bombing. But no one buys 'homicide bomber': criminality without a political agenda. My friend Bryan, a lanky and laconic Canadian with a blond ponytail, starts calling them 'SBs'. At least I hear it from him first. That is what they become, two simple letters defining an event. Neutral. A shorthand that requires no implicit judgement of the act. Only later do I begin to understand that wars are as much defined by the weapons that are used in them as they are by the nature of those who fight, or by their causes or histories. They are given a unique shape and texture by poison gas, the trench, the flame-thrower and cruise missile, by the helicopter seeding mines. Each lends colour to the special fears that different conflicts and weapons induce. These, my wars at the beginning of the twenty-first century, are framed by the suicide attack.

I learn the particularities of the SB, the sound and smell and consequences. The muted, sickly colours: drained yellows and greys of bomb-amputated limbs. Dead, bruised faces sagging like sodden plaster. Blown-out windows and the scattering of keys and shoes and human fragments. Most of the time I hear them at a distance, until one day a bomb explodes fifty metres from where I am eating dinner outside my hotel on Jerusalem's Nablus Road, opposite the Damascus Gate that leads into the Old City. It is a premature event, the bomber detonating his load on being challenged in his car by soldiers at a random checkpoint. At this distance there are no nuances to be imagined in the sound, only a total immersion in its exclamation, and in its after-math, the underwater silence peculiar to explosions. I grab a notebook from the table and run outside. But there are soldiers charging at me who push me back into the restaurant garden. Angry faces follow me in and shout at the handful of guests frozen over their food. As if by eating in an Arab-run hotel, the soldiers imply, we are admitting some obscure complicity.

The fear of SBs imposes new rules on working in the city, which will later be replicated in Baghdad (until it is impossible to go out there at all). Common wisdom, as well as evidence, has it that there are risky times. And there are dangerous places. I won't eat in a restaurant in Jewish West Jerusalem that has a glass frontage or lacks security at the front door. Where there is security I find myself rating the efficiency of the bored young men with their metal-detecting wands: how well they search a friend's handbag or pat me down. There are discussions about the best place to sit in those Jewish places we do frequent. Do I want to be close to the door? Behind a pillar or on the first floor? Food stalls are out. I avoid places too where people gather in the open like bus stops, cinemas or queues. Public celebrations.

The idea of the SB leaches into the culture in unexpected ways. A suicide bomber disguised as an observant Jew explodes next to Bryan's apartment overlooking Ethiopia Street, a pretty thoroughfare of ancient limestone buildings, after being challenged by a soldier. It is the fifth bomb in Jerusalem in two days. The bomber's head flies off and rolls into the courtyard of the Lycée Français, visible from Bryan's balcony. His cock and balls, however, all in one piece, are plastered across the windscreen of a car parked outside the school. A rumour that goes round the West Bank for some months after – put about, some people claim, by the Israeli spooks – says that the genitalia have not been buried. And so the bomber will not be able to enjoy the fruits of martyrdom in heaven with the virgins promised to the *shaheed*. After that I hear from a cop that the male SBs are strapping their cocks up tightly to keep them with the torso when their bomb goes off. Finally, I hear the event recycled as a joke by Palestinian men. It goes like this: an Israeli and the suicide bomber who has killed him are ascending to heaven in a lift. The suicide bomber is boasting to his victim about the virgins he has been promised for his act. The Israeli is smiling. 'What's your problem?' asks the SB. 'I've just killed you.' 'I don't have a problem,' replies his smirking victim, 'but you do. Your dick is in my pocket.'

It is a week after the bomb on Jaffa Road and I am perched opposite the stretcher in the back of another ambulance, one of several lined up, autistically neat, at the end of one of the broad thoroughfares of Ramallah, on the West Bank. The ambulances this time are painted with Red Crescents, not the interlocking scarlet triangles of the *Magen David*. We are around a corner from the *muqata* – the broad, walled compound of the Palestinian leader Yasser Arafat, where soon enough he will be trapped under Israeli siege. Which eventually will be his mausoleum. It is close enough to the action that I can run around the corner and be in the thick of it in seconds. By now the clashes seem grimly familiar, the stone-throwing boys, the Israelis with their gas and rifles, as choreographed as an exchange of spears in the *Iliad* or on a tribal battlefield. The drivers smoke cigarettes and wait. Sometimes a vehicle creeps forward out of the line, ready to speed into the crowd to retrieve a casualty.

I have crossed the Second Intifada's conflict line, the century-old front between Jews and Palestinians, but an easy enough car journey in January 2002, to sit with Nasser Ahlam in the ambulance she crews. Compact and slender, she sits next to the driver, brushing away the brown hair that falls over one cheek. Her face is almost as pale as those of the Hasidic Jews who had gathered the human remnants from the recent bombing. The hair frames pretty but pinched features that crowd the centre of an oval face. The effect is a permanent appearance of being concerned: a slight young woman, hunched and small behind the windscreen, spine bent and shoulders tense.

We do not have to wait long for the first stones and the first shots. But I am here to ride with Nasser, not to see the injured boys with their broken limbs and fractured skulls. A few days ago it was Nasser's friend Wafa Idris, the woman she worked with on these ambulances, who walked on to Jaffa Street at 12.15 p.m. with a backpack containing ten kilos of explosives. It was Nasser's co-worker, Wafa, with her dark falling curls, who blew herself to pieces, killing an eighty-one-year-old man and injuring a hundred others. I want to answer a question: whether I have met this woman and her dead friend before on my visits to this ambulance station. Whether, in recalling that vague encounter, I can understand. But when I watch Nasser I realise that I can't recall her face. There is no connection. All that is left is to ask Nasser what made her friend do this.

'**T**eh-RAW.' Ariel Sharon, Israel's Prime Minister, strangles the syllables when he spits out the word in English. His vocal chords squeeze the letters into strange new shapes – 'Teh-ROAR' – until the word is transformed into a guttural enunciation of violence, pregnant with new sinister meanings. It begins with a sharp Te and then a breathy H that almost fades into a glottal stop. Finally, a growling rises from deep in his gullet. It is not just 'terror' now but something different appropriated through constant repetition. I hear it at press conferences. On television. Until one day he is sitting in front of me in his office, skin translucent with age, oddly insubstantial for a heavy man who occupies so much space.

The curving white spinnaker of his shirtfront, inflated by his belly, pushes through his dark jacket. Only his wrists and eyelids move with animation. A hand flaps vigorously like a landed fish gasping for air. It looks independent – severed – from the man who sits behind his desk, surrounded by his coterie of aides who slip him notes, or answer when he cannot find an English word. What Sharon means is 'Arab Teh-raw'. A word and a concept always exclusive to the enemy's behaviour – belonging uniquely to the other. 'I'll tell you what we will be doing. What we are doing now,' he says at the end of a long, rambling interview, a year after Wafa's death. 'What my grandfather and my parents have done, myself, my sons, and families here, facing Arab terror for five, six generations.' I hear the same word again on both sides of this conflict. Israeli terror. Palestinian terror. Until I believe that it is the word that gives meaning to this conflict.

Terror. A physical sensation: the sequence of responses occurring in the human body that we associate with an overpowering and imminent threat. In the rush of hormones, the heart beats rapidly. Rapid breathing occurs, flooding the blood with oxygen to prepare for fight or flight. Our skin sweats. Eyes widen and the pupils dilate. There are few things we feel as powerfully as this. Memories formed in times of fear and trauma are more readily imprinted in the brain and more easily recalled from what scientists believe is a special memory circuit designed to imprint the most frightening of our experiences. To teach us strategies for future survival.

Of all of the emotions, the human brain devotes the most physical resources to handling fear, activating a complex sequence that judges the proximity of the perceived danger and calculates the available options. In considering the faces of those around us, a crucial determinant, the brain reacts to the signals of terror significantly faster than to a smile or a neutral expression. But terror is not always short-lived and instant. Terror can last for hours or days, not quite with the same intensity. Then it is corrosive. A sickness to be suffered.

How complicated the circuit is that deals with fear and threat has been revealed in research by Dr Dean Mobbs and his colleagues at the Centre for Neuroimaging at University College London, who examined how different areas of the brain come into play depending on the distance we are from the perceived danger. The results suggest that when the threat is more distant, it is the prefrontal cortex area of the brain that deals with planning escape, concealment or negotiation – considerations for survival. When the threat is sudden and proximate, a different area takes over. Then it is the periaqueductal grey area in the mid-brain, an older section in evolutionary terms, which dominates. This area triggers quick-response survival mechanisms. It is the neurological switch that, perhaps, explains the phenomenon of the sudden fugue of refugee flight, when an urgent threat turns escape from a trickle to a general rout.

Define it again. Not the idea of extreme physical sensation this time, but terror as shorthand for terrorism. I find there is no reliable and concrete definition. Surveys of the meaning of terror in this context, conducted over two decades, have identified more than one hundred different meanings for the word, which agree only that it involves either the use of violence or the threat of its use. As Conor Gearty, the Professor of Human Rights Law at the London School of Economics, insists in his essay 'Terrorism and Morality', the meanings of the words terror and terrorism have undergone a subtle process of transformation in recent years, so that now terrorism is no longer a type of act that people commit – a tactic available to states as well as individuals – but relates to a category of person. 'The "terrorist"', according to Gearty, 'is no longer the deployer of political terror, whether as government leader, guerrilla hero or ambitious revolutionary . . . The terrorist is always now a subversive, someone who opposes the established order either in his or her nation or internationally.'

But while Gearty is right in describing how the language

of the state has tended to appropriate the meaning of terror
to serve itself exclusively, there is another localised and
mutually exclusive labelling that both parties to conflict
engage in. This is sharply underlined in the Israeli–
Palestinian conflict, where both sides have employed tactics
of terrorising the other for political ends, where both accuse
the other of terror, yet neither will accept that their own
acts amount to such.

Mohammed Awad sighs. 'After what has happened
with Wafa,' he says gloomily, 'I expect more
trouble.' Trouble. At first, it feels too inconse-
quential a word. Perhaps it is the tone he says it in. But in
protracted conflicts violence and terror become ordinary.
Problems to be negotiated like traffic jams or strikes. Late
buses. The director of emergency services for the Red
Crescent in Ramallah, Awad is sitting in his cluttered
office. He is welcoming but beneath his brisk willingness
to talk I sense a tired wariness threatening to break
through.

He asks me, politely, not to question the staff in the
ambulance station where Wafa worked about their dead
colleague. Instead, we begin talking more generally about
the psychological pressure on volunteers and paramedics
manning their ambulances, the dead and injured casualties, about the gunfire aimed by Israeli soldiers at his crews.
But even this is predicated on a shared, unspoken assump-
tion. I have come to see Awad because I know that before
she killed herself and her victim, Wafa Idris complained

about the impact her exposure to the injured of the clashes had on her. Awad knows it. 'To be honest, I am expecting them to target our ambulances even more,' he says. 'The propaganda they are putting out is that Wafa went to Jerusalem in one of our ambulances. It is not true,' he says, a hint of anger creeping in. 'She only worked on Fridays, but it gives them the excuse to come after us.' The last is said with resignation.

To explain what he means by trouble, Awad tells me the story of Firaz Samarra. Ten days before, Samarra, one of his staff from the same ambulance station, was hit in the leg by an Israeli bullet as he left his vehicle to pick up a casualty. The round damaged an artery and severed nerves. The Israeli army says it does not deliberately target the ambulance crews of the Palestinian Red Crescent, but the drivers, paramedics and volunteers who go out each day have every reason to think otherwise. In sixteen months of the *intifada* until my conversation with Awad, 122 have been injured by Israeli fire. One has been killed. His staff are convinced that they are being targeted to discourage them from assisting the wounded. The aim, they feel, is to frighten them so much that they will not come.

Although Awad has said he will not talk about Wafa, it is he who finally broaches the subject. There is a silence. 'I knew she was stressed,' he admits. He does not say her name, and I realise that he is talking about his own guilt, about having failed to help a colleague. But he is also trying to find a satisfactory meaning for Wafa's act, to frame it in the familiar concepts of a health professional's work. 'She was upset. Angry at what she had seen. She talked to me about suicide and about suicide bombings. Because of the way she was talking, I thought she was joking. I would joke back that we would save her or we would have to write her mortuary card. I never believed she would do it. Then last Sunday when I saw the body of the bomber on the television I saw it was wearing a green shirt like one she wore. I still couldn't believe it was her.'

For six months prior to Wafa's death, Munir Musa, a clinical psychologist, had been working at this ambulance station to counsel the staff. In a society that cannot comfortably discuss such feelings, Musa admits, it is an uphill task. 'The volunteers and staff here have seen terrible things,' he confides. 'Terrible things. The psychological effect on these very young people can be profound. In the worst cases they are taking bodies away that are literally in pieces. One of our women volunteers was giving first aid recently to a boy who had been shot in the head. She found herself holding his brain in her hands. It affected her profoundly. She was disturbed that she could do nothing to help. The image kept returning to her.

'Typically, the symptoms we are seeing come from feelings of frustration and hopelessness bred from having to work when you are not sure whether the soldiers opposite are going to open fire. Our staff report feeling constantly afraid and apprehensive even when they are safe at home. They complain of sleeplessness and irritability and not being able to eat. If it were not for the fact that the crisis is continuing we would be talking about the symptoms of post-traumatic stress disorder.'

I used to dream about terror. Not nightmares, but a pure, uncomplicated distillation of what desperate fear felt like. It was devoid of images or lucid memories: a plummet through darkness that would end only as I was yanked back to consciousness with a shout of 'fuck'. Then I would sit in the dark, my heart revving like a motorbike, damp with sweat, overtaken by a bleak feeling of abandonment. My eyes would search for a clue to where I was. Panicking. I recognise this now as *pavor nocturnus* – night terror – a sleep disorder that occurs between the third and fourth REM stages of deep sleep, more common in children than adults, and associated with stress. The night terrors are more bearable than the real nightmares that war has provoked that at their worst can linger like an infection even into my waking hours.

The waking dreams are worse because they are most worrying, a sign of the damage and problems I worry are yet to come. At their least shocking they are nothing more than flickering recollections that burst in the moment of the remembering. But they can solidify into more powerful flashbacks, shocking intrusions that feel frighteningly real. Among the most terrible were those that came to me for weeks after a suicide bombing in Jerusalem.

I heard the explosion far in the distance and arrived at the scene of a bus bomb as dusk was falling, the emergency services still setting up their lights and working amid a wreckage yet to be cordoned off from the media's curious gazes. Only barely registering the shapes I passed, my eyes adjusted to a gloom filled with torn body parts. A scene slowly revealed was somehow more terribly understood, burned into my recall by the delay. What I dream, I know that others dream: the product of fear and trauma in a time of conflict. That burns and scalds; that has the power to fragment. As solid and penetrating as the nails and bolts packed around explosives in an SB's vest.

I do the rounds of friends and family and scoop up the contradictory scraps of Wafa Idris's life, comparing what I have gathered with the results of my colleagues' efforts. Bits of motivation, pieced together, that do not reconstruct a living Wafa Idris but merely give shape to something dead and swollen beyond recognition by the violent act. Distorted by the force of the public examination of her personality that picks up only on the damaged and the abnormal. Or highlights suggestions of the normal placed for contradictory effect against the fact of what she eventually became. What is there to learn from this picture, from these bagged-up remains? That Wafa Idris was fond of doves, and gave a favourite niece a glass of juice before setting off on her lethal mission? That she was disappointed by a failed marriage, and was apparently unable to conceive? That the violence she had seen – and suffered – had politicised or unbalanced her? I ask myself whether I believe the inference of two French photographers who met her at the ambulance station on separate occasions in the months leading up to her death, who described her as silent and withdrawn, refusing to be photographed, suggesting that the idea of her violent death underwent a lengthy gestation. All that seems certain is that she spoke of becoming a martyr – for political not religious reasons – to a few friends, relatives and colleagues. And they, like Awad, did not believe that she quite meant the admiration she expressed for the SBs.

I go to a funeral for Wafa. But there is no corpse to bury – that is still being held by the Israelis. It is a symbolic event, as much political as a memorial for a lost life. I meet her family and fall into conversation with an uncle who gives me his number and asks me to call again when I am next in town. In the end her close relatives are as confused about the meaning of her death as I am. There is shock, sadness, and sympathy. Idealisation too of an act that social pressure insists the family must accept and embrace as a moment of national courage and sacrifice, but which they'd rather had never happened.

So I hope it will be Nasser Ahlam who will supply the missing connection. Even then I have been warned that Nasser is still in shock over her friend's death. When the questions come out of my mouth, there is a stunning triteness to them – although the circumstances demand answers. In the back of the ambulance, amid the brutality of another day among the clashes, I ask her gently if her friend spoke of what she was going to do. Her eyes flicker from side to side as if she is avoiding tears. Finally, she replies: 'No.' 'She was my best friend,' Nasser adds, and then refuses to say any more about Wafa Idris. Perhaps that is all there is to say: to insist on the severed connection, on loss, on the inability to understand what is impossible to understand – what impels us to these ultimate choices. Towards sacrifice. And suicide. Towards the act of killing.

I attempt one last question. Did she feel the same anger, working on the ambulances at the clashes? 'It has affected my daily life,' Nasser says. 'Since the beginning of the *intifada* I have seen blood and death and injuries almost daily. Yes, it does make me feel anger at those who are doing this to us. I feel every second that we are under threat and could be punished by the Israelis just for working in an ambulance crew.'

onflict's permission for violence exculpates those who use it, blaming the victims for their fate. Often its use is framed in terms coinciding with the 'supreme emergency' of the Just War theorists – that grants recourse to military action for defence against an existential threat or in pursuit of a suppressed desire for nationhood. They were arguments cynically in evidence in the brief war between Georgia and Russia in August 2008 when both sides were quick to deploy accusations of 'ethnic cleansing' and 'genocide' against the other, even as the fighting wound down, to justify their deeds.

But theory is too rarefied and distant a thing. Theory washes clean the blood and bigotry and emotion. It obscures the human tendency to hate and to construct legitimising arguments in the service of hatred that allows acts of terror – either by the state or groups – to be conceived as just and morally expedient. It is self-serving and self-justifying for the opposing communities involved, not least when using the word terror itself. Terror – it is then understood – is so terrible a thing that it requires responses outside of normal laws, even the ethics of war. When terror is invoked there is no requirement to address what led to the breakdown of peace. It justifies a new violence in kind. It explains why counter-terrorist campaigns are frequently dirty – involving assassination, torture and arrest without trial.

The self-serving way Israelis and Palestinians define terror was described by Jacob Shamir of the Hebrew University in Jerusalem and Khalil Shikaki, from the Palestinian Centre for Policy and Survey Research, in 2002. In surveys conducted among Israeli Jews, Israeli Arabs and Palestinians at the height of the Second Intifada in 2001 – not long before Wafa detonated her bomb – the researchers asked subjects to rate a series of eleven violent events and whether they would agree or disagree that they were terrorist acts. Those events included the destruction of the Twin Towers by al-Qaeda, the Lockerbie bombing, the killing of twenty-one Israelis at the Dolphinarium disco in Tel Aviv and the murder of twenty-nine Palestinians at the Al-Ibrahimi Mosque by the right-wing Israeli settler Baruch Goldstein on the day of the Jewish Purim festival in 1994.

Their research discovered that Israelis 'greatly underrated' as terror abuses committed by Jews, including police shootings of unarmed Palestinian demonstrators, while 'overwhelmingly judging as terrorism all acts of violence committed by Palestinians'. The findings were neatly mirrored when the same questions were asked of Palestinians who underrated violence perpetrated against

Israelis while giving the label of terror to most Israeli assaults. The only notable exception to this pattern was the recognition by three-quarters of Israeli Jews of Goldstein's massacre as terrorism.

And how acts are named is not simply a question of perception or semantics. It is critical to the way in which intractable conflicts develop what has been described as an ethos of conflict in the societies engaged in them, fuelling the continuation of violence. For the way in which the two communities define acts of terror — as acts committed only by the other — is decisive in determining what is permissible as a response and what targets and actions are acceptable.

Then it is mediated through the societal memory that communities in conflict develop to interpret their experiences. The historical narrative that Israel's society has fostered has been one of being under constant siege since the nation's creation in 1948, and in the decades before — both by neighbouring Arab countries, by non-state 'terrorist groups' and from the local Arab population — encapsulated in its culture in the memory of the genocidal moment of the Holocaust. Seen through this prism any action undertaken by Israel's security forces is necessarily defensive. Never to be described as terror. And since for a large part of Israel's short life 'Arabs' have been regarded as the threat, then the Palestinian population — its ideas and hopes and institutions — must be regarded as part of the 'security problem'. Terrorism exists, it is thus argued, because the population wills it so — a cultural mindset reflected in the unwillingness of Israel's courts to prosecute its soldiers for human rights abuses.

On the Palestinian side a parallel process of rational-isation is equally in evidence. It tells the story of the Nakba – 'the Catastrophe' – the counterpoint to Israel's inde-pendence myth, an account of mass flight, ethnic cleansing and brutal reprisal that culminated in the failure of Pales-tinian national ambitions. Since Palestinian statehood is the goal, violently denied, its society is able to absolve itself from the charge of terror. Instead, the tools employed – suicide bombings included – are seen as the weapons of last resort, all that is available to the weak, long suppressed by a powerful foe, armed by its equally strong friends. Because all Israelis serve in the armed forces, because all benefit and are complicit in the Occupation, and because Israeli society has yet to insist on the Occupation's end, all are targets.

My white Corsa bounces along the deeply rutted track, clipping the white knuckles of limestone and the flints exposed among the olive groves. The trees here are old, their bark thick and herniated. I am looking for a road that the residents of a neighbouring village have told us will take us by a back way into the city of Jenin and directly into the besieged refugee camp – home to 14,000 Palestinians – whose last houses terminate somewhere among these trees. It is the third day of the siege and the car is struggling with too many people in it as we traverse a loose slope of boulders and dirt. When finally we hit it, the road is potholed and narrow, leading gently down towards the city's Al-Damaj district between shallow earth banks. We creep towards a wall and rooftops in the distance, a white line drawn against the red earth. Then I see the helicopters.

They are two shapes at first at the far end of the camp, the distance dissolving their silhouettes into a pair of dark commas, which float over the cityscape of flat rooftops and the occasional spire of a minaret. But there is no mistaking the sound of their guns as they hang close above the narrow lanes. For now there is no other sound of fighting, just silence punctuated by the helicopters' cannons, a work-manlike rotation between the two, jack-hammering their rounds like nails into the roofs, launching the occasional missile. What I cannot and will not know until much later, when the battle is ended, is how these helicopters came before dawn, unleashing a deadly salvo of missiles into the houses of the sleeping camp.

We creep on, the doors of the car cracked open in case we need to escape. Ahead and to the right I can see close by the wall where the last houses of Al-Damaj run out. To the left is a cluster of low buildings. The car edges forward along the dirt, until it turns into tarmac: the city's bound-aries, and limit of the fighting. We lurch ahead in heartbeats into a scene whose colours are super-saturated by adrenaline into the colours of fear: glacial blues, haematic reds, and whites like ivory. The helicopters are drifting back towards the end of the camp we are closest to, perhaps alerted by the movement below. Their shapes become quickly clearer until they are starkly visible machines of glass and metal, encumbered with their weapons pods. The nearest swings towards us, its tail rotor rising, nose dipping, an alien mechanical intelligence examining the life below, two hundred metres distant. Seeing us. Calculating its response. I imagine communications and orders. Targeting. The 'TV' signs taped to the car's roof (letters easier to fashion with strips of electrical tape than the word 'Press') feel scant protection.

We reverse quickly and decide to follow the line of the wall and find another way to reach the camp, bumping through the same groves as before. I hit another road much wider than the first, designed to service the building of new houses, new neighbourhoods not yet begun. We are not in the camp this time but on the edges of Jenin proper. Despite my fear I am fixated on the neat parallel lines of the new kerbs that extend into the countryside, imposing a meaningless geometry. As if the city had grown this far and stalled without the resources to continue.

Where we are now, the helicopters are inaudible and invisible. So we enter a city under siege, blocked off to the media by the Israeli army. What follows is a sickeningly nervy progression familiar from the preceding weeks observing the fighting in the West Bank cities of Ramallah, Bethlehem and Nablus. We drive to a junction. Stop and look. Proceed. Halt again. Crawl forward. Never quite knowing where we are and with no guide to ask. Turning a corner, I am confronted by a scene that shocks me more by its quietness than the attacking choppers.

A pair of Israeli armoured personnel carriers is sitting in the road next to an open area. I can see a soldier, bulbous-headed in his helmet, standing at a crew hatch waving at a colleague out of sight. But it is what is next to them that disturbs me: a long line of Palestinian men queuing in the sun, heads bowed and hands crossed on their thighs in front of them. So many men and so few soldiers, that only fear could bind this scene together, imposing this lifeless picture of meekness. We are taking pictures from a distance when we are spotted. The soldiers shout at us, turning one of the vehicles to give chase. I can't hear what they are saying but it no longer seems a good idea to linger.

O peration Defensive Shield, a war in miniature within a conflict that never seems to end, whose violence peaks and diminishes and peaks again. The three weeks of heavy fighting in March and April of 2002 follow an escalation of suicide bombings in March in which seventy Israelis are murdered. Eleven ultra-Orthodox worshippers are killed in Jerusalem's Me'ah Shearim, including four children from one family. On 9 March the Moment Café in Jerusalem is hit. Eleven die in the explosion that guts a restaurant bustling with evening diners. A bus is bombed in Galilee. A shopping centre in Jerusalem. The outrages culminate in the attack on the Park Hotel in the seaside resort of Netanya during the Passover holiday on 27 March, launched by Hamas and carried out by Abdel-Basset Odeh. Another thirty perish.

Prime Minister Ariel Sharon articulates the logic of retribution in the midst of the attacks: 'The Palestinians must be hit, and it must be very painful. We must cause them losses, victims, so that they feel a heavy price,' he says. What he means is not prevention or disruption, but to

deliver a pain in kind. The biggest Israeli operation in the
West Bank in a decade will bring about the deaths of 497
Palestinians. A further 1,447 will be wounded in the incursions into six major Palestinian cities. Its conclusion will
be the siege of Jenin, a battle among the booby-trapped
lanes of the city's camp, where for the first time the intensity of the fighting drives us back, and excludes us from
witnessing at first hand what happens.

A handful of months after Wafa Idris's death, terror
follows terror as the tanks and helicopters, the squads of
troops and armoured bulldozers, enter the heavily populated civilian areas. Officially their mission is to kill or
arrest the 'terrorists'. But as the days roll on it becomes
more plausible to me that the task is to punish an entire
people as well. That it is certainly the view of some of the
Israeli troops involved is summed up in a crude piece of
graffito scrawled in English upon the wall of a human
rights organisation in Nablus and signed 'the IDF' – the
Israel Defense Forces. 'Fucking Arabs,' it reads. 'Never
mess with us again.'

It is a daily commute to the fighting from Jerusalem,
returning to the American Colony Hotel for drinks and a
late supper. On the third day of trying to edge ever deeper
into Bethlehem, I encounter an Italian friend clasping a
hotel towel as a white flag. He tells my little group he is
attempting to reach a priest close to Manger Square and
the Church of the Nativity. And so we go forward as he waves
the towel, ineffectually I think, surprising a squad of Israeli
soldiers fighting up a narrow flight of steep stone stairs,
faces dirty and distorted with fear, whom we then follow

down the street. A strange procession that is halted in one of the stone alleys by the body of an elderly civilian inside a damaged shop, his brain leaking on the concrete.

Some days we are tolerated by the Israeli troops; on others we are shouted at or chased. Sometimes fired on. A colleague from the *Washington Post* is shot not far from me while we are working in Ramallah, the bullet missing his spine by millimetres. Two weeks later my own convoy is hit attempting to reach the wife of the arrested Palestinian leader Marwan Barghouti, rounds smashing through the car ahead of us. We swing past the rapidly reversing vehicle, turning on our warning lights. But attempting to move forward we are fired on again.

And finally we reach Jenin, and its refugee camp that the Israelis call the 'The Capital of Suicide Bombers' for supplying a quarter of all SBs to that date. It is a fact that permits a cynical redefinition of the camp so that it is no longer deemed a civilian centre containing a minority of militants, but an armed military camp – despite the presence of only an estimated two hundred militants among so many thousands. Regardless of that, say Israel's military lawyers, it is subject to different rules. Terror's rules.

I catch the stink of cheap perfume and corruption the moment I leave the car. At thirty metres I can see the bodies stacked for burial outside the hospital in Jenin buzzing with photographers and reporters with notebooks. Even at this distance the smell hits me powerfully. I count thirty bodies wrapped in white material and plastic, bound with string and stained in places the colour of spilled tea. Someone is sprinkling them with more perfume, holding a handkerchief to his face and emptying small bottles over the corpses to make them easier to handle. In the heat of this dusty Friday afternoon all he achieves is to make the smell of death seem even filthier than ever.

There are two bodies on crude stretchers, slightly separate from the rest, wrapped up like delicate pieces of furniture made ready for the removal van. I notice that someone has scrawled the names in red and blue magic marker on the shrouds. A small crowd of men has gathered silently around the bodies. Two boys are kneeling in the dirt beside the shrouded bodies. The elder is dressed in a black polo shirt and jeans. I take him to be twelve or so. He crouches, his knees pulled to his chest, his hands clasped together in an attitude of prayer, oblivious of the men around him, eyes fixed still on a point far in the distance, as if trying to solve a puzzle. The other boy is much younger, hunched up a few feet from the second corpse, hands covering his face, and quietly weeping. One of the men speaks gently to the older boy. A voice that cannot penetrate his world.

The hospital workers, busy nearby with the rest of the neatly ordered dead, tell me that some of the bodies have been excavated from gardens and yards where they had been hastily interred, and from a mass burial plot close to the hospital where they were placed in the midst of the heaviest of the fighting. They are awaiting reburial now that the violence has ceased. Most, the staff concede, were fighters from among the men of Islamic Jihad, Hamas, and the al-Aqsa Martyrs' Brigade who fought in the bitter battle in the camp, rigging the lanes with the bombs that, at their most deadly, wiped out an entire patrol of thirteen Israeli soldiers. I meet Yassin Fayed whose two brothers, Amjad, aged thirty, and Muhammad, twenty-one, both fighters with Hamas, are lying among the dead. He is angry. He tells me that Israeli soldiers shot them after their arrest. It is impossible to check. But it is not beyond credibility. In this dirty operation in the West Bank's cities I have seen the bodies of five members of Yasser Arafat's elite guard in Ramallah being carried from the building where they died, stiff with rigor mortis. Their wounds told the story. Injured in the fighting they had been finished off, each with a single close-contact shot to the head or neck. But it is not the presence of the dead of Jenin that shocks me. It is what the Israeli military has done to the camp.

I take a short walk to the Hawashin neighbourhood, passing a small area of grass, another block of conflict-damaged houses, until I turn a corner and I am confronted by an expanse of bulldozed rubble the size of a football field. It is all that remains of more than one hundred houses, smashed and scoured to nothing. In the centre of the devastation the bulldozers have pushed through a crude route, leaving on either side head-high banks of broken concrete, seeded with clothes and broken furniture, and tangled with metal reinforcing rods that have burst free to protrude like picket stakes. Everywhere I look there are smashed sinks, pictures, cooking utensils and children's toys.

But the rendering of a whole neighbourhood to fragments of rubble, a grey and amorphous lunar uniformity, is less troubling than the small pockets where the destruction is not so utterly complete, where the scraps of a life destroyed tenaciously adhere. Among the banks of flattened houses is a partly collapsed building. I can see at once that the house's front has been sheared off by the passage of the military bulldozer as it widened one of the camp's narrow passages – now gone – to allow in the Israeli armour ahead of the wholesale destruction at the conclusion of the battle. The demolition of the front supporting wall has caused the roof to slide forward and cave into the upper rooms in a wide sagging 'V'. The cleaving has also left exposed a solitary internal room, still square amid the sliding planes of walls and roofs.

The room is fringed by several large remnants of concrete wall that hang on their steel rods above a pile of ruins, unsupported columns suspended perilously in space. The room is small, perhaps no more than fifteen feet across where it is open to view. A red and dusty carpet, which someone has spread across the floor, is too big for what remains, falling in a wide drape over what is now a deep lintel of ruined concrete. Sitting defiantly on the carpet on plastic chairs overlooking the destruction are three women with their children, occupants of a royal box above the drop of the scarlet. Those with a solitary room surveying the homeless.

There are others sitting among the rubble, men dusty to the waist from the effort of trying to recover anything from their smashed houses. Some have been marginally more

successful than others in their excavations. At the remnants
of one house, whose roof has been collapsed to waist height,
some bedding is still visible beneath the sandwich of
concertinaed floors. Three women are tugging at bed covers
pinned by the rubble, patterned in pretty stripes of orange,
red and white. They are, I discover, the daughters of
seventy-year-old Khalil Talib who has brought a mattock
to dig out his blankets. As the eldest of the daughters pulls,
her back bent like a crow pulling at a worm, an awkward
group files past an area flooded with water from a broken
main. At its head is a young woman wearing a long black
coat with a floral pattern on the arms. She leads two men
who are carrying a third young man in a wheelchair on which
someone has painted the words 'Swede 24' on its solid
wheels.

I have come to the ruins of Hawashin looking for
evidence of a massacre, following rumours – reported as
fact – of up to five hundred dead. The dead I can account
for number fewer than sixty, thirty fighters I am told, and
twenty-two civilians. It is not Sabra and Chatila, as some
have been suggesting, referring to the massacre of
Palestinian civilians by Israel's Christian allies in the
Lebanese war – nor Srebrenica. But other crimes of war
are powerfully evident. What is obvious is that the severity
of fighting does not tally with the scale of the destruction.
What it speaks of is a behaviour almost as reckless of the
lives of the camp's civilian residents as Wafa Idris's bomb
was for the shoppers of Jaffa Road, and to the same end.
To post a message, written in fear and blood, in pursuit of
a political agenda.

Wandering through the camp I am approached by Mr G, as he asks me to call him, and we fall into a conversation in English. Mr G wants me to be aware that a handicapped 'boy' was 'buried alive by the Israelis'. By now I am surrounded by a small, curious group of men. One of them pulls at Mr G's elbow and insists that he explain what he is saying. He translates his story back into Arabic to the men pressing in on us, and they 'correct' him. When he begins again it is to tell me that it was not one but five handicapped residents of the camp who were buried by Israel's bull-dozers. The conversation dribbles out into an embarrassed silence on all sides. Later I learn that Mr G is talking about Jamal Fayid, aged thirty-seven, who lived with his family in the neighbourhood next to Hawashin and could neither speak, eat nor move without assistance, and who was bulldozed in his house despite the pleas of his family.

A few minutes later I am reminded of the prohibition on the 'wanton destruction' of civilian homes by Miranda Sissons, a researcher with Human Rights Watch. I stumble across her, a slight Australian with boyishly cropped hair and glasses, as she criss-crosses the rubble banks with Manaf Abbas, a human rights worker with the Palestinian group al-Haq. Both of them – like me – are interviewing the survivors. She digs into a pocket to remove her Palm Pilot. What Sissons wants to show me among these ruins is Article 147 of the Fourth Geneva Convention. I screw up my eyes against the glare of the sunlight to read what is written on the screen. I jot down the words 'extensive destruction or unlawful appropriation of property, not justified by military necessity committed either unlawfully or wantonly', aware that even as I write them their meaning is made evident by the remains of the houses on which I stand. It mentions other crimes that may be applicable to Jenin: the taking of hostages for human shields by the Israelis and the same army's refusal of access for humanitarian and emergency medical assistance; the targeting of civilians, particularly by Israeli snipers. There is a barely controlled rage in Sissons' voice. 'There have been very serious violations of the rules of war that need to be investigated. The disproportionate use of force. The excessive use of force. And the extensive destruction of property. There has been a total lack of respect for the rights of civilians. And those breaches are still continuing. Israel is still blocking the facilitation of humanitarian access and continuing to shoot on civilians here.' There is nothing more to say. We stand, dazed in silence.

An hour later I run into Eyad and Jawad Kassim, two brothers who lived with their family in four houses at the edge of the destruction. Eyad's house and his mother's have been reduced to nothing. Jawad's still stands but one outside wall has been demolished and two missiles hit the building. Eyad and Jawad deny that they are fighters. 'We had four homes,' says Eyad. 'Now they're destroyed.' He admits that there were fighters and heavy fighting in the camp, but believes his house and those of others were destroyed in retaliation for the deaths of the twenty-three Israeli soldiers killed during the battle. 'They are lying when they say there were gunmen in all of the buildings they destroyed.' He appears a gentle man. I believe he is. But away from the violence they all seem like ordinary, gentle people with ordinary concerns: the soldiers and the gunmen, each with his reasoned, insistent argument for terror and destruction. All of them reasonable killers. After examining the ruins, Eyad lights a cigarette and walks away to cry.

The Contaminated Wound

The man is executing a jarring pimp roll of exaggerated angular motions as he approaches us. He is thin as a Giacometti bronze, wearing a dirty shirt half buttoned from the waist, which flaps over his hips. As he comes closer I can see he is unshaven, his eyes bloodshot and yellow. He halts to talk to us, head held slightly to one side. But I can't understand what he is saying. He smiles a crooked grin revealing a mouth full of cigarette-stained teeth and extends his hands shakily as if to reassure us. His expression, too forced and curiously voluptuous, threatens danger. I am worried. Questions pile up. Cards to be turned over. Is he out of it? One of the crazies who have flocked on to the streets after Saddam's fall – the same people I have seen fire RPGs into buildings for fun? In a city febrile with looting – which the Americans have done nothing to control – anyone out of their homes in these violent days following the Iraqi capital's fall is to be treated with caution.

The man's expression, as it turns out, is only the look of pain that the Old Masters, depicting the martyrdom of saints, elided with the religious rapture. A taut smile-that-is-not-a-smile, rather a contraction of the muscles. I stay back, keeping him at arm's length until it is clear he does not have a weapon. He is asking for help. Sensing our fear, the man dramatises his predicament, gingerly lifting a corner of his shirt and pulling it above his abdomen to reveal a hollow, famished stomach beneath protruding ribs.

He has been gut-shot. There is stuff caked on his stomach, painted in a couple of smears, palm-wide, like marks from a tribal ritual. Mud or ashes spread from the fire. I imagine his hand moving something that is wet and dripping in slow, thick increments. Smoothing it thin with long fingers to help it dry. There is a bad smell. A mixture of shit and something worse: mortality.

The wound has been crudely dressed with a section of cotton wool taped to his stomach, now stained and bloody. The adhesive on the dirty, white micropore tape has come unfixed where the wound is wet, allowing him to lift the pad on its upper hinge of tape to reveal a hole the size of a golf ball. There is something bulging greyly through it. A loop of intestine, I think, the colour of a drying, sea-washed pebble. I stare at the wound as he looks at me. Someone has clumsily fitted a colostomy bag that is now fat and leaking out material mixed with what looks like clotted dark blood. We establish that what he wants is for one of us to change his dressing, and replace the bag, tasks far beyond the resources of either our small medical kit or first-aid skills.

Through Magdi, our Iraqi guide, we suggest that he goes to one of the hospitals at the nearby Baghdad Medical City for treatment. We offer to transport him. At the mention of the hospital a look of alarm crosses his face. He is terribly afraid of going there. Perhaps he is one of the foreign fighters who came to fight the American invasion who, we've heard, have been dragged from wards in some parts of the city and summarily shot by other Iraqis. I give him a bottle of water. There is nothing else to do.

We are by the river in one of those blank modern city spaces, the hemmed-in, useless interstices of walls, roads and flyovers – urban remainders and dead ground. In Baghdad, Saddam's oversized public buildings and monuments squat, beached in these shadowlands of redundancy. We are in a baffling cul-de-sac of concrete and tarmac that leads only to a meaninglessly short walk along a waist-high concrete balustrade beside the river, lacking shade or anywhere to sit. I look down at the river. There are some snags and a handful of little wooden boats, like skiffs. Not even a good view. In the brief inter-lude between the invasion and the emergence of sectarian warfare, only courting couples will supply it with a meaning.

The man wanders off towards the steep river slope where he has been hiding. As he does I notice that something as beige as incinerator ash has settled on the concrete wall, thick enough to write my name in with my finger. It is not ash but a thick layer of dust, soft as talcum powder, deposited by the huge sandstorms that accompanied the invasion. The dust has covered everything – houses, shrubs and windscreens – infiltrating the defects in the concrete walls and the brick joints, and gathering at the bottom of the hotels' empty pools. It has coated palm leaves and bushes with a dull and gritty frosting the colour of floods and high-water lines. The colour, it seems to me, of headaches and defeat. Now the storms have finally passed, they have left behind a jaundiced yellow sky contaminated by the sand and particles of oil from damaged, flaming wells and refinery towers. Together, they contrive at evening to colour the sky into a panorama of inflamed oranges and reds.

Across the Tigris, where the Third Infantry Division has halted its advance, I can still hear from time to time the sharp little exchanges that have dwindled in the six days since the city's fall. They are the small furious engagements that mark the US troops' efforts to clear the river's far bank, a wide littoral of scrub and mud and reeds, and the buildings that line it, of the last holdouts. The sound jabs in the consciousness like the pain from an abscessed tooth. But most of the gun battles now are between the rival gangs of looters tearing the city quite literally apart, ransacking museums, schools and government buildings. Stealing the wires from high-tension electric cables. Jacking cars. Scooping up the huge stockpiles of hidden guns, explosives and artillery shells to be hidden and reburied, fuel for the future war: the real conflict of the insurgency that will not be won so easily.

The sound of these exchanges is ragged: too long blasts of automatic-weapons fire in contrast with the rhythm of the American skirmishes with the remnants of the Saddam Fedayeen, the regime's last bitter-enders for now. It is all that is left of the invasion and the Battle for Baghdad. Scattered gunfire and the handful of towering columns of dense, black smoke. The piles of the discarded uniforms of the Iraqi troops, sloughed off like lizard skins on the street corners where they fled the advancing US tanks and helicopters on their 'Thunder Run' into Baghdad. Every-where American soldiers.

I am looking for the Medical City – the *Madinat at-Tibb* – a huge and sprawling area of teaching hospitals, to hear the stories of the Iraqis injured during the Coalition's advance. It was once the Middle East's best and most modern medical facility. Now it seems to be decaying in the way that ageing concrete perishes, as rock itself degrades, cracking and exfoliating. I am not looking for the fighters' stories but those of ordinary civilians. I want to ask the doctors how they coped under the bombing and how they managed under the international sanctions regime, and under Saddam. It is then I encounter the gut-shot man, the man who stinks of his own slow death. The entrance to the complex of hospitals must be close by. It is how we have got stuck in this dead end.

The violence between the gangs of looters has been so bad in this area that even yesterday the Red Cross's cars were driven back attempting to run supplies to the chil-dren's hospital. For now, however, a momentary quiet has descended. I get out to walk around and try to work out how to reach the hospital, whose twenty-storey buildings are visible a little further along the river. I am with Sharon Abbady, my friend and companion of two conflicts, a tough Venezuelan-American photographer.

A few minutes later we are finally inside the Al-Mansour Paediatric Teaching Hospital in Medical City, waved into the complex by a couple of American soldiers. Outside the Paediatric Hospital I pass a cluster of doctors and male nurses, still in their pale blue scrubs, standing guard with

AK-47s against the gangs of thieves who have already stripped the hospitals here of X-ray machines and drugs, cardiac monitor screens mistaken for television sets. I enter a corridor crowded with victims of the violence, and when I ask the doctors I am told a quarter have been injured by the looting. The corridor opens into a wider space, perhaps once the waiting area, which has been set up as the main area for treatment. It is not quite so crowded but the cases are more serious.

A middle-aged man in mechanic's overalls is walking carefully into the hospital. He is walking as if on slippery river stones, or on an icy pavement. He holds himself too stiffly, erect and starched as a maître d'. The man, I can see, is heavy-set, running to fat, with his dark blue boiler suit unbuttoned at the top to reveal a bare chest, a tangle of body hair matted with red clots. A thick moustache, just turning to grey, on his upper lip. I notice that his hands are wetly bloody. One, oil-dirtied, supports his chin, his fingers spread delicately across his throat. The man does not speak and when, a little later, I see him lying on a gurney, I ask about his condition and the doctor beckons me over. The man's overalls have been pulled back enough for his wounds to be visible. He has been shot twice in the chest, shallow wounds perhaps caused by bullet fragments.

The man looks at me through soft and shocked brown eyes, still holding his neck. Gently, the doctor peels away his fingers. The skin beneath his chin, where he holds it to his Adam's apple, is dark and glistening, sectioned by horizontal creases of fat where the colour of the skin pigment is darker. I don't understand what is going on at first until carefully the doctor tilts back the mechanic's head. All at once I can see what the man was holding so desperately. A bullet has severed his throat as neatly as a blade, opening a wide slit above his larynx. I am struck by how oddly bloodless it is, this wound that gapes like a second mouth as his head rocks back, exposing his windpipe. He has been clutching at his life.

This hospital is a place of dreadful injuries. I see another man carried in by friends with blood pouring from a bullet wound that has pierced his foot like a solitary stigma. A young doctor (I never get to ask the surgeons' names amid the chaos) leads me by the elbow to see this man with the bullet wound to his lower ankle. I watch, fascinated, as he probes the wound with what looks like a letter opener, digging for hidden fragments deeper than I want to imagine. We walk away so I can ask the question that I want to ask: the chances of survival for these men. 'We are short on antibiotics,' he explains with a fatalistic shrug. 'Many of these people will die from infections.'

When a standard, rifled spitzer bullet – a conical 'ball' from a modern small-arms weapon – hits the soft tissue of the human body, the entry wound has a margin of abrasion around it. The round, forcing inwards, scuffs the surrounding skin, creating a halo of tenderness that only seems to emphasise the hidden grossness of the injury. Because of the elasticity of skin and muscle, the circumference of most entry wounds tends to be smaller than the projectile's as it contracts almost instantly around the initial cavity. Water closing around a sinking swimmer's head.

The point about a rifled bullet is that it rotates at a high speed, spiralling around an axis that extends from tip to tail. The same way an American football is thrown. This high-speed spinning gives the bullet its stability, its accuracy over a long distance. The result is that conventional wounds caused by high-velocity bullets – where the round does not fragment – appear as vicious pricks, often smaller than you would expect. But rounds can behave in different ways. When the bullet has travelled a long distance, and the ball loses energy and the spin that maintains its stable trim, the round begins to flutter in its progress – an effect called yawing. What hits the target is not a head-on – the high diver's feet following the head and shoulders in a line, causing minimal splash – but a projectile tending towards a flop, the feet and legs catching on entry.

The entry wound created by a yawing round is different in shape, deformed into a flat letter 'D' shape and often exhibiting an associated tearing of the abrasion ring. It opens a deeper cavity inside the wound. This characteristic is not only visible in bullets losing energy and spin, or ricocheting off another surface before impact. It is a feature, too, of the very lightweight high-velocity rounds used commonly by both NATO and the Israel Defense Forces, small balls that are designed to fragment easily and cause maximum damage to enhance their lethal capability. The low mass of the round itself increases the chance that the bullet as a whole – or fragments of it – will tumble or sharply change direction in contact with tissue, or in passing from one density to another.

If the weapon is fired at very close range, however, a different kind of wound shape results. The gases expelled from the weapon's muzzle explode into the cavity created by the bullet, stretching and ripping the tissue so that the entry wound is stellate in appearance. A bloody star of tears extending from the centre, radiating from a faint, burned oily ring imprinted on the body.

It is not simply the kinetic energy of the bullet itself as it penetrates organs, bursts bone and severs veins and arteries, which is the only issue with gunshot wounds. A secondary consequence of being shot or hit with shrapnel is the high risk of infection, even from a graze. As the round and associated gases enter the body they suck in atomised fragments of cloth and material the bullet has hit before entering the victim; tiny fragments of car door and cinder block, wood, glass and earth, dead tissue from other casualties nearby; the lingering, ever-present bacilli found in soil. A passage of dead and dying tissue is created in the body, into which is sucked the filth of our environment by the vacuum behind the projectile travelling at supersonic speed. It is often more dangerous than the damage caused by the destructive energy of the round itself.

And in conflict it is not always the fact of the fighting – the fact of invasions and offensives, skirmishes and battles – that actually destroys societies. It is what is sucked into the necrotic cavities war creates – into the dead spaces – that weakens and overpowers resistance to the violence itself. In the Iraq of after the invasion, of after the 'cure', of after the experiment in democratisation of a brutal regime by illegal force, it begins with the looting, with resistance to Occupation, and with al-Qaeda's suicide bombings. It ends with sectarian extermination and a collapsing state.

My laptop won't play the DVD that my fixer, Wael, has brought me. So we sit — Wael, Tariq, my driver, and myself — in the cramped little business centre beneath one of the towers of the Hamra Hotel. There is no sound. But the images draw the other Iraqis working in the office into a tight and silent huddle around the screen broken only by the occasional tut-tutting. It is a sibilant and wet flicking at the palate, which I associate with stable girls and horses. Three moist and separated clicks. I have learned, here in Iraq, it carries a meaning of tremendous disapproval.

The colours are washed out into ghostly dark-shaded hues like photographic film that has been bleach-bypassed. The quality of the video too, which I suspect has been copied multiple times, is fuzzy at the edges. But there is no escaping what this show-and-tell is all about. It opens without preamble: a body is being washed in a mosque prior to burial. The camera pans across the corpse. I know, because Wael has told me, that the body is that of Hassan an-Ni'ami. I know too that in life he was a slender and good-looking man, with deep-set eyes, a face of chiselled planes with a neatly trimmed dark beard. He dressed in the dark robe and white turban of an imam at a mosque in Baghdad's Adhamiya district. He was a Sunni cleric and a senior official of the Association of Muslim Clerics. I know all this because we met in his office, after the invasion.

The cameraman lingers on the minute details of what happened to him after his kidnapping a few weeks ago. There are police-issue handcuffs still attached to one of his wrists, from which it appears Hassan an-Ni'ami was hung long enough, from an overhead pipe I guess, to cause his hands and fingers to swell with fluid. In the underwater blues of the screen, the hand ceases to be human but something dredged from the ocean bottom. An obscene anemone. One of the men in the video produces an angle grinder. He tilts it at the wrist to cut off the remaining cuff. It spits out a shower of sparks, as if from the wrist itself.

The camera moves around his body, pausing to record the injuries. Its coldly cruel eye stops on what looks like a large burn mark on the side of his chest, where the skin has become plastic and hardened, raw and red. It has the smooth pliability of something that has been shifted, or spread easily with a knife, as if his torturers placed something searingly hot near his right nipple and pushed it around. We freeze the images to examine each of the details, peering into the screen to try to understand the marks left upon his body by the men who tortured and murdered him.

The sense of horror wears off. It becomes an exercise in understanding the meaning of violence, strange as a half-learned language. A little lower on his body are a series of horizontal marks, multi-coloured bruises that wrap around his back and chest. Where they end the skin has been broken into open welts. He was beaten with something flexible that curled around him. The tip of whatever was used to beat him was travelling more quickly than the rest of the implement. Looking at these marks, it is clear to me that he was beaten with something heavy and flexible, perhaps an electrical cable, as he hung by his arms. There are other injuries: a broken nose, and small, ugly lesions that look like burns from a cigarette. An arm lies awkwardly, broken, describing the same shapes as my own broken arms from childhood. I remember the nausea of that pain.

Other injuries are less obvious. One of the higher vertebrae appears to have been pushed inwards and out of place by a heavy blow, leaving a hollow where none should be. There is a cluster, too, of small, neat, circular wounds on both sides of his left knee. At some stage an-Ni'ami has been efficiently and excruciatingly knee-capped, not once but several times. It does not look to me as though it has been done with a gun. The knee is too intact. There is none of the damage you would expect with a proximity gunshot, where gas and metal tear into tendon and bone. No scorching. Instead, it seems to have been done with something more deliberate, like a drill, a torture of which I have heard horrible rumours. But none of this killed him – that was accomplished by bullets fired into his chest from close range. The last two hit him in the head.

Looking at his body, picturing his pain, I am forced to recall the man he was in life. And my suspicions. When I first interviewed Hassan an-Ni'ami, a year before his death, it was because he was suspected of contacts with the insurgency that I went to see him in his mosque. Certainly, he made no bones to me about supporting armed resistance to US forces. More recently, I had heard that an-Ni'ami had dropped out of sight. Then, a little over a month ago, his relatives say, paramilitary police commandos from the Shia-dominated 'Rapid Intrusion' unit – sectarian thugs controlled by a Ministry of the Interior run on Shia sectarian lines – discovered an-Ni'ami at his family home in the Sha'ab neighbourhood of northern Baghdad. His capture then was reported on television as that of a senior 'terrorist commander'. Twelve hours later his body turned up in the morgue.

All open wounds are rapidly contaminated with bacteria from the environment, frequently with the rod-shaped bacilli of the clostridia family whose members include those that cause tetanus, gas gangrene and botulism. But deep, dirty wounds – the kind of injuries associated with ballistic and blast injuries – are those most susceptible to dangerous infections. Low in levels of oxygen – or completely devoid – these ruined cavities of dead and dying flesh provide the best environment for rapid proliferation of clostridial infections. Left unchecked, the clostridia produce powerful toxins capable of destroying the walls of neighbouring cells, eventually killing the cell itself. A chain reaction is set in place, cell after dying cell, until the result is a lethal cycle of infection that leads rapidly to sepsis, toxaemia and shock. It is the gas produced by the dying cells that gives off the bad smell, the smell of gangrene. Corruption. It is the odour that undertakers call tissue gas — the smell of death and of the gut-shot man whose own bacteria, living in his bowel in the faecal matter, have been driven out into his body by whatever struck him.

With infection the skin changes its colour, a sickening hue radiating from the initial site of the wound, the surface growing warm to the touch. Later the skin discolours to a coffee shade, experienced with increased pain and swelling. In the case of those bacteria that live without oxygen at all, the infection takes hold rapidly. Sometimes a thin, brown substance is exuded from the wound. Infected muscle becomes swollen with fluid, changing colour to dark red or grey. As the condition accelerates, casualties experience high fever, irregular heartbeat, shock, and finally the multiple failure of organs. While some infections are treatable with antibiotics, others are multi-drug resistant, among them the T strain of *Acinetobacter baumannii*, a virulent bacterial infection which contaminated the American field hospital system and evacuation chain back to Germany and the US. Able to swap DNA with other strains, it constantly evolves. Becoming more dangerous.

Without recourse to effective treatment it is simply a matter of observing the symptoms' progression: measuring how deeply the infection has set in, and how serious the fever. Of tracking the violence as it morphs. Watching as the institutions of an already damaged state fail one by one. Sunni jihadist groups lay bombs at mosques, markets, the other places where the Shia gather. They blast ceremonies and celebrations and queues of men waiting for work. Shia militias, attached to the proliferating parties and factions, the sub-factions and gangs, begin their own murderous campaign. It starts with reprisal killings of former officials in Saddam's Ba'ath party blamed for the murder of Shias while Saddam was in power. In a tribal society that insists on retribution what begins as scattered tit-for-tat events gathers its own momentum with each atrocity, establishing a culture of hate. And with the rise of Shia power following the elections, Shiite death squads become synonymous with the police and the Ministry of the Interior, kidnapping and murdering Sunnis in reply, at first for the bomb attacks, and then simply because they are Sunni. They dispose of their tortured and murdered victims on rubbish dumps, in culverts and rivers. In the end the US soldiers weld down the sewer covers in some areas of Baghdad to prevent bodies being hidden.

It is not only the infecting agent but the pre-existing health of the patient that is critical. In the Iraq of after the invasion, in the Iraq of after the attack intended by its authors to transform it, I grow used to the symptoms of the infection that has been sucked in behind it, into a state already sick from three decades of Saddam's dictatorial rule, from an international sanctions regime imposed after the first war, designed to hurt Saddam but which only damaged Iraqis. It is a slow poisoning that hollows out an Iraq not strong enough to resist, its institutions enfeebled, non-existent or, like the old Ba'athist organisations, including the army, pointlessly cut away. An act of politically motivated debriding by Iraq's new American masters excises the live, healthy tissue along with the dead, weakening Iraq still further.

I try to track the occult spread of the contaminating agents, flowering like bacterial cultures, invisible and lethal. In war's culture of death and permissive violence, the conflict creeps into schools and hospitals and universities, where the intelligent and independent are targeted or driven out. It fuels a culture of criminality and corruption, of 'taxes' imposed by the militias, of rape, and the imposition of behavioural rules, not least for women. I am left to monitor its symptoms: through killings, kidnappings, and through the increasingly secretive and exclusive conversations between my Iraqi friends, both Sunni and Shia, who, once open with each other, now retreat into whisperings about the other's sect.

On the same disc there are images of other victims too, all arrested by units of the Shia-controlled Ministry of the Interior. I slog through them with my notebook, the sordid business of examining death, in the hope that by recording these details I can both understand what is happening in Iraq and excavate some meaning from the violence. The post-mortem images show a dozen or so farmers from the insurgent hotbed of Medayeen, seized by police as they slept in one of Baghdad's markets, whose bodies were discovered on a rubbish dump to the north of the city. Like an-Ni'ami, their bodies also bear the marks of extensive torture before execution, most with a bullet to the head. The face of the first body is blackened by strangulation or asphyxiation. Another has bruises to his forehead where he was hit repeatedly with a heavy object. Yet another, his hands still tied with cord, has been punched in the eye and had his ankle fractured. There are

signs of burning on one man's body similar to those on
an-Ni'ami's. The last two have identical puncture wounds,
a fist-width apart, the signature of a spiked knuckle-
duster.

What I want to say about violence I have been unable
to say in my own newspaper. We subscribe to a curious
convention, all of the media, that when we write about
war and violence we largely ignore the detail of the consequences – what bullets, bombs and knives do. We are
happy to watch crime procedurals on television, and
graphic horror films, yet it is still regarded as bad form
to describe the reality of the everyday horror of conflict.
But to understand conflict one must confront what people
do when they kill and mutilate – because in the texture
and the detail of them there exists meaning.

The use of the drill I understand. It is an old horror story
made real. Revisited and reinvented. Trailing around Iraq
I hear endlessly repeated the stories of the brutalities from
Saddam's time. In particular, I hear the story of the drill.
People tell me of the ever more complex instruments of
torture they believe were used in Saddam's jails – chairs
rigged with drills that moved into the body, complex
contraptions like modern iron maidens. Only some of it is
true, even recalling the awfulness of Saddam's long rule.
But in the telling and retelling, it grows into a powerful
myth. A commonplace. Now that Saddam is gone, the stories
permit an assault on those deemed guilty by association
with the horrors of his jails. This encompasses all of Iraq's
Sunnis, the minority that dominated Iraq under Saddam.
Who dominated the Shia, with brutal consequences. The

stories allow the drill and iron and electrical cabling, the penetrating wounds in an-Ni'ami's legs.

Like the military surgeons, swabbing the wounds of the injured, I find myself growing my own cultures collected from Iraq's wounds. It is a flora of testaments and observations of brutal events that – as they bloom – become more powerful, contaminating, more dangerous and more difficult to contain.

Sheikh Nadhum, a Sunni preacher at a mosque in Baghdad's Abu Dscheer district, crosses and recrosses his elegant wrists. He touches things distractedly, picks at a hem. He loses track of what he is saying or drifts into the reassurance of a formal style of speech. His hand, lying in his lap, is bandaged where a bullet hit him in the drive-by attack that killed his twenty-year-old son and son-in-law as they sat in their car outside a nearby mosque, sprayed with bullets by the occupants of a blue Opel.

It is March 2004, a year after the invasion. I struggle to find the mosque I am looking for in the uniform grid of the suburbs. Instead, I stumble across a neighbouring Shia mosque. By this mosque's gate a nervous huddle of men is gathered. Palms are pressing the last corner of a long black banner painted with white lettering to the wall while it is hammered up with masonry nails. Directions are given to lead me to find Sheikh Nadhum. I ask what the banner reads. One of the men traces out the words: 'We severely attack the dirty, criminal act that targeted Sheikh Nadhum az-Zayeedi and his son and son-in-law which led to the martyrdom of the last two.' I am struck all at once by the feeling that it is not simply an expression of solidarity, but also a plea: 'Not us. We did not do this.'

But someone did. In two weeks ten Sunni mosques across the city have been attacked and twenty people killed. In reply Sunnis in mainly Shia areas have attacked Shia mosques and shrines. When I describe to the US and British officials what I have come across, they wave it away as an irrelevance, unwilling to recognise their plans to reinvent Iraq may be unravelling. That the infection is setting in. It is the beginning of Iraq's sectarian war, the war that will run in parallel with the other war between insurgents and the Occupation, which eventually will run in parallel with other conflicts – Sunni nationalists against al-Qaeda; Shia faction on Shia faction; gang on gang, the cells of violence replicating and mutating.

I find the sheikh wearing a long white dishdasha robe in a corner of the mosque's main room. Other sheikhs sit in their brown cloaks and headdresses with their backs to the walls, or arrive in little groups to clasp his uninjured hand and whisper a few formal words. I notice that behind him stands an AK-47. I am beckoned across to offer my condolences, and speak with him. 'I was expecting this,' he says. 'I had a strong feeling we might be hit or injured because I knew people from other Sunni mosques were being attacked. But we have heard from Jesus,' he explains in a low voice, almost a whisper, 'that if someone slaps you on the cheek then you must turn the other.' I suspect that he has framed the Christian metaphor for my benefit alone.

He pauses, then says: 'I lead these people here. I will not permit hostility against the Shia. '

'My personal opinion,' he says more loudly to the room, to reinforce the point, 'is that this is not sectarian. Someone is trying to stir up problems between us. We are all from the Zayeedi tribe [originally from the south]. We are a very mixed tribe with a lot of intermarriage. I can only accuse the enemies of Islam of committing these crimes.' When I ask who, the sheikh blames 'foreign elements' and blames the Americans for failing to seal the country's borders. He blames Iraq's 'many enemies' for trying to provoke chaos. 'I have been here for thirteen years,' he insists again, 'and throughout all that time the Sunnis and Shia have joined together.' His words are a cue for a group of Shia sheikhs to rise as one. 'God knows,' says one, 'these are not Iraqis who did this. We are brothers and not criminals. At school we played together.' But it is Iraqis who are doing this. Sheikh Nadhum is wrong.

It becomes ever more difficult to focus on individual tragedy, on the everyday horror. On the cruelty of the phone calls that follow disappearances saying Don't bother to look, or You can have the body in so many days. I become jaded by stories of death, disappearance and mutilation. Until only the extraordinary stands out – the 'spectacular' attacks. Or, paradoxically, the tiniest detail. I am drawn to stories that reflect the ordinariness of life: how children go to school, babies are born. I hear of young couples putting off marriage so as to avoid the risk of having children in the middle of the war; teachers and professors fleeing into exile; parents who will no longer let their children go to school. The poison of conflict creeps into everything. I talk to actors who cannot act; painters who cannot paint; women who cannot teach or work in their hospitals. Children who cannot play outside, whose world is confined to the house next door, or the one across the street.

In the late autumn of 2006 I visit Hossam al-Din al-Ansari, principal violinist and composer in residence with the symphony orchestra in Baghdad, at the Al-Shaab Gallery. It requires a dangerous trip across the city, thirty long minutes in the car, unnerving even the guards who clutch their hidden weapons.

There is no electricity in the rehearsal space, so a few arriving musicians head for an area beneath a high skylight. I stumble in the darkness, tripping over blue folding chairs. Two violinists, one a man in his sixties, set up their scores on a couple of music stands, extracting the music from plastic shopping bags. It is stifling. The little evening light there is pools weakly around the men, who peer through the gloom, turn pages, and play short broken measures. Other musicians head for the 'kitchen' – a small room with a counter and a kettle – but with windows that make it lighter than the rehearsal hall. As more musicians arrive it becomes clear there is insufficient space for the whole orchestra. The cello squeezes behind the counter with the bigger brass. Elbows touch elbows as the strings attempt to play.

The orchestra has played in Baghdad only a handful of

times since war broke out. Ten of its members have emigrated while others only manage a fitful attendance. I find Hossam al-Din al-Ansari in his office working on notation. He is a compact man with a neatly clipped grey moustache beneath a tall, balding dome of a head. He sets his violin beneath his chin and improvises arpeggios, while I take his portrait – a moment of unexpected beauty and release after the fearful journey. We meet the day after International Music Day. 'We played yesterday at the National Theatre,' he says brightly, and then admits that only invited government officials were able to attend. 'That was the seventh or eighth concert – I can't remember. In the last six or seven months, since the security situation deteriorated so badly, we've played abroad.' Before that, he concedes, their biggest concert was for officials in the Green Zone. Another couple of concerts were held for Baghdad's elite in the city's two biggest social clubs, one in the Hunting Club and the other in the Alawiyah Club.

'We try to avoid the complicated symphonies,' he explains. 'It's mainly overtures that we play now.' He attempts a brusque optimism but there is something sad about his descriptions of the orchestra's recent achievements: concerts played in Kurdistan and Jordan, or for a select minority. 'It is a very difficult time. But we are challenging the situation and trying to be . . .' he sighs. 'Not too far from the public. We are trying to perform concerts every month. But . . . circumstances. If we wanted to submit, we could just stop work. Or we could all go to the West. We are trying not to let things go back with the level of our playing. Which would be natural, in the circumstances. We are working to keep our standard up.'

He has his violin across his knee. 'The players fight hard against what is happening here. You know, in an orchestra, it is not the individual player. So day and night the player builds himself up over a period of time through long work and practice. He does not give in that easily. He does not relinquish his art. In the 1950s we used to get these Russian films here in Iraq. We were talking about this a quarter of an hour ago. Someone was talking about running. Then someone recalled there was a film about the German attack on Leningrad. And this film showed the orchestra, the symphony there, broadcasting during the fighting. It showed the different players. How they came to the concert and the difficulties that they had. Because of war . . .' he articulates the word at last. 'We felt we were reliving their circumstances.'

He pauses. He is quieter now, deflated. 'Personally. I spent three hours reaching the concert on Sunday. There was a bomb on the road. Some of the players couldn't come at all.' He tries to remember who. 'Percussion. One of the drummers. Two of the violinists, I think. Those who did show up had the same difficulties as those that did not show. We feel like we are battling in a war.' He tells me about some of his recent compositions, written during the conflict: Beloved Leave Taking and The Good Land, a chamber piece for two violins, oboe, viola and cello. I ask him whether he still believes that Iraq is a 'good land'. 'This is still a good land,' he insists. He halts again to give it further thought. 'Maybe the land is good,' he adds, 'but sometimes the people are not good . . .'

One day Wael spots a paragraph among the small ads of the *Al-Taakhi* newspaper over our break-fast of Nescafé in my room at the Hamra Hotel. It is our dawn patrol, hunting among the lines of text for the signs that will tell us how the texture of the war is being slowly transformed. How life is being changed. Randomly, Wael reads out headlines and we talk about what the stories mean. In these pages, among the adverts and football results, are stories of disappearances and bodies found, a gauge that allows the temperature of the conflict to be taken.

We have the papers spread out on my unmade bed. Wael finds what we are looking for on page ten. It is not news stories that we focus on today but a little paragraph among the public announcements telling us that Umar Salman is planning to change his name. None of us knows Umar Salman, but the fact is startling all the same, the few lines required by the office of National Identity in Al-Rusafa. If there are no objections within ten days, the notice reads in the formal grammar of officialdom, then Umar asks to be known as Samir.

The problem, Wael explains, is the name Umar itself. It is a very 'Sunni' name. Being Sunni it is a dangerous name to have in Baghdad's neighbourhoods that are controlled by the Shia militia checkpoints, and patrolled by Shia death squads, many in the uniform of the police. Umar: the second

Caliph who reigned after the Prophet Mohammed. It feels too early in the day to be struggling with the complex history of the emergence of the two branches of Islam and their hostility. But Wael persists, explaining patiently how Shias regard the three Caliphs as usurpers of the Prophet's inheritance, which they believe had been promised by Mohammed to his cousin and son-in-law, the figure Shias revere as the Imam Ali. How perilous a name is evidenced by the alleged discovery by police, in Baghdad's Al-Adil neighbourhood, of a dozen or so corpses of young men, killed and dumped by the death squads. It is a story that gains currency. All were young Sunnis shot with a single bullet to the head and left on a garbage heap. All called Umar. Left with their ID papers on their chests.

We continue to dig through the announcements in *Al-Taakhi*. It is not only Umar Salman. Others wish to change their names to disguise their sectarian identity. Salman Aggal wants to change his daughter's name from Ayisha. A pretty name, I had always thought. Now I learn that it, too, is regarded as being 'very Sunni' because it was the name of the daughter of the first Caliph, and a wife of the Prophet Mohammed, similarly reviled by Shias. In the same half-page Abdul Karim announces his intention to change his tribal name from Ithawi — a large and well-known Sunni tribe — to the neutral al-Barri. It is not only the Sunnis. In the adverts too there is a Christian applying to change his son's first name — from Michael to Ali.

The green gates of Karima Mohammed's home open on to a small courtyard covered with a roof made of palm leaves. It is two weeks before I come across the announcements of the name changes. There are a few plants in pots set against one wall. A rose bush has been dug into a hole the size of a football that has been excavated from a concrete yard still damp from being hosed and brushed. A single wilting bloom, its petals turning brown at the edges, hangs heavily from one of three stems. Someone has taken the television set outside and set it up among the propane gas tanks used to power the oven, and the tool boxes that line the white-painted walls of Karima's single-storey home. Except for the noise of the TV news, which Karima turns off when we arrive, there is only the sound of birds.

Karima is a small and solid woman, well into middle age. I know her sectarian affiliation before I arrive at her gates. Karima and her family are Sunnis in a largely Shia street, in a predominantly Shia town whose largest mosque is a base for Shia militiamen. I am here to meet her because her husband, Saleh Ahmed Mahmoud, a driver with the Ministry of Agriculture, and her son, Ghazan, aged seventeen, were taken by 'police commandos' close to the nearby petrol station run by the Jaish al-Mahdi militia loyal to the Shia preacher Moqtadr al-Sadr.

Her men, she says, were taken on 5 September. The day after they disappeared, her husband's brother received a threatening phone call. He would not tell Karima what the caller said, only that it was sectarian in nature. Since then she has heard nothing. Karima fears the worst. 'We have heard no news at all except for that first day,' she says, surrounded by four younger children. 'We have not had threats from the Shias in this neighbourhood, because we are neighbours. We know each other. There is no one here who would hurt us.' It is a terrible and familiar story, the third I have heard this morning in this street. What is memorable is not the facts of Karima's loss. I notice on the wall that Karima has affixed two of the highly stylised pictures of Imams Ali and Hussein, large-eyed and cartoon-like. Shia images of devotion in a Sunni house, hung up as a belated protection for what remains of her family from the killers.

A tactic I had not noticed before becomes obvious over the following days: physical objects being used as modern shibboleths, conferring invisibility in the world of war. I hear of Sunni drivers in Baghdad, who hang from the windscreen mirrors of their cars the Shia religious symbols you can buy for a few pennies in the marketplace, fearful of the armed thugs on the roads threatening abduction and death. Little pictures of Imam Hussein in gaudy cases that are hung from a chain of plastic beads. Others tie the green headband worn at Shia religious festivals around the top of the gear stick. I hear of Sunnis purchasing tapes of Shia religious music and sermons to be slipped quickly into their cassette players as they approach checkpoints: all good for a quick glance; a fleeting encounter with a bored gunman. But it does not alter the deeper issue of identity.

One day I am told the story of 'Abu Amir', a Sunni who lives in a Shia neighbourhood in the western suburbs of Baghdad. A friend of a friend recounts it. Abu Amir runs a small grocery shop near his house. Most of his neighbours, like his customers, are Shia, who like him, know what he is and protect him as they can. Abu Amir avoids the local Sunni mosque to prevent being marked out as a Sunni in a Shia area. When the fear becomes too much he furnishes himself and all his family members with forged Iraqi national IDs that suggest in the details of his birthplace and name that he is definitively Shia. The real ones he buries in the hope of safer times when it is possible to revert to who he really is. He is too frightened, however, to bury them even in his own garden. For now he is inoculated.

Things Fall Apart

I ask the driver to slow down as we approach the first houses of Khan Younis. There has been clan violence here as recently as this morning. A hurried conversation follows and I'm told, where I am sitting in the back seat, that it is better to pass through the town as fast as possible. We are on our way south, heading out of the choked and claustrophobic urban sprawl of Gaza City, towards Rafah and the Gaza Strip's southernmost extremity. Between the towns and camps and neighbourhoods is what passes for Gaza's countryside.

To my left are fields that extend up towards the nearby border fence with Israel, an unapproachable zone indicated by a few dark trees. The driver points out the polluted wetlands of the Wadi Gaza nature reserve, where kingfishers perch on the fly-tipped garbage and families picnic. It quickly gives way to more buildings and balding, rubbish-littered paddocks and orchards of citrus and olives. As we head further down the Strip, banks of prickly pear appear more frequently in the fields of run-down farms that sit beside scrapyards.

From time to time smashed buildings are visible from the road, which the Israeli bombs and artillery strikes have rendered back to their constituent parts. Gangs of metal pickers live off these ruins, their sharp clack-clacking audible before you see them. Like stonechats calling amongst the rubble. They chip out the iron reinforcing rods in the concrete with hammers and chisels to sell for a few shekels, or cannibalise the wiring they pull out of the fallen blocks for copper. They are most in evidence in the ruined wasteland of the old industrial zone just beyond the Erez Crossing in the north – one of the entry points to Gaza – several acres of factories and workshops destroyed by the Israelis on their evacuation of the settlements from the Strip.

I notice inexplicable redundancies as well, symbols of a society in decay. Not far from Khan Younis, the shells of two wheel-less buses without glass or seats sit neatly stacked, one upon the other, as if arranged on the floor of a child's bedroom. Their paint, once red and grey, is weathered to the dull matt of primer. Gutted and useless things, saved for no discernible reason.

Entering Khan Younis it is clear from the tension in the car that trouble is anticipated just ahead of us. It is obvious in the absences that Khalid and the driver immediately tune in to. There are no walkers or boys thrashing their donkey carts. No cars. Missing too are the children playing marbles in the sand. Although there is no sound of fighting, I recognise it: the deadened, airless space that exists between periods of combat. With good cause my Palestinian companions are concerned that armed and invisible watchers are picketed around, jumpy and overlooking the streets. The driver is anxious that no one should mistake us for what we're not – fighters from a rival family – and anticipate that gunfire might be directed from our car by firing at us first.

We are speeding down a long street lined on both sides by the town's distinctive eucalyptus trees – called *kanyia* by the Palestinians and pronounced 'Kenya' – planted for their shade. Beneath the branches, shaggy with leaves like hanging blades, patches of grass scab loosely to the sand. Suddenly the driver brakes, lurching me forward. There are burned, still-smouldering remnants of tyres, a handful of wrecked vehicles and scatterings of concrete littering the road ahead of us, not quite blocking one of the main junctions. We are forced to weave carefully round the obstructions, slowing as we do. What I want to see is to our right: one of the strongholds of the warring clans.

I am looking out at an area of streets opening on to the main road, a few blocks close to a small pharmacy controlled by the al-Masris of Khan Younis who are presently at war with the al-Tahas. We keep moving as quickly as we can through the smoky haze of burned rubber, rubbish, car paint and oil – the familiar stink of violence that sticks to your clothes, tenacious as the odour of an autumn bonfire. As the driver guns the engine and accelerates again, I can see how this area of houses has been turned into a temporary stockade. The mouths of the streets have been choked with ramshackle head-high barricades, sandbags, breeze blocks and furniture, even vehicles. On the flat roofs of the houses more sandbags have been set round aerials and water tanks to build firing positions overlooking the street. It is not a place to linger. The smoke from the tyres is a reminder that armed clashes between the two families ended only a little while before.

On my first visits to Gaza, the violence's nature was defined by the confrontation with the Israelis, as the Oslo Accords unravelled into the bloodshed of the Second Intifada. There were rivalries and murders then within Palestinian society, largely invisible to outsiders' eyes. But they did not fit the template of Arab–Israeli violence and so were regarded as an irrelevant sideshow. All changed within two years. The Jewish settlers inside the Strip, for long sustained by troops and by-pass roads, are gone. They were evacuated in 2005 by Israel's Prime Minister Ariel Sharon in a unilateral withdrawal. Farmers and the soldiers who guarded them; housewives, commuters and zealots, even the handful of Israeli surfers who used to hang out in the dunes and ride the breaks on beaches open only to them. All gone. The long-shouldered winter waves, grey as porpoises, now barrel in unridden.

But what followed was not a relief of the crushing pressure on Gaza. The fragmenting zones of exclusion that once existed around the settlements and settler roads and bases were replaced by a different kind of encirclement by an enemy out of immediate reach but still controlling all the facts of Gaza's existence – fuel and goods, access to work and markets for its products. Still Occupied, even at arm's length.

It is January 2006, a few days before elections that the Islamist group Hamas will win against the Fatah movement of the late Palestinian leader Yasser Arafat. For so long Fatah has represented the mainstream of Palestinian ambitions, but now is regarded as self-serving, worn out, ineffectual and corrupt. In Gaza these days a different kind of conflict is going on from the one I witnessed two years before with the boys and their blast bombs.

An *intifada*, that on the West Bank is exhausted, plods on here in a slugging, weary and unequal rope-a-dope sustained by a population hemmed in and under siege. The Qassam rocket teams fire their home-made projectiles, pieces of scaffolding tube equipped with crude fins, over the Strip's boundaries. Most often they fly into the Israeli town of Sderot, almost adjacent to the Gaza town of Beit Hanoun. Over the years they have killed only a handful. But they are still terrifying as they fly into factories and kindergartens and homes. In return, the Israelis bomb with jets or reply with artillery fire. Sometimes they send in tanks in their dozens in incursions. Palestinians – both militants and civilians – die in the hundreds. But it is the toxic violence that forms a backdrop to this desultory tit-for-tat with Israel that I have come to see: the conflict between Palestinian factions allied to the rival political groups, and between Gaza's clans themselves.

I am on my way down south to Rafah for a meeting with Alaa al-Hams, a leader in Fatah's al-Aqsa Martyrs' Brigade. It is not without nervousness that I am travelling to see a man accused of kidnapping the family of a British activist in Gaza. This targeting of foreigners to dramatise local complaints and rivalries is a new thing. Most often these events are short inconveniences, then the BBC's Gaza correspondent Alan Johnston is seized and held for almost four months by militant members of the Dogmoush clan to use as leverage in a dispute.

Alaa has called the meeting too close to sunset for my

liking. Common sense tells me it is a bad idea to be having a rendezvous with a purported kidnapper with darkness so near. But if I don't see him now, after a series of phone calls to intermediaries to make contact, I'm not sure whether he will agree to meet again. So I pass through Khan Younis, where its warring families are in the middle of a brief *hudna*, a cessation of the violence that is not quite a truce, but, literally, a 'pause'. Reaching Rafah we park the car. There are more phone calls. Directions are supplied. It appears we cannot drive where we are going, so we abandon the car to walk to the designated apartment house.

When I am taken into the room to meet Alaa, I am surprised by how young he looks. He is dressed neatly in a beige rollneck and a fashionable interpretation of a leather flying jacket with a heavy collar of fake greenish wool, thick and textured like carpet. By Gaza standards his clothing looks expensive. His black hair and beard are cropped to an even length over a round head. But it is his eyes that command attention: dark and intense, set beneath heavy brows in an almost child-like face, so large they have the appearance of being permanently astonished. It is a face that could seem spoiled and petulant, except for a hardness Alaa carries with him.

There is a wiriness about him that is apparent despite the heavy jacket. He is like a boxer, tense with the fighter's awareness of the possibility of violence. Alaa's lieutenants hustle in and out, all of them older than him. They are battered looking, wearing the hardship of their lives on their faces. One in particular catches my attention: a cadaverous man, balding, with a long face and caved-in cheeks, missing some teeth, who stays close to his leader.

Days before our meeting Alaa was under arrest by Palestinian security officials who grabbed him from the street and accused him of snatching Kate Burton, aged twenty-four, an international volunteer in Gaza, and her parents in an argument over unpaid wages for his men. Several hundred of Alaa's armed and masked fighters then stormed the Rafah border crossing with Egypt, commandeering bulldozers, smashing holes through the fence to demand his freedom.

Now Alaa is free. He sits behind a desk in a safe house fiddling with his phone, fearful of being assassinated both by the Israelis, whom his group attacked before their unilateral withdrawal, and by rival Palestinian factions within Gaza. He gets up to shake hands then settles uncomfortably back into his chair. It puzzles me, this meeting. I am not sure how he thinks it can benefit him, unless to demonstrate his authority to his own men – how journalists come courting him. Either that or it is necessary – for reasons I can't fathom – for him to publicly deny the charge of kidnapping once again.

'Angry? Am I angry at being accused of kidnapping? The accusation was aimed at my group . . .' He attempts to appear unfazed by the affair. But it is belied by his words. 'Being picked up on the street and accused . . .' Alaa's grammar – clauses, verbs, subordinate clauses – is in the process of being levered violently apart by his fury. Broken up into half-finished thoughts. 'The Israelis destroyed my dream of going to live in Europe one day,' he says abruptly.

I find it hard to follow this random train of reasoning. He becomes aware of my confusion. 'I used to live there,' he adds.

Two of his men are in the room with us now. I decide that I am safe enough although it would be easy for them to take me if they wanted. No one knows that I am here. His men stand and listen deferentially while I struggle to keep up. I wonder: Is he always like this? Or have I caught him at a bad moment? Under stress and struggling. Then I realise that he is as anxious to present the right impression of a thoughtful leader as I am of meeting him.

I try to probe again into the circumstances of what happened. 'It was the evening,' says Alaa. 'I had told my bodyguards to leave me. I was carrying some apples and some bread, and walking near the mosque in the centre of the city. I saw this Mitsubishi full of men wearing masks. They grabbed me and put something over my head.' He exhales. 'I thought at first it was the Israelis kidnapping me, but then they took me to the central jail. On the second day at 2 a.m. a colonel from intelligence came to see me and I asked what I was being accused of. He said: the kidnapping of the British people. I told him I did not do that. And he said he was only there to implement the law. That is when I said: "Why don't you uphold the law? There is no law! Before the kidnapping of the British or after."'

I would like to believe in his exasperation. If it was not his group responsible for the kidnapping, why was he picked up? Alaa slips back into a haze. 'It was a misunderstanding. There are problems. Internal problems between myself and . . . others. Different parties.' He holds me in a steady, defiant gaze that challenges me to delve more deeply into private matters. 'This is about authority within the city. It is about the vacuum in the Palestinian National Authority. Caused,' he adds, lest there be any misunderstanding, 'by the Israelis.'

Because it is commonplace to blame everything on the Israelis, I at first miss that Alaa – perhaps unwittingly – is making a significant point, one I will hear repeated in the following days. Slowly I grasp it. The Israelis inside Gaza provided a focus for resistance, an outlet for the frustrations. With the enemy moved beyond the reach of easy harm, and confronted by a corrupt and weak Palestinian Authority, the gunmen, whose status and power relied on resisting the Israelis, have turned upon each other.

Alaa continues. 'It is the absence of law that is creating anarchy. It has allowed individuals outside of the organised groups to have access to guns – people who have no sense of responsibility. Now there are guns being used in the streets. Power is with individual groups. In my group, we are against barricades in the streets, kidnapping foreigners, shutting the roads and turning them into fortresses.'

'You understand,' he says, 'that the departure of the Israelis from Gaza does not mean the end of the Occupation. The Israelis are only five kilometres away. And we still live in a . . . If anyone had dreamt of things getting better. Of the ending of the Occupation. Liberty. Stability. A better life . . . You know, I'm sorry. It's getting worse. It is becoming a nightmare for us.' There is a regretful tone in this tough young man. 'I hope we will have peace. I hope to have the opportunity to take my children and . . .'. He searches for an image representative of ordinary hope. 'To a garden. Or in the street. I can't, you know. Get in a car without fear. This issue,' he says, referring to the spiralling instability that began with the death of Yasser Arafat, 'makes me think hard before putting my weapons down. I don't feel secure.'

We exit into a dusk the colour of week-old bruises, a soft grey that bleeds into yellows and damson. To rumours of yet more clashes in Khan Younis. I can hear the sound of distant, sporadic bursts of fire as the *hudna* crumbles. It is not safe to return the way we came, so we take the coast road back, past the ruins of the abandoned settlements among the dunes, torn down in the immediate aftermath of the evacuation. A brisk wind is blowing, but we stop to look out at the sea on a beach once forbidden to Palestinians. As we do I consider Alaa's remark: how strange it is that even this violent man with his scores of armed followers cannot feel safe in Gaza any more.

Prolonged conflict leads to social disintegration. The speed of the breakdown depends on unpredictable factors: the strength of group solidarity and resilience, the coping strategies available, and whether the new internal tensions created by conflict — and the pre-existing ones exacerbated by it — can be resolved. No society is immune to conflict's power to atomise over extended periods. As bonds once strong are severed, a kind of exothermic reaction takes place, a release of energy and heat, described in discord and competition.

The social frictions in Gaza's society were shaped by six decades of experience of strife. As they played out, they expressed themselves in yet more conflict and further social fragmentation. First was the war of 1948 that transformed Gaza's society – then under Egyptian control – setting up the conditions for the tensions in Palestinian society that would emerge. An original population of around 80,000 was overwhelmed by the sudden influx of twice that number of refugees fleeing the creation of the Jewish State. Their long-term future would be a life within camps run by the United Nations, vast slums that pooled round Gaza's original towns and villages.

Over the decades, as a detailed historical and social analysis by the International Crisis Group in 2007 depicted it, kinship relationships among the incoming, largely rural refugees were weakened by the experience of flight and long-term displacement. Existence in the camps was socially levelling too. It guaranteed for many access to universal education and health care for the first time. Confronted with this influx, native Gazans reinforced clan associations as a mechanism for insisting on their social, political and economic supremacy.

An already complex situation was exacerbated by Israel after its conquest and Occupation of Gaza in 1967 following the Six Day War. Fearful of the radicalising conditions within the camps, Israel chose to manage its rule in Gaza by dealing with clan leaders even as Israel's other policies, particularly economic, were undermining the very system it was trying to prop up. In particular Israel's demand for day labourers – drawn largely from the refugee population – enriched the incomers, who looked to the Palestine Liberation Organisation for leadership, at the expense of the original inhabitants.

There were other motors for change and for building social friction. Two *intifadas*, reliant on youthful popular committees, also undermined efforts to maintain the old social order. These periods of uprising would produce successive generations of fighters who insisted on being rewarded and politically accommodated for their struggle. But in the end it would be the Palestinian Authority itself, in the wake of the Oslo Accords, which contributed the final accelerator to a volatile mix. Seeking quickly to entrench its rule, the Fatah-led Authority took a leaf out of the Israeli Occupiers' book, wooing the prominent families and further incorporating them into the Authority's new power structures. Most dangerously of all, Yasser Arafat undermined any notion of the primacy of the rule of law by creating a Department of Tribal Affairs to oversee an informal justice system in parallel to the formal one, allowing the powerful families to dictate their own system of reparations.

All of the elements were in place for the collapse which would follow: a chain reaction set in motion by the combination of the Second Intifada and Israel's disproportionate response. An economic siege of Gaza, allied with poverty, inefficiency, corruption and the destruction of the Palestinian Authority's security establishment, would lead to the breakdown of law and order. In the prelude to the violent purge against Fatah by Hamas in the summer of 2007, families and clans would emerge as powerful actors again. Taking old rivalries on to the streets. Privatising Gaza's violence.

T he killing in the town of Beit Hanoun in Gaza's north, my host explains, began like this. Hussein al-Kafarna was driving his wealthy uncle's Mitsubishi 4x4 when the driver of a donkey cart from a rival clan, the al-Masris of Beit Hanoun – not the al-Masris of Khan Younis – crashed into him. Enraged, Hussein went to the al-Masris to demand compensation. A hothead by reputation, he drew his pistol and fired it twice into the air in the argument that followed, then used the gun to club the donkey driver. I am sitting in the house of a member of the Popular Front for the Liberation of Palestine, whose family is mediating between the warring clans. For now there is a truce after days of clashes that have kept his family trapped inside the home. Their fear is such that he insists on not being named, and I am hustled into his house. I sit in his small, blue-painted room beneath a cheap print of Che Guevara, while my host – an engineer by trade – explains the history of the family's worsening feud.

'It was last month. Late November. The owner of the car was a very tough young man. There was a shot fired at a house owned by the donkey man's family. Within three days, four people had been killed. In mid-December, I believe it was. Family members were being followed into Gaza City itself. A Kafarna was going to the bank when he was followed by an al-Masri who saw that he could shoot and kill him.' My host offers me a cigarette, which I refuse. He lights his own, ready to continue. 'Women and children have been hurt and killed in these clashes. It was made worse by the fact that both the al-Masris and the Kafarnas supply a third each of the police and security forces in Beit Hanoun. So the police refused to get involved to stop it.'

A day later Nasser Shabat fills in more of the details. Although he is a community leader in Beit Hanoun he does not want to meet there. Instead we meet in an apartment in a tower block in Beit Lahiya, overlooking Beit Hanoun. It belongs to his brother Said whose nephew was hit by a stray round during the fighting between the two families. Said, a heavy-set man with large glasses sitting on a bulbous nose, asks me to wait for a moment and digs through a drawer. He fetches the bullet extracted from his nephew.

He holds the round up to the light between his index finger and thumb. His other fingers are spread out in a delicate fan so I think he is showing me something precious. In his thick fingers, tips stained from cigarettes, the sharp, copper-coloured thing looks like an extracted tooth; a thorn pulled from a footpad. Even as we speak, the sound of gunfire is audible nearby, carrying across the houses from where the al-Masris and Kafarnas are firing from their rooftops, random and persistent as a child's cough. 'You have to ask,' says Said, his face set into a mask of bitterness, 'why the same families with long histories of friction were under control for generations? Through the time of the British Mandate, Egyptian rule, the Israeli Occupation and the most recent *intifada* there were almost no killings. Then, the Palestinian Authority allowed everyone to carry guns and closed their eyes to the groups fighting the Israelis. It ignored the reality that many of the groups fighting were under weak control. It ignored the problems unless they were on the doorsteps of members of the leadership. If the law has been implemented here at all, it has been only against the weaker clans.'

'This is a stupid problem,' says Nasser contemptuously, 'that reflects badly on the leaders of the families. The donkey carriage was the start. But there has been a history of problems between these families. It goes back a long time. You know, originally they were not from Beit Hanoun. They weren't from here. In the beginning the al-Masris were the smaller family to the Kafarnas. They felt they lived in their shadow, that they were minor. This was back at the time of the British Mandate and Egyptian rule. The Kafarnas had the lobbying power. But the two families lived very close. Then came 1948 and the numbers doubled after they . . .' he struggles to find an appropriate expression, '. . . transferred from the Other Place.'

I listen to this gossip relating the ancient rivalries between these families – a recitation involving culpability so far in the past. I attempt to grasp this encapsulation of the hidden social narrative of conflict, ebbing and flowing with the setbacks of Gazan life. It has a barbershop – or pub – conventionality in its description. Except the events it frames are still being played out within earshot: a murder in Khan Younis; a car crash and a beating in Beit Hanoun, each leading to new blossoming of violence. My fear of being in this block of flats reminds me he is not describing a soap opera or gangster fable on television, but detailing in its slow unravelling the disintegration of Gaza's life.

Nasser picks up the story again. 'During the Occupation the al-Masris built up a good financial base. Eighty per cent of all al-Masri men married more than one woman. The al-Masris,' he continues, 'were doing very well. They wanted to increase their numbers. That is what they are famous for in Beit Hanoun. That was their vision. Previously there were problems between the Kafarnas and other families, but not the al-Masris. So the area was divided into four main blocks of family control with smaller families looking towards the bigger families.' Nasser pauses for breath. The hiatus is punctured by another burst of distant gunfire that only serves to underline his contempt. His tone, when he begins again, suggests the opening of a new chapter in his long explanation.

'During the Occupation in Gaza itself, then, you see, everyone was too preoccupied to look at what was going on internally with the families' rivalries. The difficulties really began with the coming of the Palestinian Authority. That is when the al-Masris grew in political power. But after the first five years of the Palestinian Authority it is clear there was a vacuum here. People lost their feeling of security. The institutions were slowly collapsing. Then the families came to the conclusion that no one was being protected. So they felt they needed to do that themselves.'

Nasser calls one of the head nurses at an intensive care unit who lives in Beit Hanoun. 'Iyad' the man calls himself although it is not his real name. He is from a small family, scared of talking out of turn in the midst of a clan feud. The phone is turned to speaker. We've barely started to speak. 'They're shooting now!' His voice is overtaken by a quality I recognise, high, breathless and climbing, a child gasping at the end of a tantrum. A tone I recognise as fear. 'They were firing outside my house just now.' There is a crack, distinct even on this line that pops and crackles like an old record. 'That was a bullet,' he gasps. 'I'm looking out my window . . .'

The fighting subsides again. Iyad begins to tell me what has happened to break the temporary truce. But I know a large part of it already, having driven through the contested areas the evening before. How among the crowds on the streets, celebrating the festival of Eid, young men in black appeared in little groups, moving purposefully towards the buildings they had occupied as firing positions during the previous fighting, and had given up as part of the peace deal. How some had clambered up a water tower overlooking the crowds and fired straight into them. 'They were on the high buildings,' says the nurse. 'Shooting out of the Kafarna blocks. I can't look out of the window any more,' he says. 'There are wounded. They cannot be evacuated.' I am not sure whether the last two comments are even linked. Whether he means there are new wounded. Or wounded still trapped from before. I think the former. But I can't ask him. Nasser is speaking gently to Iyad. 'Don't come,' he says. 'Don't try to come out now. They're shooting everything.'

I hear a young woman has been shot in the latest round of fighting a few minutes after I passed the street she was standing in. I decide on a different approach. If the staff of the hospitals cannot come to me, I will go to one of the clinics where the wounded are being treated. It is not necessarily a safer option than going to Beit Hanoun. Clan members have sought their enemies to murder them in hospital, forcing the Palestinian Authority to designate one hospital for the Kafarnas and another for the al-Masris. But I head for the al-Awda clinic in Jabalia whose catchment area is Gaza's north. There are police posted not far from the ambulance ramp. They slide into cover as we arrive, then, seeing the 'TV' stickers on the car, they reappear with a fake bravado. We bump down the ramp. There are more figures who slip behind concrete pillars and walls, with masks pulled over their faces. They are wearing civilian clothes. Not police, but the clan fighters who have so far refused to meet me. There is an injured fighter in the hospital. These men have been posted here to protect him from attack.

I approach carefully. The men are still jumpy from the recent violence, scared of an attack, and not willing at first to speak about the feud. I'm told sharply that it is a 'private matter' between the Kafarnas and the al-Masris, not something for outsiders. By now the police are waving away cars, and pretending to do their jobs, so the men relax a little. There are three of them. One of them, an overweight young man in his mid-twenties, is sent to cover the car park and tries to jog with his weapon but only manages a brief plodding trot before running out of steam.

The leader peels back his balaclava to reveal a sweating face marked in places with the seams left by the tight wool on his skin. Pink furrows and frowns. The others do the same. It becomes quickly apparent that they are members of the al-Masri clan. The leader calls himself 'Abu Nahed', a second introduces himself as 'Abu Khalil', although I hear the others call him Yassin. It is Abu Nahed who does most of the talking. He tells me his relative has been hit in the kidney, by a shot fired from above. He will not name him. 'This will never end,' he says, but I sense a self-conscious drama in his words, as if he does not quite believe what he is saying and is only playing a part. That an end to this feud would be possible if fighters did not need to say words like this to one another as confirmation of a fatalistic manliness. 'The Kafarnas will never keep their agreements. The weak will be hurt by the strong and no one will prevent them. It all comes from a lack of authority here. They think that we are weak and so they want to show their power.' Yassin grows angry again and interrupts to end the conversation. He shouts at me: 'Hey! This is a matter between the families! We're fighting for our survival here!'

I am not done yet. The injured woman is not at this clinic and so I call the Shifa hospital, and finally I track her down. A nurse tells me she was hit in the right hip by a bullet that damaged the femoral artery and veins. He adds that the targeting of the woman appeared deliberate. He digs out a name. Reem al-Masri. Aged twenty-two.

he fragmentation is visible across Palestinian society. Its effects are tangible in government institutions, social networks and political parties – in schools, universities and on the street. While the clan conflict is not alone in defining the nature of Palestinian society's crisis within the Gaza Strip, neither is it framed entirely by the political dimensions of the struggle between Fatah and Hamas that escalates after the Palestinian Legislative Council elections on 26 January, 2006. Rather, the two combine to carve out complex new possibilities for confrontation.

On the factional front it is not only about the getting and holding of power but about the emergence of sharply competing visions. On one side is the centralising and socially and religiously conservative Hamas that refuses to recognise the legitimacy of Israel's existence. On the other is the more secular Fatah: chaotic, nepotistic and sometimes West-leaning, an organisation that has negotiated peace settlements with Israel, trading land in the hope of securing a future Palestinian state for no appreciable movement towards genuine statehood.

Competition between Hamas and Fatah – played out in two sets of elections in 2005 and 2006 – sees Hamas emerge as the victor. It is a changing of the guard in Gaza that occurs as the relationship between the powerful clans and the Fatah-dominated Palestinian Authority is becoming ever more fraught. With the collapsing Authority relying ever more heavily on the families to deliver votes and to exercise their influence in an escalating internal security crisis, killings, kidnappings and revenge attacks fuel an arms race amongst the clans. When Hamas moves brutally to insist on its sole authority in the Gaza Strip in June 2007, the scene is set. It is an action that pits it not only against the security organisations of the Palestinian Authority, still

Fatah-dominated, but also against the Fatah-supporting clans.

Shahab al-Akhras comes into his cousins' house in Rafah while his grandmother, Sada al-Khalil, is showing me three rockets fired into their home by Hamas fighters. She keeps them in a yellow plastic bag, green things with twisted fins that seem too insubstantial to cause much damage, until I go out into the street to see the impacts that the missiles have left upon the house. Sada lays them down upon a low, large table in the centre of the room. There is a farmyard scene of plastic toys arranged in a hollow space beneath the table's glass top: a picket fence, three cows, a sheep and a chicken. They are all Fatah people in this family. Her son Youssef was a member of the Palestinian Authority's Preventive Security Force, formerly run by Gaza's security chief, a figure hated by Hamas. During the 'Internal Fighting' as everyone calls it, Youssef fled across the border to Egypt with a group of friends. Sada hasn't seen him since. Despite Hamas's claims to me to the contrary, the struggle between the two parties is not over. And Shahab is a combatant.

Shahab is eight years old. His ears stick out beneath his winter hat. As we talk, his face shifts between different moods. Sometimes it resembles the child he is, but at other times – it seems to me by a deliberate effort – he hardens it. It is the same expression worn by Alaa al-Hams, a toughness coalescing among the gentler curves of Shahab's face into a learned, defiant look. Another of the al-Akhras family, an older cousin named Thair who was arrested by Hamas for being a member of Fatah, calls Shahab over. The boy, it emerges, was beaten on the hands and threatened by masked men of Hamas's Executive Force for wearing the Fatah movement's black and white checked *hata* scarf. He is wearing it when he comes in the door, tied like a football mascot over his denim jacket. It says the same thing – which team he follows. Thair says he needs to interpret for Shahab – that he is not so easy to understand since the beating two weeks before.

'There were four of them,' explains Shahab. He is standing in front of me with Thair's hand on his shoulder, his thumbs pushed in the back pockets of his jeans, shifting his weight from foot to foot as if in front of a teacher. 'I saw them on the street and they grabbed me and pushed me in a corner. They took off my shoes and put them on the scarf and stamped on them. Then they told me to put out my arms in front of me and beat me with a stick.' Later he shows me how they did it. A hand placed in the middle of the chest to push him roughly against a wall. His arms then pulled straight, with the backs of his hands upwards. 'They said if they saw me wearing the scarf again they would shoot me in the legs. I hate them!' After this I start seeing boys and girls with their *hata* scarves everywhere I look: boys with the yellow Fatah flag tied to their bicycles, even a pair of giggling teenage girls dressed in the *hata* and the colours of the Palestinian flag who squeal they are: 'Fatah!'

I want to search out the opinions of 'Hamas children' to balance those of the Fatah kids. The answer seems to be to head to the house of Fatima an-Najar, a fifty-seven-year-old grandmother and Hamas activist who blew herself up and wounded five Israeli soldiers in 2006. These days she is a Hamas icon. The anniversary of her death is celebrated by the movement. My plan is to seek out and speak to her grandchildren as I spoke to Sada's in Rafah. When I arrive at Fatima's house in Jabalia there is a frigid, heavy rain descending. It is so cold that I feel certain it will be falling as snow up in Jerusalem. The wind blows the rain into arcing waterfalls as it pours out of the gushing gutters. The streets are flooded axle-deep in places, a grey and murky tide. Fatima's family house is opposite a grove of lemon trees that is sunken a few feet. The exterior walls are papered with posters of her martyr picture. All the colours except blue have been washed out of them, leaving a faded monochrome woman, wrinkled under her headscarf, clasping a rifle.

In a bare, cold room decorated only by images of pages from the Koran, Rafat, aged thirteen, does not give Hamas's point of view. Instead he rejects both it and its rival. 'I don't want to belong to Hamas, or any party. There is sometimes trouble at school between the parties. There are arguments and fights. And there is pressure from other students to join their side. The first day of term they'll hand you the time-tables they've made up to show how good their party is, or get your books, or they ask you to sit with them. If you do that and the other side recognises you sitting with people from the other party then they won't talk to you again. It bothers me that politics is coming into my school. It should only be for learning. But since the internal violence between Hamas and Fatah, it is happening much more.'

Iyad Sarraj, the psychologist I met four years ago at his clinic, comes to visit me at Gaza City's al-Deira Hotel, where the city's small elite — still largely Fatah followers — come to lunch and smoke *narguileh* above a little beach that curves round to the fishing port's breakwater. It is January 2008, two years since the elections that saw Hamas defeat Fatah. Seven months after Hamas used arms finally to vanquish Fatah inside Gaza and disarm the clans. And it is seven months into Israel's blockade of the Gaza Strip. These are bad times that threaten worse. There are power cuts and shortages of sugar and flour and meat, not enough to starve but sufficient to lead to rampant inflation. The supply of cigarettes runs out until Hamas blasts down the Rafah border wall with Egypt and briefly breaks the siege, triggering a massive rush by Palestinians into the farmland of Egypt to buy goods in short supply.

The doctor does not look well, bundled up against the damp winter chill in his hat and scarf and heavy overcoat. He complains of recent illness and about his prostate. He orders a mint tea and greets the well-wishers who come by from time to time to shake his hand and ask his opinion about different events. I want to hear his views on the serial fragmentations in Gaza's society. He answers my questions with a story. 'Two days ago there was an explosion at the police headquarters in al-Jawazat Square. I was at home. It was a big explosion. At first people said the Israelis had bombed the Islamic University. But it was a roadside bomb. I had a young boy of fifteen staying at my house. He said: "I hope some of Hamas were killed!" I said: "How can you say that? They are Palestinians . . ." And he said to me:

"I hope they have been killed. They have done so much damage." It shocked me. And it reminded me of when the son of Mahmoud Zahar [a senior Hamas leader] was killed a few weeks ago. I heard both women and men say they wish that he had died.' There is a tired sadness in this clever, humane man. It is a weariness born not simply of illness, but because Palestinian life has come to this.

He sips at his tea, cupping the glass in his hands. 'We have seen a lot of things. There was a series of politically motivated clashes between Fatah and Hamas during the Internal Fighting last year. Since then, we have seen that process transferred to the family. Children are preoccupied with the story of Hamas or Fatah. When you visit children's homes they ask you if you are Fatah or Hamas depending on who they are. But even families are divided. When Hamas confronted the Hillis clan, a few people in the family were also Hamas. So some ended up being divided from their relatives. There are some people who believe that this is only superficial, that we can go back to living together the way we did in the past. I believe,' adds Sarraj gloomily, 'that it is much more serious than that.'

Instead, he believes the divisions now are about fundamental issues of identity. 'Hamas believes that those outside the movement are infidels – *kafirs*. I first came across it when I was in prison. Imprisoned by Yasser Arafat,' he adds with bitterness. 'I was in prison with people from Islamic Jihad and Hamas. I asked them what the difference was being in an Israeli and a Palestinian jail. They said that being in a jail in Israel was like a medal of honour on the chest – here in a Palestinian jail it was painful. But another man, a Hamas member who was listening, said: "It is like a double honour. The Israeli's are still 'People of the Book', people of faith. These people are infidels." That was 1996.

'What has happened to us? That is my question.' He answers the question himself. 'Hamas is not simply a political movement. It offers a separate identity to young people, not just an ideological framework. It creates a barrier between the group and the rest. That is why it is easier for them to hurt and kill Palestinians who are not members of Hamas. Because they are not the true faithful.'

Sarraj describes a Palestinian society that over the decades has been incrementally weakened. We return to the subject we discussed several years before when the Israelis were still within Gaza rather than patrolling its walls – the issue of the breakdown of parental authority. The difference this time is that we are not talking about the boy blast-bombers out of their families' control, but the toxic consequences of the collapse of respect of children for their parents. 'The children are looking for a replacement, something powerful to identify with. They find that in the militants who offer a sense of security unavailable elsewhere, a strong identity they can't find in the home. The result is a fragmentation that has gone deep into Palestinian society.'

A squall of rain blows in across the sea, the drops ticking at the plastic awning that serves as the restaurant's winter roof. Dr Sarraj shrugs into his coat more deeply, shivering. 'I have a boy of two years old. He is fascinated by Yasser Arafat and by Fatah. He wants to know what party people are. His half-brother is eight. He considers himself already to be a strong Fatah supporter. What's happened?' Sarraj sighs. 'Palestinians feel defeated. And we cannot accept defeat here. So we have created new victims within ourselves who we can win over. It explains all of the brutalities.'

I t is not only violence but also the suggestion of it that is deployed in this fratricidal struggle – the threat of being diminished in the public gaze. Ibrahim Abu Najar knows it. An elderly Fatah leader from Khan Younis, the men who came for him at nine o'clock one December night took him away to cut off his moustache. Ameera, my translator, whispers sharply at me. 'It's so embarrassing for him. You understand? To cut off his moustache.' When he speaks he is barely audible, fiddling with a cigarette in a holder, a tube of brown, ivory and black polished by use, which he holds between his index and his second finger. 'They knew me in person,' he complains. 'I had helped Hamas. They didn't have to deal with me in this way. Men in masks. There were so many people. They put me in a military car and took me south to Deir al-Bala. They took me to a place underground where they cut my hair and moustache with a knife and scissors. Then they took me home. It was to humiliate me.' He screws his cigarette in slow circles into the ashtray and puts his head into his hands. 'Before there were different parties here and different colour flags. Now Hamas wants all the people to belong to them.'

I am invited to lunch by the clan elder – the *mukhtar* – of the Hillis clan at his home in Shuja'iya. It is the family Dr Sarraj has told me about, one of the most powerful, locked in a fitful confrontation with Hamas, and bitterly split in its struggle with the organisation. When I reach his house I find that Abu Mousa al-Hillis is troubled. Two of his grandsons, a boy of fifteen and another of seventeen, have been arrested in Egypt by the security services for trying to smuggle explosives back over Rafah's suddenly open border. He is furious with the boys' uncle, who has encouraged the venture. 'How long do you think they'll be in prison there?' he asks the men in the room. He answers himself. 'I think, perhaps, we will not see those boys again.'

Abu Mousa wears a long black coat and a grey wool hat that is not pulled tight over his skull but instead has been pulled up into a rounded point. It reminds me of the soft white hats the older Kosovo-Albanian men wear, elongated white felt domes that sit upon the head. I first meet him in his *diwan* – the family's meeting area – the day before our lunch. It is unfinished, a large concrete room opening on to the street, unadorned, and unlit save for the daylight coming through an unglassed area high in the walls through which the rain occasionally blows. The Israeli blockade has halted any further building work. Abu Mousa is sitting with other family elders around a brazier the size of a kitchen sink full of glowing embers, on which the coffee is being stewed in a blackened pot. He has an official-looking document printed on grey paper, which he shows me – the terms of the current truce between the Hillis and Hamas that has just ended four months of intermittent violence. But truces have been violated several times.

Over two days I piece together the story of the clashes between Hamas and the Hillis – the most serious since the official end of the Internal Fighting. How in September 2007 members of Hamas's Executive Force had tried to enter the streets of Shuja'iya that were populated most densely by the Hillis clan to arrest its members. It was an attempt that saw some of the Hamas fighters themselves seized and disarmed. How a second attempt by Hamas a month later triggered major street battles in which a large Hamas force pounded Hillis houses with rockets and artillery. And how in that battle other clans sent fighters to the Hillis' assistance.

'It is important for our sons to know,' says Abu Mousa at our first meeting, 'that it is not a political party but the family that can protect them. We had to use force,' he adds, 'because this is largely a Fatah family. Which is why Hamas attacked us, even though there are members of this family who are Hamas. Some of them came closer to the family during the fighting, but there were others who refused to fight. We exiled them. Three members of the family so far. We ignore them in the street. No one is permitted to speak with them.' I ask if it would be improper to ask the names of the exiled men. There is a tut-tutting around the fire. Abu Mousa interjects. 'It is better to die than live in this kind of exile. We live in the age of the families not of the political party.'

Abu Mousa welcomes me the following day into his house. It is warmer and more comfortable than the *diwan*, a place full of the sound of children. The room I am led into is decorated with soft toys and martyr pictures. There is a tiger and a long-haired toy dog. Three teddy bears are mounted on a wall, surrounding a picture of one of the family's many 'martyrs' from the fighting with Israel. They number fifty in total, Abu Mousa says. As we wait to eat, one of his sons arrives: Dr Mousa Hillis, a lecturer in social sciences at Al-Azhar University. After some pleasantries I realise that he has come to tell the family's side of the story of the battle with Hamas.

'One of the family members was riding in a car belonging to a colonel in the Preventive Security called Abu Ramsi. It belonged to the Palestinian Authority before Hamas took over and seized all of the cars. The Executive Force stopped the car and told him to hand it over and fired shots at the tyres. There were phone calls between us and Hamas,' adds Dr Hillis. We are picking at a huge roast chicken with our fingers and drinking soft drinks. The other men who crowd the sofas are largely silent, nodding their heads in agreement from time to time. 'They told us to hand over all of our weapons and a member of the family they wanted to arrest. We told them that our weapons are only used for the struggle against the Israeli Occupation.' I can see in these confrontations the reality of Gazan life laid bare – negotiations over issues of status and power represented by cars and guns and the right to employ violence. Dr Hillis continues: 'The *mukhtar* went to the police station. They asked for thirty-five weapons and we said we would give fifteen. There was an agreement signed at 7.30 p.m. By eight o'clock Hamas was bringing in its forces to attack our neighbourhood again. They said: "Someone started shooting at us." It wasn't true. We fought for two days before we reached another agreement.'

I am scooping piles of rice from around the stripped ribs of the bird as I listen to his matter-of-fact account, conscious of the greasy smell of the meat coming off my fingers. 'When they came again it was to three families who lived a little more distant from the rest of us, including a doctor at the Shifa hospital. Dr Hassan. They said he would be safe with them and ordered him to come out. When he did come out they shot him.' I listen to his voice, its warm cadences, the rise and fall of words in this comfortable parlour with the sound of the women and the shouting children in the background and attempt to connect these men with the bleak attrition that Dr Mousa Hillis is describing. That ceased so recently. 'Then a member of the Qassam Brigades was shot. This time Hamas surrounded and attacked the whole area again. But they failed to break us. That was before the present agreement. Now we have people watching them and they have people watching us to make sure that the agreement holds.' I ask Dr Hillis why he thinks Hamas wants to destroy the Hillis family. There is a moment of thought. 'For me,' he says, slowly, 'you have to understand, they did this because they feel angry. It is a social issue. They are low-class people. They are jealous of the things the Hillis family has.'

I see the Hillis men again in television images six months later, overwhelmed at last by Hamas and fleeing from Gaza towards exile in Israel after a day of clashes that left at least nine people dead. I try to make sense of the sequence of events: an explosion at a seaside café in the preceding week that had killed five Hamas men and a six-year-old girl. All I am left with are echoes of my conversations with the Hillis men. The talk of the boys arrested smuggling explosives into Gaza from Egypt, which I had assumed was for use against Israel. Now I ask myself whether it was for the struggle with Hamas instead.

I examine the pictures for faces that I know, men wounded on ambulance gurneys waving the cameramen away or standing naked with bound hands and blindfolded eyes en route to interrogation by Israel's security services. And I recall Abu Mousa's dining room and its martyr pictures; the boast of how many Hillis had died in the struggle with an enemy they had now been forced to run to for help. The end-point of Gaza's disintegration.

No-Man's-Land

For a youth who has been smoking heroin not long before, Mahmoud Hussein climbs the wall above me with surprising agility. His fingers grasp at things I cannot see in the cladding of smooth and streaky yellow marble, made doubly slippery by a fine coating of dust. Soon he is above me. As a climber, I'm at once impressed. I am amazed too by his recovery. An hour or so before I had watched Mahmoud nodding in a corner of the ruined Russian Cultural Centre in Kabul, his eyes glassy as a liquid morphine capsule, his head drooping on his chest, deep in his drug dreams. He was so out of it I wondered how close he was to overdose. His only movement then was to stagger to his feet to puke a stream of grey, watery vomit into a hole.

The complex of buildings I am in is a shell-wracked ruin, a monument to violence in a city still dotted, even seven years after the Taliban's collapse, with evidence of Afghanistan's long legacy of war. I come across them all over Kabul: the old king's palace; a ruined cinema; remnants of neighbourhoods. Structures reduced to nothing but façades, more sky than substance. Peeled back with a coroner's precision to reveal what lies below – rooms and staircases, toilets and meeting places. The vast majority, however, were not damaged in the fighting with the Soviets, or even in the war that displaced the Taliban, but in the internecine conflict that followed the Soviet retreat between the rival groups of mujahideen who fought for control of the spoils. I try to imagine beyond the damage. But there is little left to suggest what the centre must have been like before its various metamorphoses began: combat position, ruin, home for refugees. Now this. A fetid shooting gallery. It is a place of living ghosts who inhabit a smack twilight.

There is one thing left to suggest the complex's first incarnation. Beneath the dust, in what must once have been the central foyer, I find a damaged mural. It is dominated by the ruined face of Lenin, done in the Socialist Realist style – a monument to a failed experiment. His features have been chipped out of his face, removing the figure that the artist intended should reconcile two ideals of socialism displayed in two wings. The left side of the panorama is dedicated to Soviet triumphs of modernity. Russian doctors, scientists and steel workers who toil beneath a floating Soyuz astronaut. On the right are depicted the virtues of their former Afghan communist brothers. This section, in contrast, is rural and conservative. Afghans are portrayed at prayer and bringing in the harvest. A figure I can't recognise is riding a rearing horse, while a group of bearded, turbaned men hold up their guns. A junkie jokes that it is the mujahideen ready to fight the Russians. Only a beard and section of the lower jaw of Lenin have survived the vandalism. I wonder who removed his face – the mujahideen after the Soviet flight, or some Taliban dutifully obliterating a face not because it was Lenin's but because it was a human representation.

I had met Mahmoud outside, looking youthful in a blue sports shirt and with a flop of dark, greasy hair. Only his filthy feet and soiled trousers gave him away as homeless. We had talked after a fashion and later he had followed at a distance as I poked around a building I realised was lousy with addicts, staggering from room to room, or sitting in little rooms in rank bunker-like basements chasing the dragon, smoking 'scorpion', a mixture of hashish and smack, or mainlining.

I'm careful where I walk. There are drifts of used syringes, ankle-twisting rubble and hidden holes revealing depths into which men briefly, and furtively, disappear to get high. In one basement, once a generator room, I stumble across a man, blind in one eye, who has squirrelled his way into a turbine feeder tube, orange with rust. His face is lined and wrecked, his hands filthy. I watch him smooth out a piece of foil from a cigarette packet, careful not to tear it. He sparks a match to light a piece of string – a makeshift candle – which gutters yellow beneath a tiny heap of heroin, brown as the dirt he's squatting in. Only once as I sit on my haunches at the tube's mouth does he raise his head to make contact with his one good eye, a connection dull as a faint sonar echo. He repeats the process several times then disappears deeper inside the pipe to move his bowels, a sound horribly amplified by his shelter's shape. There are several hundred addicts living here among these gutted buildings. The smell of human shit is overpowering.

With Mahmoud in tow, I climb a set of stairs I have not come across before. They lead up and out of a kind of roofless auditorium at the centre of the building. It is the shell of the open-air stage in what was once the centre's symphony hall. Later I re-imagine these ruins: the tennis courts outside, the swimming pool, rooms once occupied by studios and a cinema. The cramped basements – favourite congregating places of the addicts – were artists' studios. As I ascend the steps in the half-light I cannot quite see what is supporting them.

Mahmoud is following more closely, more mobile and capable than before, in the hope, I suspect, that I will give him some cash. I have already given money to Gharib, the young man with the freshly slit wrists and forearms, crudely stitched and in need of new dressings. A self-confessed thief, Gharib admits in a distracted way that he had considered robbing me 'two or three times'. But with his sliced-up arms, and shambling, smacked-out gait, I figure him as ruined as the building. No threat at all.

All at once I am out of the stench and gloom and able to see the terraced levels of the rooftop, covered with pale gravel. Below are the prone forms of addicts scattered under the trees like victims of a massacre, curled uncomfortably. Above me is the 'spire' of the centre where the two angles of its roof converge. I am suddenly aware of a skinny Hazara junkie whom I came across two days ago with a dark scarf obscuring his face. He is clambering up the bullet-and-shrapnel-pitted marble facing of the wall above a drop of forty feet or so. He hauls himself finally up to a higher level where he now stands, a solitary figure. Mahmoud begins climbing too, this time just above me where I am standing on a kind of balcony. His ascent is less alarming than the Hazara's – only fifteen feet or so – but a slip would mean a broken leg or ankle on landing in the rubble. He moves right, heading for a shell hole three feet high and four feet long, shaped like an eye, a cave-eyrie high on the building's side.

I decide to follow him. Despite the dust on the chipped marble cladding that makes the holds as slick as verglassed rock on an alpine ascent, I discover small positive edges for my trainers – footholds polished with long use. Higher up there are pieces of steel reinforcing rod protruding from the exposed concrete in spikes and loops, useful for my hands. When I touch them, the metal rods are slick and warm from Mahmoud's hands. Quickly I come level with the youth where he is sitting, his knees pulled to his chest at the lip of the opening.

Behind Mahmoud is a long, narrow space illuminated in places by a few rents in the pitched roof. Where the roof has been blown in, the blocks of concrete have fallen to lie among the smaller segments like boulders on a foreshore. Mahmoud says this is where he sleeps for safety. The conversation is translated by my translator, Muhib, on the balcony below, who warns me to be careful as I hang by a metal hold taking pictures with one hand. The boy is drained of energy again, his face sad and pensive despite the drug. I think for a moment he will cry, sitting like a gargoyle at the lip of this once secular cathedral. He says

249

he is seventeen although I guess he could be older. He is not bad looking, despite his life. I sense the multiple dangers of sleeping in the cellars with the older, stronger men.

I already know his story. I heard it from him in the moments after he took the drug, his words and thoughts bubbling slowly through the numbing rush of the heroin like pockets of marsh gas. 'My mother and my brother and my sister were killed during the civil war. I had an uncle. Who had . . . an uncle. He was . . . But he's gone too.' He gropes for relationships so complex that I lose track. Mahmoud believes he has an uncle who survived. He would like to find him but is not sure where he lives. What I understand is that Mahmoud is alone. He tries to form a timeline of his life but that disintegrates as well.

There are memories that coalesce into something more meaningful. He tells me he was in Iran, which means that he fled from the Taliban's regime. It was while he was there that Afghan friends encouraged him to smoke opium, saying it would help him 'stay awake' – counter-intuitive but a story I hear many times. One day he was coming back from work to where he lived, caught by the police carrying the drug, and sent to a place the junkies call the 'barracks' for deportation home.

I become familiar with this account – of returnee refugee addicts from Iran and Pakistan – from those washed up in the Russian Cultural Centre. On a hunch I start counting as I go around the shooting gallery, sitting on the ground to talk with the groups of addicts as they smoke and inject. After dozens I lose count. All picked up their addiction in

Iran save one. All were sent to the barracks and deported. And gravitated here. Lost boys. Lost men. Who cannot find their families. They supply their own rough estimates of the addicts in the barracks with them. Two hundred out of three hundred, says one.

For many, the Russian Cultural Centre is a waiting room. Several men show me admission slips for the Nejat Drug Rehabilitation Clinic five minutes' drive along the road. They smooth out the scraps of paper in their palms, long held safe among possessions that amount to the clothes they stand in. The men complain about the waiting lists for a residential bed. With junkie logic they declare that they are desperate to shake off their addictions but then either announce that they cannot be bothered to wait for a bed, or, with a fatalistic shrug, insist that since they will 'never be treated' there is no point in pursuing it.

A week later I am confronted by another group of addicts, this time in a clinic in the dusty southern city of Lashkar Gah in Helmand province, centre of the new Taliban insurgency. Dr Rozat ullah Zia, its director, tells me a curious story about the addicts in his province, rejected by their families. I am familiar with the basic treatment methods in this clinic – the same used in the clinic I have visited not far from the shooting gallery where Mahmoud lives. It is a progression in small groups through a series of identical, bare rooms with only their fellow users to rely on. The men here sit passively – save one who thinks he can hear voices – their heads shaved like recruits in uniforms of blue or black, their cheeks caved in, skin sallow.

I learn that only those supported by their families can qualify for treatment. The relapse rate is lower, says Zia, so given the chronic lack of resources they are preferred. But I want to know about the ghosts, the rejects and dirt dwellers. What of these men? In his little office Zia considers the question. 'We have some homeless addicts in Lashkar Gah,' he admits. 'But most of them joined the police.' I am not dumbfounded only because a Western counter-narcotics official has already described the widespread criminality and drug abuse in Helmand's police. Of 356 recruits sent for police training, the official told me 195 were drug users. 'They are outcasts. So they go to the police,' says Zia. Rejected by family and tribe they have two options – to find a new belonging in the company of other junkies, or with the security forces. 'They take the unpopular assignments in places where people do not want to go,' he says. Where the Taliban and the insurgency are. Assignments where the risk of death is high.

T wo years into the Taliban's renewed insurgency that began in 2006, I find an Afghanistan that is neither fully at war nor close to peace. Instead it is stumbling ever closer towards looming catastrophe. Afghanistan exists in a halfway state, as disoriented as the junkies in the Cultural Centre, trapped in their no-man's-land of self-anaesthetisation. Nothing here is rooted: not the economy nor the sham of democratic politics – party-less, self-interested, lacking any legitimacy.

Every conversation with Afghans revolves around the same concerns – a seamless narrative, shared by all. I hear the same complaints from the brick makers out on the plain outside Kabul, from intellectuals, and from the unemployed labourers who gather at the roundabouts with their lathes and plastering equipment in the hope of a day's work. I hear it from the artists and youth workers. They complain about security, unemployment and the faltering economy; about corruption and the return of the warlords; about roads that cannot be travelled because of thieves or the Taliban or both; of checkpoints manned by police who steal from travellers. About a government they say is too weak or corrupt, made up of exiles preferred by the international community.

'Dog washers' the Afghans call them. A term coined for the returnees from Florida and Melbourne, Paris and London, who have come back to profit from the uncertain peace. It is used with withering contempt. I ask a couple of Afghan journalists one evening over a dinner in Kandahar for a precise definition. The 'dog washers' fled Afghanistan's wars to settle in the West – choosing not to stay and fight. Their jobs were often menial – 'working in a supermarket or pumping gas' – but after the Taliban's fall they lorded it over those who remained. 'It was like they owned those supermarkets, and everyone who remained was nothing,' said one friend. The dog washers in chief are those in the cabinet of President Hamid Karzai, anointed by the US and the international community. Not Westerners, but no longer quite accepted as Afghanis.

A state of not-one-thing-nor-the-other permeates Afghanistan. Officially, it is designated a post-conflict state where the business of state-building, reconstruction and peace-making is in full flow, to pump it up like the overblown figures on the Kabul gym signs – aid dollars as steroids. But post-conflict in the traditional sense has no meaning here. In this post-conflict state, the conflicts supposed to have been brought to an end by the US-led invasion go on.

For now the idea of the War in Afghanistan has as little meaning as the idea of peace. There are fierce battles across the dusty poppy fields and mountains, but these are largely localised and seasonal. Instead, the country exists in a no-man's-land, a limbo where peace-building efforts impinge on the dynamics of the violence, and where the conflict forces its own incursions into the zones of relative peace. The war is stalled but the peace is faltering. The figures supplied by the military and by foreign civilian agencies – which areas are 'insecure' and which are 'secure' – have little meaning on the ground compared with the accounts of ordinary Afghans. The country's real trajectory is measurable not in propaganda or empty statistics but in deflating hopes.

I have arrived to a warm Kabul spring with my friend and colleague Antonio Zazueta, discovering the Afghan capital in the midst of a crisis. Two days ago a group of Taliban infiltrated the city under the eyes of the intelligence ministry to try to kill the country's

President, Hamid Karzai. They launched a desultory attack on a parade ground in the capital as he reviewed the troops, accompanied by ambassadors and other VIPs. In retaliation, a few days later, hundreds of police and troops launched an assault upon a house in the Guzargah district, the hideout, they claimed, of some of those involved in the attack.

We turn up to find the shooting over and the area still sealed off by army and police. We wade across a little river sucking with banks of raw, stinking sewage to find yet more police. Outside a pharmacy, smoking their cigarettes, I see two well-dressed men in late middle age whom I take for the shop's owners until I spot the automatic weapons propped behind their legs. One is wearing a white suit. There is something in the combination of the weapon and his dandyish insouciance that unsettles me.

Ahead of us is the scene of the battle, a steep hill embedded with small crags, interspersed with a jumble of poor houses, a neighbourhood that tumbles down the hill. High above us tower the walls of the Koh-i-Thoop – 'the Cannon Fort' – where children go to run their hoops made of old bicycle wheels, sometimes on the fort's walls themselves, above a dizzying drop. Crowds line the roofs of the houses and the fort's walls, hundreds of figures who have come out to watch the fighting. Visiting one of the partridge fights that take place on Friday mornings in the Cinema Park near my guesthouse, I am supplied with a sharp reminder of this scene: the lines of watching silhouettes, waiting patiently for something to happen.

The violence of the events is most damaging in its impact on the city's fragile psychology, already jarred by an earlier suicide attack that penetrated the heavily fortified Serena Hotel a handful of months before. By the realisation that there are 'ghosts' – as the Russians once called the mujahideen – flickering among Afghanis in new shape, that of a new insurgency. Even the country's safest city is not immune.

A few days after the attempted assassination I go to mingle with the weekend crowds in the recently reconstructed Babur Shah Gardens, close to the scene of the gun battle. Here I come across the Nareed family having a picnic on an area of grass below the cafeteria, a white-painted pavilion serving food few can afford after they have paid the admission. The gardens are a haven from the dirt, stink and bustle of Kabul. Modelled on the mausoleum grounds commissioned by Zahiruddin Muhammed Babur in the sixteenth century, they sit on what is left of the private park he commanded he be buried in. The modern incarnation is a more egalitarian affair. Situated on a steep slope, the ground is sectored into a patchwork of little terraces that descend the hill, falling from the garden's highest wall. Above the wall the ground continues its ascent up to the impoverished neighbourhood of Guzargah.

In a city short of facilities and beset by grinding poverty, the gardens are a place to come and sit in the shade, beneath avenues of new-planted planes, walnuts and mulberries. Elsewhere there are almond and pomegranate trees, apples, apricot and quince planted over eleven hectares of land.

Jostling gangs of youths run up and down the stone-flagged stairs, or sit playing on the carom boards that boys hawk out for rent for a handful of Afs. Others sit and stare out beyond the park towards the rooftops of Kabul below, the city's pollution turning the snowy peaks of the Paghman Mountains opposite into grey-gauzy layers.

When I encounter the Nareeds I am watching a group of gardeners chase a pack of younger boys off a forbidden area of grass with home-made truncheons wrapped in black tape. Ahmad, his mother, Najeeba, and father, Kabir, and Auntie Abeda are returnees – like Mahmoud – this time from Pakistan where the family fled just before the Taliban finally swept to power in 1996. They returned in 2005 after being hassled by police in Rawalpindi into ending their exile.

'In Pakistan the government and police wanted to harass us. Otherwise we were happy. We don't have anywhere to live here. We rent,' says Ahmad gloomily. 'None of us are working. My sister is out of the country. She lives in Canada. And she sends us money – $100 a month.' There is a commotion among the boys milling around the pavilion above us, scattering one laughing group. 'I worked for four years in an internet café,' continues Ahmad, pleased, it seems, to recall a more productive time. 'I know about computers.'

Two granddaughters I had not noticed before, a pair of toddlers, burst through the family group. 'The situation is not good. We are not agreeing with the situation here. We were happy in Pakistan,' adds Ahmad's father, Kabir, quietly in stilted English. He echoes his son's emotions.

'We were nervous when we returned. There is rarely electricity. No gas. Everyone in the family is jobless.' Abeda mutters: 'Problem. Problem,' adding something in Urdu. 'You don't understand Urdu, do you?' she says in English. 'But you know what I am saying.' Ahmad picks up his story again. 'We left because of the war. Like a lot of people we lost our home. By the time the Taliban came to Kabul we had already left.' I ask them about the recent fighting in Guzargah. A look passes between the group. 'We feel this is our home,' insists Abeda. 'But every day we are making plans to leave.'

There are conflicts whose root causes are not repaired simply because the fighting ends. Regimes like the Taliban or Saddam Hussein's are easier to topple by external intervention than to replace. Easy victory suggests that the problems will be just as easy to solve. But seven years after the Taliban's fall, Afghanistan's divisions remain – caustic and dangerous. The same divisions have driven rebellions and wider war: between the centre and the periphery; between tradition and a desire to modernise society; between the city and the countryside, most powerfully represented by the Pashto-speaking south's sense of disenfranchisement.

The Afghanistan I encounter on this visit – despite the billions in aid and the army of foreign experts, advising on everything from growing paprika as a replacement for opium to law and local government – is in danger again of slowly ungluing. They are the same officials who drive

4x4s through Kabul's congested streets, dine at the now heavily protected Serena Hotel, speaking their aid and diplomatic speak, while distorting Afghanistan's society in unintended ways. In a country where barely 10 per cent of the population has a university degree, the international organisations' ability to offer far higher salaries than government ministries has further deprofessionalised the institutions of a society that had seen successive regimes attack the educated classes.

Far from bringing stability to the country, a divided international community has simply overseen a new crisis. The Afghan people have little confidence in their country's future, confronted by a political vacuum, widening insecurity and a rampant opium economy growing to occupy the space left empty by what is still insufficient economic aid to rebuild one of the world's poorest nations. There are precious few encouraging signs. Free speech and the media are under threat not only from the Taliban and their supporters in the south but also from warlords in even the most 'stable' areas of Afghanistan. A scheduled new round of democratic elections deepens the sense of impending crisis as individuals – guilty of all sorts of crimes during the civil war – are brought into the government in an attempt to neutralise their harmful influence but then jockey for power.

The consequence is a dangerous nostalgia for the days of the Taliban. A lorry driver from Lashkar Gah tells me a proverb that is rendered roughly to me as: 'The old thieves are better than the new.' Except it is more horrible than that. Accurately translated, it offers an even more grim analysis: 'The old stealers of the white grave clothes are better than the new.' The most powerful metaphor comes from a Western agricultural expert working in the dangerous south. Wearing an assault rifle over his shoulder for protection, he offers a new insight to why people prefer planting opium poppy to fruit trees. 'Planting trees requires time and effort,' he explains. 'To plant a tree you have to be confident about your future, to be sure that you will be there to pick its fruit when it matures. If you are not certain about where you will be in a year's time, then poppy is the more certain option.'

After the attack on Karzai, a nagging sense of fear permeates Kabul. At the Olympic Stadium, the grandiosely named sports hall out by the city's fringes, I spend an afternoon with the Afghan National Women's Basketball Team – an equally grand name for a group of keen secondary-school girls with precious little competition to play against. They are a symbol of the new, or at least reinvented, Afghanistan. They take their training seriously but the team is necessarily selected from a small pool. Many of the girls' families do not want them to come to train because of fears about security.

Even at the brickmakers' kilns at Dah-e-Sabz at the edge of the Shomali plain on the city's outskirts – the far end of the social spectrum from the smart young women shooting hoops at the Olympic Stadium – the same anxiety persists. Early one morning I follow a dirt track towards a pair of rough chimneys – portable it turns out – bulging at the bottom and tapering at the top like two towering pupae, pegged down to the kiln's dirt-piled surface with hemp ropes.

The chimneys inject a black smoke into the narrow plain's lightening, magenta dawn as a small group of men, filthy with ashes, shovel coal into holes dug on the kiln's surface. I can feel heat radiating beneath my feet. The surface is covered with the openings – *moori* – each covered with a round pan lid which the men lift every few minutes to check the baking temperature inside. It is done with a long metal hook, which the men twirl dramatically. On top of some of the *moori* sit the large kettles the men use for heating their washing water, or for boiling their green tea. When the men flip the lids to pour in more coal, hot mouths of heat and jets of flame are revealed.

The men are *mussafer*, single men living together away from home. After the shift they wash methodically, pushing the dirt down their arms towards their hands in a rough surgeon's scrub, squatting in the dust. I am invited into the hut shared by four of them. A low door leads into a single mud-walled room. They have laid a cover on the floor. Around the edges is their bedding, greasy with use. For all that the hut is surprisingly clean. On my second visit I notice some plastic flowers fixed to a wall and the mobile phone numbers of friends and family scratched into its surface.

Samiullah, aged twenty-three, pours me tea and offers some of the flat bread they are eating for breakfast. He has a serious face framed by his full beard. The other men, I notice, are shyly quiet when he speaks. 'Afghanistan is in chaos. Remember what happened three days ago.' He is referring to the attack on Karzai. 'Three people were killed!

We're sick of that. I was a refugee. My home [his Pakistani home, it turns out] is in Peshawar. I work three or four months here and then I go back home with the money.'

Samiullah's other home – his Afghan home – is a farm an hour's drive from the brick kilns in a village called Sohrobai. The area is not secure, so his family remains in Pakistan. 'Sometimes the Taliban attack. Sometimes the Coalition bombs, so I will not take my family back there. I go to look at it sometimes,' he adds ruefully. 'There is a farmer who I gave the land to look after. He grows poppies for opium sometimes, and sometimes wheat. He gives us some of the money.' But even the kilns are not entirely safe. 'Three days ago thieves with guns came to this place and stole our money and SIM cards.' Samiullah becomes gloomy. 'I am not optimistic,' he says. 'I think I would be happy to die.'

I hear a story doing the rounds of the translators in Kabul, which reaches me via some of the Afghan translators. 'Sean from the BBC' – 'tall Sean' – has gone missing. I realise with a ghastly sinking feeling this means Sean Langan, a documentary film-maker I knew in Baghdad. I check with the embassy and find he was reported overdue by his production company two weeks before, and is missing somewhere near the Pakistan border, the Taliban's stronghold. I check back through the emails I sent to Sean trying to hook up; and those to his translator Samiullah, who had expressed an interest in working for me, but from whom I had heard no more. I find a note also from one of Sean's friends whom I had contacted before coming to Afghanistan telling me Sean was up a mountain but expected home shortly.

Although the portent of this news remains ambiguous, I feel depressed even by the suggestion that this brave, funny, self-deprecating man might have come to harm. It amplifies a feeling of my own discomfort: that I feel trapped in a no-man's-land of painful indecision. After the years of chronicling violence, part of me is tired and finished with war, anxious to put the conflict zones at last behind me. Each time the moment to quit comes I find another excuse to return, still drawn to my unhealthy fascinations. But with each visit the weariness grows greater, the little bravery that I once had to employ becomes more friable and worn. When I was forty, I said it was a younger man's game and set a limit of forty-five. At forty-five I went back to Iraq. At forty-six to Gaza and Afghanistan.

I am in Kandahar again. And scared. So much of my adult life has been parcelled out in these passages of being afraid, where time seems either frozen or horribly dilated by fear's gravitational pull. I am doing my best to pass unobserved, wearing local Pashtun clothing and sporting a scratchy beard. I know that this visit is perhaps even more dangerous than my last, with the risk of kidnap or worse. The rumoured going rate for ransom being demanded by both the Taliban and criminal kidnap gangs is $10 million – the alleged amount paid for an Italian reporter. The likely outcome for any Afghans with us is a

263

quick execution. The only concession that I have not made is to disguise my shoes, a pair of battered trainers. I'm not sure I could run, if I needed to, wearing sandals.

Seven years have passed since my last visit and I hardly recognise the city with its tiny rooftop mosques and lines of praying men silhouetted against the sky. Only the mountains' coxcomb ridges remain in my memory, overlooking the area that was once Mullah Omar's house, an area now fenced and appropriated by US Special Forces. The difference is the unsettling knowledge that the Taliban are resurgent in the city and not on the run. But the war here — if not in the countryside of 'Big Kandahar', as the Afghans call the wider constellation of the south's four provinces — lies largely beneath the surface. It is played out in suicide bombings and attacks and a more subtle campaign of intimidating politicians, police and local journalists. I am warned that no one is to be trusted entirely and that even anti-Taliban politicians have been forced to make accommodations with them, both to survive and as an insurance against the risk that some day they might come back to power.

I try to construct a mental map of danger areas from the stories I hear in the city, obsessively collecting the fragments to impose a sense of order on the danger. Even then I do not manage to avoid those neighbourhoods. There are no truly safe zones, only different balances of ambiguity in a conflict-that-is-not-a-conflict. It is a point reinforced immediately after I leave when one of the routes we travelled is hit by bombs three times in two days.

Even equipped with the warnings of places to avoid, I find myself one evening driving through Loyah Wallah on the outskirts of the city, a neighbourhood of low houses and poor shops close to the canal. It is here, I am told only as we pass the neighbourhood's ramshackle graveyard, that fighters from Helmand, Zabul and Rozgan have moved their families. Officially it is not a Taliban-controlled area, but ask the government if it is safe to go there and they say no. The facts don't lie. A school has been burnt down and others targeted with grenades. A local police commander was killed in a suicide attack. The unpaved road we are driving on has been the scene of a series of landmine attacks. Even local Kandaharis avoid this district at night.

Another area, Arghand Dab, lies just beyond the city. We halt at its edge, at a sculpture park filled with dolphins and horses rendered in shapes featureless as Japanese anime figures. The park, a place popular with picnickers, marks the beginning of an expanse of heavily wooded farmland, groves of mulberry trees bisected by a river, which the Taliban have entered in force on several occasions or attacked.

The feeling of exposure is intense. Apart from the Canadian soldiers who pass through on their patrols, or overhead in helicopters, and the few people at the heavily guarded Provincial Reconstruction Team, there are only a handful of Europeans and Americans inside the city. A smattering of journalists come to make discreet visits, but a tiny number in comparison with those embedding with the US, British and Canadian troops to tell their version of the war. When they do they dress like me in local clothes and maintain a low profile on the streets.

One day I am on the other side of Loyah Wallah at a small, unfinished shrine beyond the ugly barracks-like structures of the university. Outside the shrine's walls the wooded plain leads to the mountain ridge. Piles of bricks litter the paths that lead to the shrine's open dome and unplanted flowerbeds. A workman comes across, apologising for the construction's slow progress. Despite its unfinished appearance this remains a quiet place and a handful of students come and go, to sit against the walls or on the shallow steps of the shrine to read. I assume it is dedicated to a religious figure until Hayatullah Raffiqi, whom I am accompanying, explains it is for Abdul Shakoor Rashad, a Kandahari poet and historian, famous in modern Afghan literature, who argued forcefully against a separation of Afghanistan into tribal and ethnic interests. Raffiqi is a poet and historian himself.

In his hand he has his own life's work, a series of poems from his unpublished collection *Purandi*, chronicling Afghanistan's troubled heritage. The word means 'what lies under the ash'. Embers, I take it to mean in a literal sense, but what he means is the country's experience of conflict and its hollow peace. 'He was my teacher,' Raffiqi says reverently about Abdul Shakoor Rashad. 'I knew and respected him.' I have asked him to read some poems for me from his workbook, an old-fashioned, brown A4 notepad, at a place of his choosing. And he has selected this place. But when we arrive he is shy, awkward.

It is early morning, just after 6 a.m., and the oppressive, clammy heat of the day has yet to impose itself. We are close to the wire-enclosed area that was once Mullah Omar's house. A few slender brown pigeons roosting around the shrine are startled when a Chinook and a Kiowa helicopter fly past, low against the nearby mountains, drumming away the silence. Raffiqi begins to read, and when he does the words come out in a deep but hesitant voice which becomes stronger as he continues. He reads three of his poems. His voice suggests a special attachment to the first, whose metre beats warmly and strongly with the same insistence as the Chinook's double blades. Muhib quickly whispers a translation.

> *Who took my precious life in secret? Thief!*
> *Stranger and enemy, who moved against me secretly.*
> *Robber!*

I understand it is a poem about autumn and the passage of time. But it is underscored by other meanings. Among them is Raffiqi's mourning for a life spent waiting for a brighter future Afghanistan was never able to enjoy. He says sadly to me after the reading: 'I remember the revolutions because I witnessed them all. Every one since the time of the king.' As we walk, I ask him to assess the current times. 'We live now in a time of disappointment. The worst of the times I can remember.' I am surprised he believes it to be worse than the war against the Soviets, the internecine fighting of the mujahideen and the coming of the Taliban. But it is the collapse of the slender hope that came in the years after 2001 that is felt most painfully.

I had first met Raffiqi at the offices of Afghan Azad Radio, a local station where he comes to write in a poorly lit and borrowed room, sitting in the corner of a battered sofa, scribbling his lines into his brown 'Karachi' notebook. With his greying hair neatly combed back and his trimmed beard he looks younger than his sixty-six years. 'I stayed here all the time,' he says when I ask him if he ever fled. 'If I had not faced the time of the Taliban I would look younger still!' Despite the joke there is an aura of depression that hangs about him. 'The way people are living! You only have to consider the psychological situation of these circumstances. People are wondering. They are exhausted and they feel lost. The economic situation has got worse as the security has worsened too. Recently we had almost one hundred and twenty killed in just one suicide attack. Because of that people cannot make the decisions that they need to make. They cannot decide. It is hopeless.' He is quiet, turning his book of poems in his hand, running his palm over the worn surface of the cover. 'For myself, I live only for my poetry these days.'

Returning to Kabul I meet Mahmoud for a third and final time at the Cultural Centre. It is a Friday and boys are playing soccer and cricket amid the ruins, oblivious to the addicts around them. I am looking again at the mural in the entrance hall when he appears. We talk about the spaceman on the Russian half and I ask him the identity of the rider on the horse. He looks blank and shrugs, then asks me a question about Lenin being 'the father of communism'. I try to explain.

Mahmoud seems more together than before and more animated. He looks genuinely pleased to see us. He announces, unbidden, that he has cut the amount of heroin he's been smoking, ahead of going in to take the cure in a fortnight's time. 'I've got a bed,' he says, referring to the nearby drug treatment centre. I want to believe that he really means to clean up. I ask more about his life. He says he collects used Pepsi cans and scrap metal to sell, and begs outside a mosque to fund his habit. He appears more boyish than before and I can believe he is really seventeen, his face not sagging, pale and sweating from smoking heroin. I inquire about his family again, painfully aware of the rules at the drug treatment clinics. He is clear this time. About the uncle he mentioned at our first meeting. He is not even sure if he is still alive.

'It's boring being like this,' he volunteers. 'Being an addict and being here. I am only living in this place because I must. It's like . . .' He searches for a word. 'Compulsory,' he says. 'It's just a place I've been waiting for so long. I don't want to spend another winter here.' He is wearing different clothes, a black shirt and clean combat pants. I figure there must be somewhere he hides some possessions, perhaps in his cave, although I did not see them – saw none of the men's belongings as I wandered the building. Mahmoud talks about wanting to get a job, not labouring he says, he is not strong enough for that, but perhaps work as a waiter.

He tells me about his schooling lest I should think he is stupid. But I don't think that. We are back in the ruined concert hall watching the pigeons fly. He is standing where the orchestra's chairs must once have been. His upbeat mood is broken by a complaint. He says he is suffering from diarrhoea, pulls a face and clutches his stomach and asks me for 500 Afs for antibiotics. Ten dollars. I start to walk away across the open space of the symphony hall. But I feel sorry for Mahmoud and in the end I give him the money. As he runs off, I'm certain that it's to buy more drugs.

Afterword

I n the end I begin to lose the ability to document the hurt of war honestly. The damage I have seen accumulates like drifting snow, piling deeper and deeper still. Cold and numbing. The danger is that I can no longer find a unique place to hold each of the individual stories. Over the years they have blurred into classes of things seen, categories of the dead and the injured, killers and the killed, the lost and the fleeing. An overfilled and disorganised bookshelf, I am no longer certain quite where to put my hand on the volumes. I am only aware that they are there. My taxonomy is complete and in being complete it is robbed of any meaning. It becomes harder to make distinctions and to maintain the small, intimate and necessary perspective that reveals the humanity of each person I encounter, each story I hear. This is the final trans-formation war performs. Over time and through exposure it diminishes the power of each individual voice, dulls us to experience. The result is that I am reduced to being nothing more than a stenographer. It is what war does to all of us. It is what makes it possible.

I listen to terrible stories too familiar now to be shocking. I know that courage is finite but I now discover that empathy may have its limits too. What I once felt deeply, viscerally, like a knife across the skin, I now feel only as a dull ache, a bruise. I know that this means I should bring an end to my journeys through the realm of war, give up my passport for that country of broken shapes. At last, I'm ready.

London,

August 2008

Acknowledgements

First and foremost, I would like to thank the *Observer*, my employer for almost two decades. During that time I have worked for six editors: Donald Trelford, Jonathan Fenby, Andrew Jaspan, Will Hutton, Roger Alton and now John Mulholland. Most of this book was written under Roger's editorship.

It has been assignments for the *Observer* and, more recently, also for its sister paper the *Guardian*, that have allowed me to spend as much time as I have observing how people behave in times of conflict. Paul Webster, the *Observer*'s deputy editor, has been a constant source of encouragement, support and friendship over the years, as have foreign editors Leonard Doyle and Tracy McVeigh. I have also been fortunate to work with a group of colleagues who have been as honest in their criticism as generous with their friendship. Among them I would like to single out Martin Bright, David Rose, Robin McKie and Paul Dunn. The late Arnold Kemp taught me much – not least about humanity and the importance of humility. At the *Guardian* I owe particular thanks to Harriet Sherwood and to David Munk and David Hearst.

My agent at ICM and later Curtis Brown, the indefatigable Karolina Sutton, not only persuaded me to commence *The Secret Life of War* but read the chapters and made suggestions – too many to count – on how to improve them.

I also could not have asked for a more attentive publisher than the team at Harvill Secker – first among them my meticulous editor, Stuart Williams, whose suggestions during the editing process felt invariably correct.

There are many people without whose help I could not have written this book. Fiona Beaumont gave so much in the years when the bulk of the travelling took place. Many other friends were instrumental in getting me to write about my experiences in the first place. They include Burhan Wazir, Sandra Jordan and Barbara Gunnell. I was encouraged too by friends who read and commented on the work in progress, among them Myles Quin, Will Postlethwaite, Campbell Stevenson and Antonio Zazueta.

Travelling in conflict zones I have made a large number of friends, all of whom have made the journey easier. I shared cars and adventures with Sharon Abbady, Bryan McBurney, Andrew Testa, Emma Daly, the unstoppable Steve Farrell, Inigo Gilmore, Mitch Prothero, Kim Riseth and Harald Henden, Gary Calton, Kai Wiedenhofer, Joao Silva and Stephanie Sinclair. No one could have asked for better companions in the field than David Guttenfelder, Jonathan Steele, Rory Carroll and Rory McCarthy, Suzanne Goldenberg, Andrea Bruce, Ghaith Abdul-Ahad, Aram Roston, Sean Langan, Pete Norman, James Hider, Lulu Garcia-Navarro, Declan Walsh, Andrew Lee Butters and Ron Haviv.

It was always a pleasure to find Lindsey Hilsum and Tim Lambon of Channel Four on the same story. One friend to

THE SECRET LIFE OF WAR

many of us did not make it through: Marla Ruzicka – a remarkable woman who was killed while working in Baghdad.

This book has been a much more time-consuming business than I had anticipated and has inevitably encroached on time when I should have been doing other things. My children Indigo and Al have been remarkably patient, even when their father has been sneaking in an extra hour of work on his laptop when we should have been doing something fun.

Finally, none of this would have been possible without the love and support of my partner Emily Harding, who not only read the drafts but has also been a citizen of that country called conflict.

Chapter Notes and
Further Reading

Adetailed and sympathetic account of the experiences of Staff Sergeant Garth Sizemore's unit in Baghdad – and the consequences of the high death toll among them which in the end led to near mutiny – is to be found in Kelly Kennedy's superb 2007 series for the *Army Times*, 'Blood Brothers'. At the time of writing it could be found at: www militarytimes. com/news/2007/11/bloodbrothersredirect/

In attempting to understand the physical changes that take place in the brain following repeated exposure to acute stressors like combat, I relied on the wealth of new research that has taken place in the last decade and a half. Much of it has been inspired by the ground-breaking work of Douglas Bremner at Emory University, Atlanta, in the mid-1990s with Vietnam veterans. Chris Brewin at University College London kindly took the time to talk me through some of the issues. I found *Neuropsychology of PTSD*, edited by Jennifer J. Vasterling and Brewin – although technical – immensely useful.

Clues

There are numerous books describing the run-up to the war in Afghanistan. One of the best is by my colleague at the *Observer*, Jason Burke, who has written the invaluable *Al-Qaeda: the True Story of Radical Islam*. Also excellent are: *The Looming Tower: Al-Qaeda's Road to 9/11* by

Lawrence Wright; *Holy War, Inc: Inside the Secret World of Osama bin Laden* by Peter Bergen and *The Osama Bin Laden I Know: An Oral History of Al-Qaeda's Leader*, also by Bergen. *Taliban* by Ahmed Rashid is an outstanding account of that group's rise to power.

Blast Waves

I was fortunate in coming across E.F. Kunz's seminal work from 1973 – 'The Refugee in Flight: Kinetic Models and Forms of Displacement', published in *International Migration Review* – describing what pushes refugees out of their homes. Although I had already settled on the idea of comparing the energy of a blast wave from an explosion to the pressure on a civilian population for refugee dispersal, the discovery of Kunz's work on flight patterns in times of acute pressure confirmed that I might be on the right track in trying to understand what happens at the moment when individuals decide to escape.

My understanding of the pathology and mechanics of blast injuries benefitted enormously from reading 'The Pathology of Primary Blast Injury' by Douglas D. Sharpnack, Anthony J. Johnson and Yancy Y. Phillips, which was contributed to *Conventional Warfare: Ballistic, Blast and Burn Injuries* (1991) published by the Borden Institute as part of its series of military medical textbooks.

Hate Studies

I found a number of essays, books and articles useful in building a picture of how hatreds in rival communities function, both in relation to each other and individually as an expression of social values during conflict.

An excellent general overview of the work being done in

understanding how hatred works is Evan R. Harrington's 'The Social Psychology of Hatred' (2004) for the *Journal of Hate Studies*.

With specific reference to the Israeli–Palestinian conflict, Neta Oren, Daniel Bar-Tal and Ohad David's chapter for *Psychology of Ethnic and Cultural Conflict* entitled 'Conflict, Identity, and Ethos: The Israeli–Palestinian Case' (2004), is remarkable for its many insights, not least its discussion of an ethos of conflict. I also found Shifa Sagy, Sami Adwan, and Avi Kaplan's 'Interpretations of the Past and Expectations of the Future Among Israeli and Palestinian Youth' (2002) for the *American Journal of Orthopsychiatry* invaluable.

Weapons

I came by chance across an intriguing essay for the *Journal of Consumer Research*, 'My Favourite Things: a Cross-Cultural Inquiry into Object Attachment, Possessiveness and Social Linkage' (1988) by Melanie Wallendorf and Eric J. Arnould. While not related specifically to the ownership of weapons, it did, however, make me think more deeply about how people become attached to particular objects, and how that attachment validates ideas about themselves.

The psychological processes involved in the use of weapons – in killing – are clinically laid bare in two books to which I owe a considerable debt. Joanna Bourke's *An Intimate History of Killing: Face to Face Killing in 20th Century Warfare* (1999), which I have read three times since I bought my first copy, is unrivalled in the breadth of its historical research and its humanity. *On Killing: The Psychological Cost of Learning to Kill in War and Society* (1995) by Lt. Col. Dave Grossman was equally useful and – as acknowledged in the text – I have relied on Grossman for his description of both the psychological phases experienced before, during and after killing, and for his ideas on how the remorse engendered by killing operates differently for different weapons systems and over different killing distances.

Terror

A helpful description of the processes that occur in the human brain – and where – when confronted with immediate, close and terrifying danger is to be found in *Science 317* (2007), discussing the work of Dean Mobbs and his colleagues at University College London: 'When Fear Is Near: Threat Imminence Elicits Prefrontal-Periaqueductal Gray Shifts in Humans'.

The definition of terror – in the broad sense of violence for political ends, largely by a non-state actor – is considered by Dr Jeffrey Record in his 2003 monograph *Bounding the Global War on Terrorism* for the Strategic Services Institute of the US Army War College. I also found helpful the discussion by Conor Gearty of the London School of Economics of the changing application of the word 'terrorist' in his essay 'Terrorism and Morality' (2003).

But perhaps the most useful essay that I read while considering how terror is differently defined within competing communities was 'Self-Serving Perceptions of Terrorism Among Israelis and Palestinians' by Jacob Shamir and Khalil Shikaki, published in the journal *Political Psychology* (2002).

Thanks are due to my friend Suzanne Goldenberg of the

Guardian whose article drew my attention to the graffiti in the Mattin centre in Nablus.

The Contaminated Wound

The title of this chapter was suggested by one of the section headings in the previously mentioned *Conventional Warfare: Ballistic, Blast and Burn Injuries* which contains a concise overview of both the management of infection in soft tissue injuries and a history of the understanding of tissue infection as military medicine developed.

My description of what happens when a modern small-arms round is fired, its flight and the consequence of it hitting the human body was assisted by the chapter on ballistics in *Conventional Warfare: Ballistic, Blast and Burn Injuries* (1991), 'The Physics and Biophysics of Wound Ballistics' by Ronald F. Bellamy and Russ Zajtchuk. Forensic literature contains numerous descriptions of typical and atypical entry wounds. *Gunshot Wounds: Practical Aspects of Firearms, Ballistics, and Forensic Techniques* by Vincent J. M. Di Maio (1999) offers a detailed overview of the subject. I also found useful the depiction of different entry-wound types in *A Physician's Guide to Clinical Forensic Medicine* (2000) edited by Margaret M. Stark.

A full and chilling account of the infection of the US military's medical and evacuation chain in Iraq by *Acinetobacter baumannii* can be found in Steve Silberman's February 2007 investigation 'The Invisible Enemy' for *Wired* magazine.

Things Fall Apart

The International Crisis Group's report of 20 December 2007 *Inside Gaza: The Challenge of Clans and Families*, Middle

East Report Nº71, was deeply helpful in clarifying the political context of both the re-emergence of clan competition and its relationship to the struggle between Fatah and Hamas. Published between my first visit to examine clan violence and my second trip, it helped me enormously to understand the historical background to the rise of different clans and the tensions this created in Gazan society.

No-Man's-Land

Six months after my visit to Afghanistan to research this final chapter, the situation has deteriorated. As I write, senior British military officers are talking of a war that cannot be won. It might have been tempting in these circumstances to re-work No-Man's-Land to appear prescient. But the intention of each of these chapters was to capture how things stood at certain periods of time, and to throw light on different aspects of conflict.

The starting point for this chapter was the paradox expressed by Kaja Borchgrevink and Krfistian Berg Harpviken of the International Peace Research Institute, Oslo, in their 2008 paper *Afghan Civil Society: Caught in Conflicting Agendas*. They talked of a conflictual character to the Afghan peace process – pinned between forces leading the country to renewed violence and those attempting to bring an end to the decades of killing. I also found useful Astri Suhrke's 'Reconstruction as Modernisation: the "post-conflict" project in Afghanistan' for *Third World Quarterly* (2007) which identified similar contradictions.